# STUDIES IN LITERATURE

## FIRST SERIES

CAMBRIDGE UNIVERSITY PRESS

C. F. CLAY, Manager

LONDON : FETTER LANE, E.C. 4

BOMBAY ⎫
CALCUTTA ⎬ MACMILLAN AND CO., LTD.
MADRAS ⎭

TORONTO : THE MACMILLAN CO. OF
CANADA, LTD.

TOKYO : MARUZEN-KABUSHIKI-KAISHA

Copyrighted in the United States of America
by G. P. PUTNAM'S SONS
2, 4 and 6, West 45th Street, New York City

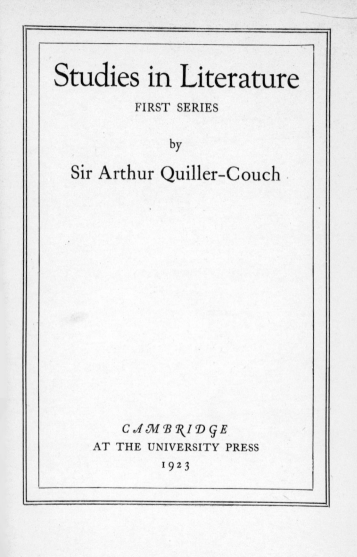

# Studies in Literature

FIRST SERIES

by

Sir Arthur Quiller-Couch

CAMBRIDGE
AT THE UNIVERSITY PRESS
1923

First Edition 1918
Reprinted 1919
,, 1920
Pocket Edition 1923

PRINTED IN GREAT BRITAIN

# PREFACE

THE first of these 'studies,' *The Commerce of Thought*, was originally read before an audience at the Royal Institution of London. *Coleridge* and *Matthew Arnold* have appeared as Introductions in 'The World's Classics' series, and I thank the Oxford University Press for allowing me to reprint them. *Swinburne* was written for 'The Edinburgh Review,' and *Charles Reade* for 'The Times Literary Supplement' on the centenary of Reade's birth.

I cannot quarrel with any critic who may find the word 'studies' too important for a volume which consists, in the main, of familiar discourses: and will only plead that it was chosen to cover not this book alone but a successor of which some part of the contents may better justify the general title. For example, in the lecture here printed *On the Terms 'Classical' and 'Romantic'* I purposely contented myself with discussing some elementary and (as I believe) mistaken notions, reserving some interesting modern theories for later treatment.

I must here, however, avow my belief that before starting to lay down principles of literature or aesthetic a man should offer some evidence of his capacity to enjoy the better and eschew the worse. The claim, for the moment fashionable, that a general philosophy of aesthetic can be constructed by a thinker who, in practice, cannot distinguish Virgil from Bavius, or Rodin from William Dent Pitman, seems to me to presume a credulity almost beyond the dreams of illicit therapeutics. By 'poetry,' in these pages, I mean what has been written by Homer, Dante, Shakespeare and some others.

ARTHUR QUILLER-COUCH

*May* 10, 1918

# CONTENTS

|  | PAGE |
|---|---|
| PREFACE | v |
| THE COMMERCE OF THOUGHT | 1 |
| BALLADS | 22 |
| THE HORATIAN MODEL IN ENGLISH VERSE | 48 |
| ON THE TERMS 'CLASSICAL' AND 'RO-MANTIC'. | 71 |
| SOME SEVENTEENTH CENTURY POETS: | |
| I. JOHN DONNE | 90 |
| II. HERBERT AND VAUGHAN | 111 |
| III. TRAHERNE, CRASHAW AND OTHERS | 137 |
| THE POETRY OF GEORGE MEREDITH | 158 |
| THE POETRY OF THOMAS HARDY | 178 |
| COLERIDGE | 200 |
| MATTHEW ARNOLD | 218 |
| SWINBURNE | 232 |
| CHARLES READE | 258 |
| PATRIOTISM IN ENGLISH LITERATURE. I. | 273 |
| PATRIOTISM IN ENGLISH LITERATURE. II. | 289 |
| INDEX | 303 |

# THE COMMERCE
# OF THOUGHT

## I

AMONG the fascinating books that have never been written (and they are still the most fascinating of all) I think my favourite is Professor So-and-So's *History of Trade-Routes from the Earliest Times*, a magnificent treatise, incomplete in three volumes. The title may not allure you; possibly you suspect it of promising as much dullness as the title of this lecture, and it is even conceivable that you secretly extend your mistrust to professors as a class. Well concerning us, as men, you may be right: the accusation has been levelled: but I shall try to persuade you that you are mistaken about this book.

For a few examples—Who, hearing that British oysters, from Richborough, were served at Roman dinner-parties under the Empire, does not want to know how that long journey was contrived for them and how they were kept alive on the road? Or take the secret of the famous purple that was used to dye the Emperor's robe. As Browning asked, 'Who fished the murex up?' How did it reach the dyeing-vat? What was the process? Was the trade a monopoly? Again, you remember that navy of Tarshish, which came once in three years bringing Solomon gold and silver, ivory and apes and peacocks. Who would not wish to read one of its bills of lading, to construct a picture of the quays as the vessels freighted or discharged their cargo?

As who would not eagerly read a description of that lumberer's camp on Lebanon to which Solomon sent ten thousand men a month by courses: 'a month they were in Lebanon and two months at home, and Adoniram was over the levy'? The conditions, you see, must have been hard, as the *corvée* was enormous. What truth, if any, underlies the legend that when Solomon died they embalmed and robed him and stood the corpse high on the unfinished wall that, under their great taskmaster's eye, the workmen should work and not 'slack' (as we say)? What a clerk-of-the-works!

Yet again—Where lay the famous tin-islands, the Cassiterides? How were the great ingots of Cornish tin delivered down to the coast and shipped on to Marseilles, Carthage, Tyre? We know that they were shaped pannier-wise, and carried by ponies. But where was the island of Ictis, where the ships received them? Our latest theorists will not allow it to have been St Michael's Mount—the nearest of all, and the most obviously correspondent with the historian's description. They tell us hardily it was the Isle of Wight—or the Isle of Thanet. Ah, if these professors did not suffer from sea-sickness, how much simpler their hypotheses would be! Image the old Cornish merchant taking whole trains of ponies, laden with valuable ore, along the entire south of England, through dense forests and marauding tribes, to ship his ware at Thanet, when he had half a dozen better ports at his door! Imagine a skipper from Marseilles—But the absurdities are endless, and I will not here pursue them.

For what other hidden port of trade was that Phoenician skipper bound who, held in chase off the Land's End by a Roman galley and desperate of cheating her, deliberately (tradition tells) drove his ship ashore to save his merchants' secret? Through what phases, before this, had run and shifted the commercial struggle between young Greece and ancient Phoenicia imaged for us in Matthew Arnold's famous simile:

> As some grave Tyrian trader, from the sea,
>   Descried at sunrise an emerging prow
> Lifting the cool-hair'd creepers stealthily,
>   The fringes of a southward-facing brow
>     Among the Ægean isles:
> And saw the merry Grecian coaster come,
>   Freighted with amber grapes, and Chian wine,
>   Green bursting figs, and tunnies steep'd in brine;
> And knew the intruders on his ancient home,
>
> The young light-hearted masters of the waves;
>   And snatch'd his rudder, and shook out more sail,
>   And day and night held on indignantly
> O'er the blue Midland waters with the gale,
>   Betwixt the Syrtes and soft Sicily,
>     To where the Atlantic raves
> Outside the Western Straits, and unbent sails
>   There, where down cloudy cliffs, through sheets
>       of foam,
>   Shy traffickers, the dark Iberians come;
> And on the beach undid his corded bales.

What commerce followed the cutting of Rome's great military roads?—that tremendous one, for instance, hewn along the cliffs close over the rapids that swirl through the Iron Gates of Danube. By what caravan tracks, through what depots, did the great slave traffic wind up out of Africa and reach the mart at Constantinople? What sort of men worked goods down the Rhone valley; and, if by water, by what contrivances? To come a little later, how did the Crusaders handle transport and commissariat?

Through and along what line of *entrepôts* did Venice, Genoa, Seville ply their immense ventures? Who planted the vineyards of Bordeaux, Madeira, the Rhine-land, and from what stocks? Who, and what sort of man opened an aloe market in Socotra? Why, and on what instance, and how, did England and Flanders come to supply Europe, the one with wool, the other with fine linen and naperies?

Now of these and like questions—for of course I might multiply them by the hundred—I wish, first of all, to impress on you that they are of first importance if you would understand history; by which I mean, if you would take hold, in imagination, of the human motives which make history. Roughly (but, of course, very roughly) you may say of man that his wars and main migrations on this planet are ruled by the two great appetites which rule the strifes and migrations of the lower animals—love, and hunger. If under love we include the parental instinct in man to do his best for his mate and children (which includes feeding them, and later includes patrimonies and marriage portions) you get love and hunger combined, and doubled in driving power. Man, unlike the brutes, will also war for religion (I do not forget the Moslem invasion or the Crusades) and emigrate for religion (I do not forget the Pilgrim Fathers): but, here again, when a man expatriates himself for religion the old motives at least 'come in.' The immediate cause of his sailing for America is that authority, finding him obnoxious at home, makes the satisfaction of hunger, love and the parental instincts impossible for him save on condition of renouncing his faith, which he will not do.

Neither do I forget—indeed it will be my business, before I have done, to remind you—that hundreds of

thousands of men have left home and country for the sake
of learning. There lies the origin of the great universities.
But here again you will find it hard to separate—at all
events from the thirteenth century onward—the pure ardour
of scholarship from the worldly advancement to which it
led. Further, while men may migrate for the sake of
learning I do not remember to have heard of their making
war for it. On this point they content themselves with
calling one another names.

To cut this part of the argument short—Of all the men
you have known who went out to the Colonies, did not
nine out of ten go to make money? Of all the women, did
not nine out of ten go to marry, or to 'better themselves'
by some less ambiguous process?

We are used to think of Marathon as a great victory
won by a small enlightened Greek race over dense hordes
of the obscurantist East; of Thermopylae as a pass held
by the free mind of man against its would-be enslavers.
But Herodotus does not see it so. Herodotus handles the
whole quarrel as started and balanced on a trade dispute.
Which was it first—East or West—that, coming in the
way of trade, broke the rules of the game by stealing away
a woman? Was Io that woman? Or was Europa? Jason
sails to Colchis and carries off Medea, with the gold: Paris
sails to Sparta and abducts Helen—both ladies consenting.
Always at the root of the story, as Herodotus tells it, we find
commerce, coast-wise trading, the game of marriage by
capture: no silly notions about liberty, nationality, religion
or the human intellect. It is open to us, of course, to
believe that Troy was besieged for ten years for the sake
of a woman, as it is pleasant to read in Homer of Helen
watching the battlefield from the tower above the Skaian
gates, while the old men of the city marvel at her beauty,

saying one to another 'Small blame is it that for such a woman the Trojans and Achaeans should long suffer hardships.' But if you ask me, do I believe that the Trojan war happened so, I am constrained to answer that I do not: I suspect there was money in it somewhere. There is a legend—I think in Suetonius, who to be sure had a nasty mind—that Caesar first invaded Britain for the sake of its pearls; a disease of which our oysters have creditably rid themselves. And even nowadays, when we happen to be fighting far abroad and our statesmen assure us that 'we seek no goldfields,' one murmurs the advice of Tennyson's *Northern Farmer*

> Doänt thou marry for munny, but goä wheer munny is.

Money? Yes: but let your imagination play on these old trade-routes, and you will not only enhance your hold on the true springs of history; you will wonderfully seize the romance of it. You will see, as this little planet revolves back out of the shadow of night to meet the day, little threads pushing out over its black spaces—dotted ships on wide seas, crawling trains of emigrant waggons, pioneers, tribes on the trek, men extinguishing their camp-fires and shouldering their baggage for another day's march or piling it into canoes by untracked river sides, families loading their camels with figs and dates for Smyrna, villagers treading wine-vats, fishermen hauling nets, olive-gatherers, packers, waggoners, long trains of African porters, desert caravans with armed outriders, dahabeeyahs pushing up the Nile, busy rice-fields, puffs of smoke where the expresses run across Siberia, Canada, or northward from Capetown, Greenland whalers, Newfoundland codfishers, trappers around Hudson's Bay....

The main puzzle with these trade-routes is that while

seas and rivers and river valleys last for ever, and roads for long, and even a railroad long enough to be called a 'permanent way,' the traffic along them is often curiously evanescent. Let me give you a couple of instances, one in quite recent times, the other of today, passing under our eyes.

A man invents a steam-engine. It promptly makes obsolete the stage-coaches, whose pace was the glory of England. Famous hostelries along the Great North Road put up their shutters; weeds begin to choke the canals; a whole nexus of national traffic is torn in shreds, dissipated. A few years pass, and somebody invents the motor-car—locomotion by petrol. Forthwith prosperity flows back along the old highways. County Councils start re-metalling, tar-spraying; inns revive under new custom: and your rich man is swept past a queer wayside building, without ever a thought that here stood a turnpike gate which Dick Turpin or John Nevinson had to leap.

For a second change, which I have watched for a year or two as it has passed under my own eyes at the foot of my garden at home.—As you know, the trade of Europe from the West Coast of America around the Horn is carried by large sailing-vessels (the passage being too long for steamships without coaling stations). One day America starts in earnest to cut the Panama canal. Forthwith the provident British shipowner begins to get quit of these sailing-vessels: noble three- and four-masters, almost all Clyde-built. He sells them to Italian firms. Why to Italian firms? Because these ships have considerable draught and are built of iron. Their draught unfits them for general coasting trade; they could not begin to navigate the Baltic, for instance. Now Italy has deep-water harbours. But the Genoese firms (I am told) buy these ships for the second reason, that they are of iron: because while the Italian Government lays a crippling duty on ordinary iron, broken-up ship-iron may enter free. So, after a coastwise voyage or two, it pays to rip their plates out, pass them under the rollers and re-issue them for new iron; and thus for a few months these beautiful things that used to wing it home, five months without sighting land, and anchor under my garden, eke out a new brief traffic until the last of them shall be towed to the breakers' yard. Even in such unnoted ways grew, thrived, passed, died, the commercial glories of Venice, Spain, Holland.

## II

Now I will ask you to consider something more transient, more secret in operation, than ways of trade and barter— the ways in which plants disseminate themselves or are spread and acclimatised. For my pupils in Cambridge, the other day, I drew, as well as I could, in the New Lecture Theatre, the picture of an old Roman colonist in his villa in Britain, let us say in the fourth century—and you must remember that these Roman colonists inhabited Britain for a good four hundred years. Let me quote one short passage from that description:

The owner of the villa (you may conceive) is the grandson or even great-great-grandson of the colonist who first built it, following in the wake of the legionaries. The family has prospered, and our man is now a considerable landowner. He was born in Britain; his children have been born here; and here he lives a comfortable, well-to-do, out-of-door life, in its essentials I fancy not so very unlike the life of an English country squire today. Instead of chasing hares and foxes he hunts the wolf and the wild boar; but the sport is good, and he returns with an appetite. He has added a summer parlour to the house, with a northern aspect and no heating flues; for the old parlour he has enlarged the *praefurnium*, and through the long winter evenings sits far better warmed than many a master of a modern country house. A belt of trees on the brow of the rise protects him from the worst winds, and to the south his daughters have planted violet-beds which will breathe odorously in the spring. He has rebuilt and enlarged the slave quarters and some of the outhouses, replaced the stucco pillars around the atrium with a colonnade of polished stone, and, where stucco remains, has repainted it in fresh colours. He knows that there are no gaps or weak spots in his stockade fence—wood is always cheap. In a word he has improved his estate, is modestly proud of it; and will be content like the old Athenian, to leave his patrimony not worse but something better than he found it.

Such a family—it was part of my picture—would get many parcels from the land they still called 'home,' from the adored City—*urbe quam dicunt Romam*—The City; parcels fetched from the near military station on the great road where the imperial writ ran; parcels forwarded by those trade-routes of which I have spoken; parcels of books —scrolls, rather, or tablets; parcels of seeds—useful vegetables or pot-herbs, garden flowers, fruit-plants for the orchard, for the colonnade even roses with real Italian earth damp about their roots. For the Romans here were great acclimatisers, and upon Italy they could draw as a nursery into which the best fruits, trees, flowers of the world had been gathered after conquest and domesticated.

For beasts, it seems probable that they introduced the ass—with the mule as a consequence, the goat, certain new breeds of oxen; for birds, the peacock from India or Persia, the pheasant from Colchis, the Numidian guinea-fowl (as we call it), the duck, the goose (defender of the Capitol), possibly the dove and the falcon. But we talk of plants.

Britain swarmed with oak and beech, as with most of the trees of Gaul; but the Roman brought the small-leaved elm, ilex, cypress, laurel, myrtle, oriental plane, walnut; of fruits (among others) peach, apricot, cherry, probably the filbert; of vegetables, green peas (bless him!), cucumbers, onions, leeks; of flowers, some species of the rose (the China-rose, as we call it, for one), lilies, hyacinths, sweet-williams, lilacs, tulips.

But these were plants deliberately imported and tended. What of wild-flowers—the common blue speedwell, for instance? I am not botanist enough to say if the speedwell was indigenous in Britain: but, as a gardener in a small way, I know how it can travel! If the speedwell will not do, take some other seed that has lodged on his long tramp northward in the boot-sole of a common soldier in Vespasian's legion. The boot reaches Dover, plods on, wears out, is cast by the way, rots in a ditch. From it, next spring, Britain has gained a new flower.

### III

I come now to something more volatile, more fugacious yet—more secret and subtle and mysterious in operation even than the vagaries of seeds; I come to the wanderings, alightings, fertilisings of man's thought.

Will you forgive my starting off with a small personal experience which (since we have just been talking of a very common weed) may here come in not inappropriately? I received a message the other day from an acquaintance, a young engineer in Vancouver. He had been constructing a large dam on the edge of a forest, himself the only European, with a gang of Japanese labourers. But the rains proved so torrential, washing down the sides of the dam as fast as they were heaped, and half drowning the diggers, that at length the whole party sought shelter in the woods. There, as he searched about, my young engineer came upon a log-shanty, doorless, abandoned, empty, save for two pathetic objects left on the mud floor—the one a burst kettle, the other a 'soiled copy' (as the booksellers say) of one of my most unpopular novels. You see, there is no room for vanity in the narrative—a burst kettle and this book—the only two things not worth taking away! Yet I—who can neither make nor mend kettles—own to a thrill of pride to belong to a calling that can fling the *other thing* so far; and nurse a hope that the book did, in its hour, cheer rather than dispirit that unknown dweller in the wilderness.

But indeed—to come to more serious and less dead, though more ancient, authors—you never can tell how long this or that of theirs will lie dormant, then suddenly spring to life. Someone copies down a little poem on reed paper, on the back of a washing bill: the paper goes to wrap a mummy; long centuries pass; a tomb is laid bare of the covering sand, and from its dead ribs they unwind a passionate lyric of Sappho:

$$Οἰ\ μὲν\ ἰππήων\ στρότον,\ οἱ\ δὲ\ πέσδων,$$
$$οἱ\ δὲ\ νάων\ φαῖσ'\ ἐπὶ\ γᾶν\ μέλαιναν$$
$$ἔμμεναι\ κάλλιστον·\ ἔγω\ δὲ\ κῆν'\ ὄτ-$$
$$τω\ τις\ ἔραται.$$

Troops of horse-soldiers, regiments of footmen,
Fleets in full sail—'What sight on earth so lovely?'
Say you: but my heart ah! above them prizes
   Thee, my Belovèd.

I believe that this one was actually recovered from a rubbish-heap: but another such is unwrapped from the ribs of a mummy, of a woman thousands of years dead.

Was it bound about them because her heart within them perchance had beaten to it?—wrapped by her desire—by the hands of a lover—or just by chance? As Sir Thomas Browne says

What song the syrens sang, or what name Achilles assumed when he hid himself among women, though puzzling questions, are not beyond all conjecture. What time the persons of these ossuaries entered the famous nations of the dead, and slept with princes and counsellors, might admit a wide solution. But who were the proprietaries of these bones, or what bodies these ashes made up, were a question above antiquarism.

## IV

But these travels and resuscitations of the written or the printed word, though they may amuse our curiosity, are nothing to marvel at; we can account for them. I am coming to something far more mysterious.

A friend of mine, a far traveller, once assured me that if you wanted to find yourself in a real 'gossip shop'—as he put it—you should go to the Sahara. That desert, he informed me solemnly, 'is one great sounding-board. You scarcely dare to whisper a secret there. You cannot kill a man in the Algerian Sahara even so far south as Fort Mirabel but the news of it will be muttered abroad somewhere in the Libyan desert, say at Ain-el-Sheb almost as soon as a telephone (if there were one, which there is not) could carry it.'

Well doubtless my friend overstated it. But how do you account for the folk-stories? Take any of the fairy-tales you know best. Take *Cinderella*, or *Red Riding Hood* or *Hop o' my Thumb*. How can you explain that these are common not only to widely scattered nations of the race we call Aryan, from Asia to Iceland, but common also to savages in Borneo and Zululand, the South Sea Islander, the American Indian? The missionaries did not bring them, but found them. There are tribal and local variations, but the tale itself cannot be mistaken. Shall we choose *Beauty and the Beast*? That is not only and plainly, as soon as you start to examine it, the Greek tale of *Cupid and Psyche*, preserved in Apuleius; not only a tale told by nurses in Norway and Hungary; not only a tale recognisable in the Rig-Veda: but a tale told by Bornuese and by Algonquin Indians. Shall we choose *The Wolf who ate the Six Kids while the Seventh was hidden in the Clock-case*? That again is negro as well as European: you may find it among the exploits of Brer Rabbit. Or shall we choose the story of the adventurous youth who lands on a shore commanded by a wizard, is made spell-bound and set to do heavy tasks, is helped by the wizard's pretty daughter and escapes with her aid. That is the story of Jason and Medea: you may find all the first half of it in Shakespeare's *The Tempest*: but you may also find it (as Andrew Lang sufficiently proved) 'in Japan, among the Eskimo, among the Bushmen, the Samoyeds and the Zulus, as well as in Hungarian, Magyar, Celtic and other European household tales.'

Well, I shall not give a guess, this evening, at the way in which these immemorial tales were carried and spread. As Emerson said

> Long I followed happy guides
> I could never reach their sides;
> Their step is forth, and, ere the day
> Breaks up their leaguer, and away...
> But no speed of mine avails
> To hunt upon their shining trails...
> On eastern hills I see their smokes,
> Mixed with mist by distant lochs.

But the camp-fires around which men told these old tales have been broken up for the next day's march, and the embers trodden out, centuries and centuries ago.

## V

Well, now, let us work back for a few minutes towards this inexplicable thing through something of which, though marvellous, we may catch at an understanding. In the beginning of the eighth century in the remote north of a barbarous tract of England, a monk called Bede founds a school. He is (I suppose) of all men in the world the least —as we should put it nowadays—self-advertising. He just labours there, in the cloisters of Jarrow, never leaving them, intent only on his page, for the love of scholarship. Between his solitary lamp and the continent of Europe stretches a belt of fens, of fog, of darkness, broad as two-thirds of England; beyond that, the Channel. Yet the light reaches across and over. As Portia beautifully says

> How far that little candle throws his beams!
> So shines a good deed in a naughty world.

Men on the continent have heard of Jarrow: eyes are watching; in due time Bede's best pupil, Alcuin of York, gets an invitation to come over to the court of Charlemagne, to be its educational adviser. So Alcuin leaves York, soon to be destroyed with its fine school and library by the Scandinavian raiders (for your true barbarian, even when he happens to be a pedantic one, always destroys a library. Louvain is his sign-manual)—Alcuin leaves York and crosses over to France with his learning. Very well: but how can you explain it, save by supposing a community of men in Europe alert for learning as merchants for gold, kept informed of where the best thing was to be had, and determined to have it?

Yes, and we are right in supposing this. For when light begins to glimmer, day to break, on the Dark Ages (as we call them, and thereby impute to them, I think, along with their own darkness no little of ours, much as the British seaman abroad has been heard to commiserate 'them poor ignorant foreigners')—when daylight begins to flow, wavering, and spreads for us over the Dark Ages, what is the first thing we see? I will tell you what is the first thing *I* see. It is the Roads.

## VI

That is why—to your mild wonder, maybe—I began this lecture by talking of the old trade-routes. I see the Roads glimmer up out of that morning twilight with the many men, like ants, coming and going upon them; meeting, passing, overtaking; knights, merchants, carriers; justiciars with their trains, king's messengers riding post; afoot, friars—black, white and grey—pardoners, poor scholars, minstrels, beggar-men; pack-horses in files; pilgrims, bound for Walsingham, Canterbury, or to Southampton, to ship there for Compostella, Rome. For the moment let us limit our gaze to this little island. I see the old Roman roads—Watling Street, Ermine Street, Icknield Street, Akeman Street, the Fosse Way and the rest—hard-metalled, built in five layers, from the foundation or *pavimentum* of fine earth hard beaten in, through layers of large stones, small stones (both mixed with mortar), pounded *nucleus* of lime, clay or chalk, brick and tile, up to the paved surface, *summum dorsum*: one running north through York and branching, as Hadrian had diverted it, to point after point of the Great Wall; another coastwise towards Cornwall; a third for Chester and on to Anglesey, a fourth, embanked and ditched, through the Cambridgeshire fens:

I see the minor network of cross-roads, the waterways with their slow freight. You may remember a certain chapter of Rabelais, concerning a certain Island of Odes in which the highways keep moving, moving of themselves; and another passage in Pascal in which the rivers are seen as roads themselves travelling with the travellers[1]. Well, I see it like that; and the by-roads where outlaws lurked; the eastern fens where a hunted man could hide for years, the lanes leading to sanctuary. Some years ago, in Cornwall, I took an old map and decided to walk by a certain road marked on it. My host averred there was no such road in the parish; his brother, a district councillor, agreed. Well, being obstinate, I followed the old map, and found that road. What is more, after tracking it for a quarter of a mile, stooping under thorns and elders and pushing through brambles, I came in the dusk upon a fire and a tramp cooking his pot over it. It is a question which of us two received the greater shock.

## VII

Now in the Middle Ages, to keep these roads, and especially their bridges, in repair was one of the first calls on godly piety: nor will you ever begin to understand these Middle Ages until you understand their charitable concern for all travellers. Turn to your Litany, and read:

That it may please thee to preserve all that travel by land or by water, all women labouring of child, all sick persons, and young children; and to shew thy pity upon all prisoners and captives.

---

[1] It is observable how many of the great books of the world —the *Odyssey*, the *Æneid*, *The Canterbury Tales*, *Don Quixote*, *The Pilgrim's Progress*, *Gil Blas*, *Pickwick* and *The Cloister and the Hearth*—are books of wayfaring.

Read the evidence collected by Jusserand, and it will leave you with no doubt that the persons thus interceded for are not mixed together casually or carelessly; but that the keeping of the roads in repair was considered as a pious and meritorious work before God, of the same sort as attending the sick or caring for the poor, or comforting the prisoners. A religious order of *Pontiffs* (*Pontifices*, bridge-makers) built bridges in many countries of Europe. The famous Pont d'Avignon was one; Pont St Esprit (still in use) was another. A bridge with a chapel on it was one of the most familiar features of medieval England—a chapel and a toll-gate—the church being no more averse then than now to 'take up a collection.' Old London Bridge, with a chapel on it—Old London Bridge which for centuries was the marvel of England—Old London Bridge which (mind you) remained until the middle of the eighteenth century, until Dr Johnson's day, the *only* bridge spanning the Thames—was begun in 1176, finished in 1209, with its twenty arches, by subscription of the charitable.

I have no time, this afternoon, to draw you separate portraits of the men and women travelling these roads: but medieval literature (and especially our Chaucer) teems with pictures of them—pictures which, if read with imagination will 'depict your chamber walls around' as with a moving frieze. I shall conclude by choosing one familiar figure and for a minute or two presenting him to you, with what he meant: the Wandering Scholar.

## VIII

He is young, and poor, and careless. He tramps it on foot, and, when his pocket is empty, has no shame in begging: and men find a religious reward in doling him a penny: he being bound for one of the great universities, of whose learning the world has heard; for Oxford or Cambridge, or for Paris, or, farther yet, for Bologna, for Salerno. The roads of Europe are full of his like. No one quite knows how it has happened. The schools of Remigius and of William of Champeaux (we will say) have given Paris a certain prestige when a mysterious word, a rumour, spreads along the great routes, of a certain great teacher called Abelard whose voice will persuade a man's soul almost out of his body. The fame of it spreads almost as pollen is wafted on the wind: but spreads, and alights, and fertilizes. Forthwith, in all the far corners of Europe, young men are packing their knapsacks, bidding good-bye to their homes, waving back to the family at the gate as they dare the great adventure and fare (say) for Paris, intellectual queen of Europe.

The desire of the moth for the star! The ineffable spell of those great names—Paris, Oxford, Cambridge, Bologna, Salamanca! These young men reach at length the city which has been shining in their imagination. The light fades down its visionary spires to a narrow noisome medieval street in which the new-comer is one of a crowd, a turbulent crowd of the wantonest morals. But youth is there, and friendship: to be kept green through the years of later life, when all this young blood is dispersed, and the boys have shaken hands, not to meet again, and nothing remains in common to Dick of York and Hans of Hungary but a memory of the old class-room where they blew on their fingers, and took notes by the light of unglazed windows, and shuffled their numb feet in the straw.

Let me instance one such scholar—William Dunbar, the great fifteenth-century poet of Scotland. He was born about 1460, went to St Andrews and there graduated

Master of Arts in 1479: at once became an Observantine
Friar of the Franciscan Order, and started to travel: very
likely took ship first from Leith to the Thames, but anyhow
crossed to France—the little passenger ships of those days
carrying a hundred besides their crew. Says the old ballad:

> Men may leve alle gamys,
> That saylen to seynt Jamys!

(that is, to St James of Compostella)

> Ffor many a man hit gramys (vexes),
>     When they begyn to sayle.

> Ffor when they have take the see,
> At Sandwyche, or at Wynchylsee,
> At Brystow, or where that hit bee,
>     Theyr hertes begyn to fayle.

Then follows an extremely moving picture of the crowded
sea-sickness on board. We will not dwell on it. Somehow,
Dunbar gets to France; roves Picardy; is in Paris in 1491
and mingles with the scholars of the Sorbonne; returns
home by way of London (and be it remembered that the
kingdoms of England and his native Scotland were more
often antagonistic than not in those days); on his way
pauses to muse on London Bridge—that Bridge of which I
spoke to you a few minutes ago—'lusty Brigge of pylers
white' he calls it and breaks into this noble praise of our City:

> London, thou art of townes A per se.
>     Soveraign of cities, semeliest in sight,
> Of high renoun, riches and royaltie;
>     Of lordis, barons, and many a goodly knyght;
>     Of most delectable lusty ladies bright;
> Of famous prelatis, in habitis clericall;
>     Of merchauntis full of substaunce and of myght:
> London, thou art the flour of Cities all.

. . . . . .

2–2

Above all ryvers thy Ryver hath renowne,
　Whose beryall streamys, pleasaunt and preclare,
Under thy lusty wallys renneth down,
　Where many a swanne doth swymme with wyngis fair;
　Where many a barge doth saile, and row with are (oars);
Where many a ship doth rest with toppe-royall.
　O, towne of townes! patrone and not compare,
London, thou art the floure of Cities all.

My discourse, like many a better one, shall end with a moral.  I have often observed in life, and especially in matters of education—you too, doubtless, have observed —that what folks get cheaply or for nothing they are disposed to undervalue.  Indeed I suspect we all like to think ourselves clever, and it helps our sense of being clever to adjust the worth of a thing to the price we have paid for it. Now the medieval scholar I have been trying to depict for you was poor, even bitterly poor, yet bought his learning dear. Listen to Chaucer's account of him when he had attained to be a Clerk of Oxenford, and to enough money to hire a horse:

As leene was his hors as is a rake,
And he nas nat right fat, I undertake,
But looked holwe, and ther-to sobrely;
Ful thredbare was his overeste courtepy;
For he hadde geten hym yet no benefice,
Ne was so worldly for to have office;
For hym was levere have at his beddes heed
Twénty bookés clad in blak or reed
Of Aristotle and his philosophie,
Than robés riche, or fithele, or gay sautrie:
But al be that he was a philosophre,
Yet haddé he but litel gold in cofre;
But al that he myghte of his freendes hente
On bookés and his lernynge he it spente,
And bisily gan for the soulés preye
Of hem that yaf hym wher-with to scoleye.

How happy would such a poor scholar deem us, who have printed books cheap and plenty, who have newspapers brought to our door for a groat, who can get in less than an hour and a half to Oxford, to Cambridge, in a very few hours to Paris, to Rome—cities of his desire, shining in a land that is very far off! Nevertheless I tell you, who have listened so kindly to me for an hour, that in the commerce and transmission of thought the true carrier is neither the linotype machine, nor the telegraph at the nearest post office, nor the telephone at your elbow, nor any such invented convenience: but even such a wind as carries the seed, 'it may chance of wheat, or of some other grain': the old, subtle, winding, caressing, omnipresent wind of man's aspiration. For the secret—which is also the reward—of all learning lies in the passion for the search.

# BALLADS

## I

THE Ballad is, of all forms of poetry, about the most mysterious and singular: singular in its nature, mysterious not only in this but in its origin and its history.

We need not, here, today, trouble ourselves overmuch with its origin, which is much the same as Melchizedek's. Yet we may not wholly neglect the question. There are, as you probably know, two conflicting theories about it; and the supporters of each talk like men ready to shed blood, though for my part I hold that a very little common sense might reconcile them; since each theory contains a modicum of truth, and each, when pushed to the extreme, becomes frantically absurd.

On the one hand we have the theory—invented or pioneered by Herder, elaborated and oracularly preached by James Grimm—that these 'folk songs' were made *by* the 'folk'; that they burst into existence by a kind of natural and spontaneous generation in a tribe or nation, at that stage of culture when it is 'for all practical purposes an individual'; that a ballad comes, or came, into being much as the floating matter of a nebula condenses to form a star.

Now there is much truth in this. A tribe meets together to celebrate some occasion of common interest—a successful hunt, a prosperous foray, the wedding of its chief, the return of the god who brings summer, the end of a religious fast, a harvest home. As Professor Kittredge puts it in his Introduction to the abridgement of Child's great collection of Ballads:

The object of the meeting is known to all; the deeds which are to be sung, the dance which is to accompany and illustrate the singing, are likewise familiar to everyone. There is no such diversity of intellectual interests as characterises even the smallest company of civilised men. There is unity of feeling and a common stock, however slender, of ideas and traditions. The dancing and singing, in which all share, are so closely related as to be practically complementary parts of a single festal act. ...And this is no fancy picture. It is the soberest kind of science,—a mere brief chapter of descriptive anthropology, for which authorities might be cited without number.

Let me add that all this rests on the early discovery of man that all manual or bodily labour is enormously increased in effect, when timed to rhythm. So a regiment marches to a band; so the tramp of a column crossing a light bridge has to be broken lest the timed impact wreck the structure; so in the Peninsular War a British regiment heaved down a wall apparently immoveable, by lining against it and applying bodily pressure in successive rhythmical waves. So I, who have lived most of my life over a harbour, have seen and heard crews weighing anchor at windlass or capstan, or hauling on ropes, to a sailors' chanty, the solo-man intoning

We have a good ship and a jolly good crew!

the chorus taking him up

And away, away Rio!

So also—as we saw in one of the lectures last term, the children in our streets help out dance with song in such primitive games as 'Sally, Sally Waters,' 'Here come three Dukes a-riding,' or

> London Bridge is broken down
> Dance over, my Lady Lee!

The 'nebular' theorists have etymology, too, on their side, for what it is worth. Undoubtedly 'ballad' comes from the late Latin verb *ballare* 'to dance,' and should mean a song accompanied by dancing. Undoubtedly *some* old ballads with their refrains are referable to that origin— the famous old one of *Binnorie*, for example, with its chorus:

> There were twa sisters sat in a bour ;
> *Binnorie, O Binnorie!*
> There cam a knight to be their wooer,
> *By the bonnie milldams o' Binnorie.*

But this only applies to *some* ballads, and these a few. The theory, pushed to cover all, exposes its absurdity in Grimm's famous phrase '*das Volk dichtet.*'

That let in Schlegel, who at first had nibbled at Grimm's theory; as it lets in all those who maintain (and I think incontrovertibly) that, after all, in the end a ballad must be composed by *somebody*; and if you think a ballad can be composed by public meeting, just call a public meeting and try! In human experience poetry doesn't get written in that way: it requires an author. Moreover these ballads, as they come down to us, though overlaid by improvements by Tom, Dick and Harry, are things of genius, individual. As for etymology, if *balada* be the origin of *ballad*, so is it of the *ballet*: and so is *sonetto* the origin alike of a Beethoven's *Moonlight Sonata* and a Miltonic or Wordsworthian Sonnet. *Sonetto* means a song accompanied by instrumental music. It is all very well to say

that in Milton's hands 'the Thing became a trumpet';
but he certainly did not attune it to an instrumental
*obbligato*.

So you get the opposing 'artistic' theory; that our ballads
were composed by minstrels, gleemen, scôps, skalds, bards;
itinerant professional singers who composed them and
recited them at wakes, fairs and feasts, from town to town,
from hall to hall. Bishop Percy, and generations of scholars
after him, ascribed the composition of our ballads to these
professional minstrels almost as a matter of course. Nor,
to my mind, does Professor Kittredge make a very shrewd
point when he says

Such ballads as have been recovered from oral tradition in
recent times (and these...comprise the vast majority of our
texts) have not, except now and then, been taken down from
the recitation or the singing of minstrels, or of any order of
men who can be regarded as the descendants or representatives
of minstrels. They have almost always been found in the
possession of simple folk whose relation to them was in no
sense professional.

Quite so: and the simple answer is that the itinerant singer
died more than three hundred years ago. Whether of
inanition, passing out of vogue, or because the invention of
printing killed him, die he did: and he left no professional
descendants, because the printing-press had destroyed the
profession. You cannot collect ballads straight from the
lips of men three hundred years in the grave. Whence in
the world would anyone expect to recover them, save from
descendants of those simple folk *for* whom they were
written and from whom they have been transmitted?

Nor again does that seem to me a wholly triumphant
objection which Dr Gummere makes in his chapter on

Ballads in *The Cambridge History of English Literature*.
Says he:

> Still stronger proof lies in the fact that we have the poetry
> which the minstrels did make; and it is far removed from
> balladry.

This, to start with, is inaccurate. We have not the poetry
which the minstrels did make: we have only some of it.
But truly you could hardly have a better example of the
root-blindness which affects men who treat literature
learnedly as a dead thing, without having served an
apprenticeship in it as a living art. Anyone who practises
writing, quickly learns that appropriateness to subject and
audience is a great part of the secret of style; and the
defter, the more accomplished, the more tactful your artist
is, the less surely can you argue (say) from his manner in
light verse to his manner in a pulpit. Let me give you an
example. Here is the opening of a nineteenth century
ballad:

> Ben Battle was a soldier bold,
>     And used to war's alarms:
> But a cannon-ball took off his legs,
>     So he laid down his arms!
>
> Now as they bore him off the field,
>     Said he, 'Let others shoot,
> For here I leave my second leg,
>     And the Forty-second Foot!'

And here is the opening of a poem of about the same date:

> I saw old Autumn in the misty morn
> Stand shadowless like Silence, listening
> To silence, for no lonely bird would sing
> Into his hollow ear from woods forlorn....

Now, supposing the authorship of *Faithless Nelly Gray* to
be uncertain, what is more certain than that a scholar of

Dr Gummere's type would demonstrate the impossibility of its having been written by Thomas Hood 'because we *have* Hood's *Ode to Autumn*, and it is far removed from *Faithless Nelly Gray*'? Yet as a fact he would be quite wrong; because Hood wrote them both.

No: the really important point about ballads has nothing to do with 'who wrote them?' even if that could be discovered at this time of day. It matters very little to us, at any rate, if they were written *by* the people. What gives them their singularity of nature is that, whoever wrote them, wrote them *for* the people: and to this singularity, this individuality, by a paradox, their curious avoidance of the self-conscious personal touch will be found (I think) in no small degree to contribute.

## II

Let us first, however, establish that the Ballad has a nature of its own among poetic forms; is a thing by itself, or, as Professor Ker puts it, 'the Ballad is an Idea, a poetical Form, which can take up any matter and does not leave that matter as it was before.' Professor Ker goes on:

In spite of Socrates and his logic, we may venture to say, in answer to the question 'What is a Ballad?'—'A Ballad is *The Milldams of Binnorie* and *Sir Patrick Spens* and *The Douglas Tragedy* and *Childe Maurice*, and things of that sort.'

'And things of that sort.' Let me read you a sample or two of the sort of thing. Here are a few stanzas from *Tam Lin*:

> Janet has kilted her green kirtle
> A little abune the knee;
> And she has snooded her yellow hair
> A little abune her bree,
> And she is on to Miles Cross
> As fast as she can hie.

About the dead hour o' the night
　　She heard the bridles ring;
And Janet was as glad at that
　　As any earthly thing.

And first gaed by the black, black steed,
　　And syne gaed by the brown;
But fast she gript the milk-white steed
　　And pu'd the rider down.

She 's pu'd him frae the milk-white steed,
　　An' loot the bridle fa',
And up there rase an eldritch cry,
　　'True Tam Lin he's awa'!'

　　.　　.　　.　　.　　.

They shaped him in her arms at last
　　A mother-naked man;
She cast her mantle over him,
　　And sae her love she wan.

Up then spak' the Queen of Fairies,
　　Out o' a bush o' broom,
'She that has borrow'd young Tam Lin
　　Has gotten a stately groom.'

Out then spak' the Queen o' Fairies,
　　And an angry woman was she,
'She 's ta'en awa' the bonniest knight
　　In a' my companie!

'But what I ken this night, Tam Lin,
　　Gin I had kent yestreen,
I wad ta'en out thy heart o' flesh,
　　And put in a heart o' stane.

'And adieu, Tam Lin! But gin I had kent
　　A ladye wad borrow'd thee,
I wad ta'en out thy twa grey e'en
　　Put in twa e'en o' tree.

'And had I the wit yestreen, yestreen,
    That I have coft this day,
I'd paid my teind seven times to hell
    Ere you had been won away!'

Here are some verses from a carol-ballad—that of *The Seven Virgins*:

All under the leaves and the leaves of life
    I met with virgins seven,
And one of them was Mary mild,
    Our Lord's mother of Heaven.

'O what are you seeking, you seven fair maids,
    All under the leaves of life?
Come tell, come tell, what seek you
    All under the leaves of life?'

'We're seeking for no leaves, Thomas,
    But for a friend of thine;
We're seeking for sweet Jesus Christ,
    To be our guide and thine.'

'Go down, go down, to yonder town,
    And sit in the gallery,
And there you'll see sweet Jesus Christ,
    Nail'd to a big yew-tree.'

.    .    .    .    .

Then He laid His head on His right shoulder,
    Seeing death it struck Him nigh—
'The Holy Ghost be with your soul,
    I die, Mother dear, I die.'

O the rose, the gentle rose,
    And the fennel that grows so green!
God give us grace in every place
    To pray for our king and queen.

Furthermore for our enemies all
    Our prayers they should be strong:
Amen, good Lord; your charity
    Is the ending of my song.

Or here two stanzas from another old narrative carol—
*I saw Three Ships*:

O they sail'd in to Bethlehem!
    —To Bethlehem, to Bethlehem;
Saint Michael was the sterèsman,
    Saint John sate in the horn.

And all the bells on earth did ring
    —On earth did ring, on earth did ring:
'Welcome be thou Heaven's King,
    On Christ's Sunday at morn!'

Here are three stanzas from a ballad in dialogue—*Edward,
Edward*:

'Why does your brand sae drop wi' blude,
    Edward, Edward?
Why does your brand sae drop wi' blude,
    And why sae sad gang ye, O?'—
'O I hae kill'd my hawk sae gude,
    Mither, mither;
O I hae kill'd my hawk sae gude,
    And I had nae mair but he, O.'

'Your hawk's blude was never sae red,
    Edward, Edward;
Your hawk's blude was never sae red,
    My dear son, I tell thee, O.'—
'O I hae kill'd my red-roan steed,
    Mither, mither;
O I hae kill'd my red-roan steed,
    That erst was sae fair and free, O.'

'Your steed was auld, and ye hae got mair,
    Edward, Edward;
Your steed was auld, and ye hae got mair;
    Some other dule ye dree, O.'—
'O I hae kill'd my father dear,
    Mither, mither;
O I hae kill'd my father dear,
    Alas, and wae is me, O!'

And here is one from a ballad with a refrain—*The Cruel Brother*. [But I should say in parenthesis that, of the ballads which survive to us, few carry a refrain: they are far fewer than to justify the stress laid on the refrain by those who trace all balladry to communal dancing. The vast majority as we have them, tell straightforward stories straightforwardly.]

There were three ladies play'd at the ba',
    *With a hey ho! and a lily gay!*
By came a knight and he woo'd them a'
    *As the primrose spreads so sweetly.*
        *Sing Annet, and Marret, and fair Maisrie,*
        *As the dew hangs i' the wood, gay ladie!*

Here are some verses of a Robin Hood Ballad which tells how Robin, having won the King's pardon on condition that he lived at the King's court, homesickened for the green-wood and Barnesdale, and at length obtained leave for a week's furlough there:

When he came to greenè-wood
    In a merry mornìng,
There he heard the notès small
    Of birds merry singìng.
'It is far gone,' said Robin Hood,
    'That I was latest here;
Me list a little for to shoot
    At the dunnè deer.'

Robin slew a full great hart;
   His horn then gan he blow,
That all the outlaws of that forèst
   That horn they couldè know,

And them together gatherèd
   In a little throw;
Seven score of wight young men
   Came ready on a row,

And fairè didden off their hoods,
   And set them on their knee:
'Welcome,' they said, 'our dear mastèr,
   Under this green-wood tree!'

Robin dwelt in greenè-wood
   Twenty year and two;
For all dread of Edward our King,
   Again would he not go.

    .    .    .    .    .

Christ have mercy on his soul,
   That died upon the rood!
For he was a good outlàw,
   And did poor men much good.

And here finally is the well-known *Lyke Wake Dirge*, so weird and wonderful:

This ae nighte, this ae nighte,
   —*Every nighte and alle*,
Fire and fleet and candle-lighte,
   *And Christe receive thy saule.*

When thou from hence away art past,
   —*Every nighte and alle*,
To Whinny-muir thou com'st at last:
   *And Christe receive thy saule.*

If ever thou gavest hosen and shoon,
  —*Every nighte and alle*,
Sit thee down and put them on:
  *And Christe receive thy saule.*

If hosen and shoon thou ne'er gav'st nane
  —*Every nighte and alle*,
The whinnes sall prick thee to the bare bane;
  *And Christe receive thy saule.*

From Whinny-muir when thou may'st pass,
  —*Every nighte and alle*,
To Brig o' Dread thou com'st at last;
  *And Christe receive thy saule.*

. . . . . .

From Brig o' Dread when thou may'st pass,
  —*Every nighte and alle*,
To Purgatory fire thou com'st at last;
  *And Christe receive thy saule.*

If ever thou gavest meat or drink,
  —*Every nighte and alle*,
The fire sall never make thee shrink;
  *And Christe receive thy saule.*

If meat or drink thou ne'er gav'st nane,
  —*Every nighte and alle*,
The fire will burn thee to the bare bane;
  *And Christe receive thy saule.*

This ae nighte, this ae nighte,
  —*Every nighte and alle*,
Fire and fleet and candle-lighte,
  *And Christe receive thy saule.*

Now I put it to you, Gentlemen, that all these extracts, with all their difference of subject, have a common note at once unmistakable and indefinable; a note which attests them all as poetical and as alike, and yet as somehow different from any other poetry we know: certainly different from the note of any conscious poet known to us. And this peculiar ballad-note persists, perseveres, even down to late imes and whether the ballad sing high or low.

It can sing high:

> Half-owre, half-owre to Aberdour
> 'Tis fifty fathom deep;
> And there lies gude Sir Patrick Spens
> Wi' the Scots lords at his feet.
>
> *(Sir Patrick Spens)*

Or

> About the dead hour o' the night
> She heard the bridles ring.      *(Tam Lin)*

It can sing low:

> Then up bespake the bride's mother—
> She never was known to speak so free—
> 'Ye'll not forsake my only daughter
> Though Susie Pye has crossed the sea.'
>
> *(Young Beichan)*

Or

> An' thou sall marry a proud gunner;
> An' a proud gunner I'm sure he'll be.
>
> *(The Great Silkie)*

It can gallop:

> O there was horsing, horsing in haste
> And cracking of whips out owre the lee.
>
> *(Archie of Cawfield)*

Or it can be merely flat pedestrianism:

> There was slayne upon the Scottès' side
> For sooth as I you say,
> Of four and fifty thousand Scottes
> Went but eighteen away.      *(Otterburn)*

But always it is unmistakable, and like no other thing in poetry.

## III

Now as we study this peculiar unmistakable note, one or two things become clear to us.

It becomes clear, in the first place, that whether or not these ballads 'wrote themselves' (as Grimm put it)—whether or not they were written *by* the people, as they certainly were *for* the people—it is no accident of chance or of time that withholds from us all knowledge of the authorship. We discern that somehow anonymity belongs to their very nature; that anonymity, impersonality, permeates their form and substance. Let me apply a test which I have applied elsewhere. If any known man ever steeped himself in balladry, that man was Sir Walter Scott, and once or twice, in *Proud Maisie* and *Brignall Banks* he came near to distil the essence. If any man, taking the Ballad for his model, has ever sublimated its feeling and language in a poem

seraphically free
From taint of personality,

that man was Coleridge, and that poem *The Ancient Mariner*. If any writer today alive can be called a ballad-writer of genius, it is the author of *Danny Deever* and *East and West*. But suppose a bundle of most carefully selected ballads by Scott, Coleridge, Kipling, bound up in a volume with such things as *Clerk Saunders, Cospatrick, Robin Hood and the Monk*,—you feel (do you not?)—you know—they would intrude almost, though not quite, as obviously as would a ballad of Rossetti's or one from Morris's *Defence of Guinevere*.

Now we must never forget that the old ballads have come down to us orally, after centuries of transmission through the memories of simple people who never thought of them as 'literature'; that in fact, barring the broadsides, they never were 'literature' or written speech at all, until Bishop Percy in 1765 started apologetically to make them literature. And so I have sometimes fancied that the impress of their authorship may merely have worn away as the impress on a shilling wears away after years of transference from pocket to pocket. There is something in this; and there is more in it when we remind ourselves that a ballad written on one memorable event will often have been recast and refurbished to commemorate another. Let me illustrate this from the fortunes of a beautiful one, *The Queen's Marie*. You all know it:

> When she cam to the Netherbow port,
>   She laugh'd loud laughters three;
> But when she cam to the gallows foot
>   The tears blinded her e'e.
>
> 'Yestreen the Queen had four Maries,
>   The night she'll hae but three;
> There was Marie Seaton, and Marie Beaton,
>   And Marie Carmichael, and me.
>
> .    .    .    .    .    .
>
> 'O little did my mother ken,
>   The day she cradled me,
> The lands I was to travel in,
>   Or the dog's death I wad d'ee!'

Now Professor Child collected and printed some twenty-eight variants and fragments of this ballad—which is a somewhat late one, if its story can be traced no farther back than 1563. Then, or about then, Mary Queen of Scots had four Maries among her gentlewomen—Mary Seaton, Mary Beaton, Mary Fleming and Mary Livingstone: and Knox, in his *History of the Reformation*, relates a tragic scandal, involving the queen's apothecary and 'a

Frenchwoman that served in the Queen's bedchamber.'
This is substantially the story told in the ballad; which,
however, in most versions makes the king himself ('the
highest Stewart of a'') to be the male sinner. But why
Mary Carmichael and Mary Hamilton in place of Mary
Fleming and Mary Livingstone? Well, we must travel to
Russia for it. There, after the marriage of one of the
ministers of Peter the Great's father with a Hamilton, that
Scottish family ranked with the Russian aristocracy. The
Czar Peter was punctilious that all his Empress Catharine's
maids-of-honour should be remarkable for good looks; a
niece of the minister's wife, a Mary Hamilton, was appointed for her extreme beauty. There followed an amour
with one Orloff, an aide-de-camp to the Czar: a murdered
babe was found, the guilt traced to Mary. Orloff was
arrested but subsequently reprieved or pardoned. Mary
Hamilton suffered execution, on March 14, 1719.

Here, then, we have a story almost precisely similar to
that of the ballad; with a real Mary Hamilton, who does
not occur historically in the scandal of 1563. *Her* date is
1719: and yet no one with the smallest sense of poetry
can put the ballad so late, or anywhere within a hundred
years of 1719. Obviously the old ballad was re-adapted to
fit a new scandal in high life. But, mark yet again, the
stanza about the four Maries is merely incidental and has
nothing to do with the scandal: and as that kind of scandal
has been common enough in courts from very early times,
there is no reason why the ballad should not reach back to
very early times, have been adapted to the business of 1563
and re-adapted to the business of 1719. Speculation, to
be sure!—But that is where you always are with ballads.

Yet—no! Our simile of the shilling worn in passing
from pocket to pocket, will not do. For it is not only that

the more a ballad suffers wear and change the more it remains the same thing: it is that the more it wears, the more it takes that paradoxically sharp impress, the impress of impersonality.

## IV

The next point to be noted of the Ballad is its extra-ordinary rapidity of movement. Rapidity of movement has been preached of the epic by Horace, and by Matthew Arnold specially commended in Homer. But, for rapidity, these innominate lays beat anything in Homer. I remember studying, once on a time, a treatise on American cocktails and coming on the following rider to a recipe for a mixed liquor entitled Angler's Punch—'N.B.—This punch can also be put up in bottles, so that the Angler may lose no time.'

Now the true Ballad is put up (doubtless upon experience) so that the audience loses no time:

> The king sits in Dunfermline town
> Drinking the blude-red wine;

and forthwith he asks

> 'O whare will I get a skeely skipper
> To sail this new ship o' mine?'

And 'What,' Professor Ker very pertinently asks, 'What would the story of Sir Patrick Spens be worth if it was told in any other way—with a description of the scenery about Dunfermline, the domestic establishment of the King of Norway, and the manners of the court?'

This rapidity of movement is constant, and (if it be not begging the question to term it so) 'professional.' There are tricks, *clichés*, always at hand to carry us from one incident to another:

> They hadna sail'd a league, a league
> A league but barely three...

when something new is ready to happen. The little foot-
page, after he has duly louted on his knee and received the
fatal message, always runs with it and has to cross a river:

> And whan he came to the broken briggs
> He bent his bow and swam...

actually bending his bow (I suppose) and laying his arms
across it while he kicked his legs, swimming: and so on.
Almost always you will find the intervals hurried over in
this way, and it would seem that the audience (easy with
conventions as simple folk are) took these formulae for
granted as the right and proper bridges over dull gaps of
narrative.

## V

Now let me draw four lines for you: the first two across
the map, the second two in historical time.

Across the map of England and Scotland I draw my
first and northerly line from the Firth of Forth to the Clyde;
my second and southerly from Newcastle-on-Tyne to St
Bee's Head. Between these two lines lie almost all the
places most celebrated in ballad poetry. They crowd
thicker and thicker as on either side they near the ancient
Border of the two kingdoms: but I draw no line here,
being cautious; because, as you know, the men of whose
deeds the ballads were written—deeds ranging from pitched
battle to the reiving of cattle and brides—drew no line at
all, either in morals or geographically: even mathematically,
none known to Euclid. Their line had breadth. At the
thinnest it was a strip; and they called this strip 'The De-
batable Land.'

Now of course all the many ballads of Border fights

and forays—from *Otterburn* and *Chevy Chase* to such things as *Kinmont Willie*, *Hobbie Noble*, *Jamie Telfer in the Fair Dodhead*—come from this region. But these are not the very best; and the curious fact is that all the very best ballads, which have little or nothing to do with forays and cattle-lifting, also come from this region, and specially among the upper waters of Tweed and Teviot. A fact is a fact, and a guess is a guess, and I can bring no evidence for what is nevertheless my sincere belief—that once on a time there lived just hereabouts a man of genius who gave these songs their immortal impress and taught it to others (also he may have taught the children of the Border the use of the Bow).

> Now these, the songs, remain to eternity,
>   Those, only those, the bountiful choristers,
>     Gone—those are gone, those unremembered
>     Sleep and are silent in earth for ever.

As Ecclesiasticus has it:

Let us now praise famous men, and our fathers that begat us....Leaders of the people by their counsels, and by their knowledge of learning meet for the people, wise and eloquent in their instructions: such as found out musical tunes, and recited verses in writing....All these were honoured in their generations, and were the glory of their times. There be of them that have left a name behind them, that their praises might be reported. And some there be, which have no memorial; who are perished, as though they had never been; and are become as though they had never been born; and their children after them.

Or as Lucian put it:

Mortal are the things of mortals: we abide as they decay.
—If you doubt this proposition, put it just the other way.

I have told you my guess. But this much is no guess.—
Folk-poetry being a large word, we do our scientific sense
of it some help by fixing the best of this form of our
literature upon a certain folk inhabiting a certain limited
region, which we find to lie between the Forth and the
Tyne.

## VI

I draw my other two lines, which are chronological, at
the years 1350 and 1550. Almost all the evidence shows
that the Ballad with the impress we know upon it, rose,
flourished, declined, within that period. The author of
*Piers Plowman* mentions 'rimes of Robin Hood and
Randolph, earl of Chester' as known to the common men
of his day: Wynkyn de Worde printed the *Lytell Geste of
Robyn Hood*, as we have it, about a hundred and forty
years later: but when, yet a century later, we come to the
Elizabethan dramatists, we find them holding the Ballad in
open derision. Nor could the Last Minstrel of that age (if
we suppose any such person) have pleaded with Scott's
that

> The bigots of an iron time
> Had called his harmless art a crime...

the truth being rather that he had delighted the company
long enough. A new poetry had come into vogue with
Wyat and Surrey, Grimald, Lodge, Lyly and the rest,
and as an artistic poem the Ballad had passed into the
shade. It has been, as we know, impersonal—curiously
impersonal—in utterance: its business had been to tell a
plain tale. The lyrical cry seldom breaks from it. When
it does, at its most poignant, it breaks forth thus, as Leesome
Brand buries the wife he has killed unwittingly:

There is a feast in your father's house,
*The broom blooms bonnie and sae it is fair—*
It becomes you and me to be very douce,
*And we'll never gang down to the broom nae mair.*

. . . . . . .

He's houkit a grave, long, large and wide,
*The broom blooms bonnie and sae it is fair—*
He's buried his auld son doun by her side,
*And we'll never gang down to the broom nae mair.*

It was nae wonder his heart was sair
*The broom blooms bonnie and sae it is fair—*
When he shool'd the mools on her yellow hair,
*And we'll never gang down to the broom nae mair.*

And this is exquisitely poignant: but it is not personal, as any stanza of Wyat's is personal: for instance

> And wilt thou leave me thus,
> That hath loved thee so long
> In wealth and woe among:
> And is thy heart so strong
> As for to leave me thus?
> Say nay! say nay!

The ballad-metre had been simple, almost to jog-trot (you remember Dr Johnson's parody). The Ballad had never philosophised its emotion. But now listen to this:

> To love and to be wise,
> To rage with good advice,
> Now thus, now than, so goes the game,
> Uncertain is the dice:
> There is no man, I say, that can
> Both love and to be wise.

Keeping that stanza in mind, let us take an old ballad which has happened to attract in its time (1) the Eliza-

bethan improver and (2) the eighteenth century embel-
lisher, and see what a mess they both make of it, with the
best intentions. It begins, much in the fashion of the *Nut
Brown Maid*, with a set dialogue—a dialogue between a
lover and a pilgrim who is returning from the shrine of St
Mary at Walsingham: and it starts in the true ballad-style.
(I may mention that it is quoted in Fletcher's play *The
Knight of the Burning Pestle*.)

> 'As ye came from the holy land
>     Of Walsingham,
> Met you not with my true love
>     By the way as you came?'

> 'How shall I know your true love,
>     That have met many a one
> As I came from the holy land,
>     That have come, that have gone?'

> 'She is neither white nor brown,
>     But as the heavens fair;
> There is none hath her form divine,
>     In the earth or the air.'

> 'Such a one did I meet, Good Sir,
>     Such an angelique face:
> Who like a nymph like a queen did appear
>     In her gait, in her grace.'

> 'She hath left me here alone,
>     All alone, as unknown,
> Who sometime did me lead with herself
>     And me loved, as her own.'

> 'What's the cause that she leaves you alone
>     And a new way doth take,
> That sometime did love you as her own
>     And her joy did you make?'

'I have loved her all my youth,
But now am old, as you see,
Love loves not the falling fruit,
Nor the withered tree.'

So there you have, with its pretty anapaests, a little
ballad-poem, fairly ended and closed. Now comes in the
improving Elizabethan with a sophisticated moral:

Know that Love is a careless child,
And forgets promise past:
He is blind, he is deaf when he list,
And in faith never fast.

His desire is a dureless content
And a trustless joy;
He is won with a world of despair
And is lost with a toy.

*  *  *

But true love is a durable fire
In the mind ever burning,
Never sick, never old, never dead,
From itself never turning.

You see how far we are getting from the simplicity of the
first stanzas? But worse, far worse, is to come. Bishop
Percy found this version in his folio: but a 'corrected'
copy was forwarded to him by his friend Mr Shenstone.
Now Shenstone was by no means a negligible poet, in the
eighteenth century manner: but tripping anapaests were
too vulgar for him and thus he emended:

'As ye came from the holy land
Of blessed Walsingham,
O met you not with my true love
As by the way ye came?'

'How shall I know your true love
    That have met many a one,
As I came from the holy land
    That have both come and gone?'...

and so on, with a deadening fist on each stanza, until we
come to this superlative ending:

But true love is a lasting fire,
    Which viewless vestals tend,
That burns for ever in the soule,
    And knowes not change nor end.

'Viewless Vestals'!

## VII

Now let me say, before concluding, that greatly as I
adore these old ballads I do so not idolatrously. They are
genuine poetry, peculiar poetry, sincere poetry; but they
will not compare with the high music of Spenser's *Epithalamion* or of Milton's *Lycidas* or of Keats' *Nightingale*. In
truth any comparison of the ballads with these would be
unfair as any comparison between children and grown
folk. They appealed in their day to something young in
the national mind. They have all the winning grace of
innocence: but they cannot scale the great poetical heights
any more than mere innocence can scale the great spiritual
heights. Tears and fasting and bread eaten in sorrow go to
*that* achievement: and who has not known and tried them
and been tried by them

He knows you not, ye heavenly powers!

I but contend today that to complain of the fifteenth
century as unpoetical, turning your ear aside from this out-
pouring of spring numbers to listen to the bagpipe drone
of a Lydgate or a Hoccleve, is to sin like—a handbook.

## VIII

I end with a ballad—*The Old Cloak*—which, as we are, with all our shortcomings, a humorous nation, deserved a long line of children, but in fact had few or none. I cannot think why. It runs in antiphon like the *Nut Brown Maid*, and is a supposed dialogue between a good man and his wife:

*He.*  This winter's weather it waxeth cold,
    And frost it freezeth on every hill,
And Boreas blows his blast so bold
    That all our cattle are like to spill.
Bell, my wife, she loves no strife;
    She said unto me quietlye,
'Rise up, and save cow Crumbock's life!
    Man, put thine old cloak about thee!'

O Bell my wife, why dost thou flyte?
    Thou kens my cloak is very thin:
It is so bare and over worn,
    A crickè thereon cannot renn.
Then I'll no longer borrow nor lend;
    For once I'll new apparell'd be;
To-morrow I'll to town and spend;
    For I'll have a new cloak about me.

*She.*  Cow Crumbock is a very good cow:
    She has been always true to the pail;
She has help'd us to butter and cheese, I trow,
    And other things she will not fail.
I would be loth to see her pine.
    Good husband, counsel take of me:
It is not for us to go so fine—
    Man, take thine old cloak about thee!

*He.*  My cloak it was a very good cloak,
    It hath been always true to the wear;
But now it is not worth a groat:
    I have had it four and forty year'.

Sometime it was of cloth in grain:
   'Tis now but a sigh clout, as you may see:
It will neither hold out wind nor rain;
   And I'll have a new cloak about me.

*She.* It is four and forty years ago
   Since the one of us the other did ken;
And we have had, betwixt us two,
   Of children either nine or ten:
We have brought them up to women and men:
   In the fear of God I trow they be:
And why wilt thou thyself misken?
   Man, take thine old cloak about thee!

*He.* O Bell my wife, why dost thou flyte?
   Now is now, and then was then:
Seek now all the world throughout,
   Thou kens not clowns from gentlemen:
They are clad in black, green, yellow and blue,
   So far above their own degree.
Once in my life I'll take a view;
   For I'll have a new cloak about me.

*She.* King Stephen was a worthy peer;
   His breeches cost him but a crown;
He held them sixpence all too dear,
   Therefore he called the tailor 'lown.'
He was a king and wore the crown,
   And thou'se but of a low degree:
It's pride that puts this country down:
   Man, take thy old cloak about thee!

*He.* Bell my wife, she loves not strife,
   Yet she will lead me, if she can:
And to maintain an easy life
   I oft must yield, though I'm good-man.
It's not for a man with a woman to threap,
   Unless he first give o'er the plea:
As we began, so will we keep,
   And I'll take my old cloak about me.

# THE HORATIAN MODEL
# IN ENGLISH VERSE

## I

BEFORE discussing—as I am engaged to do this morning—the Horatian model in English verse, give me leave, Gentlemen, to delimit the ground.

I am not going to discuss the many attempts to translate Horace—to turn him straight into English verse—with their various degrees of ill-success. They are so many, so various, as to raise one's moral estimate of Man—*improbus homo*, indomitable still—against all experience and the advice of his friends—'still clutching the inviolable shade!' The talents of the late Mr Gladstone were multifarious and large indeed in their ambit; yet we may agree that the *Odes* of Horace were not haunts meet for him:

> Piscium et summâ genus haesit ulmo...

as he translated

> The elm-tree top to fishy kind
> Gave harbour....

Or we might paraphrase—in words addressed to another Father William:

> And yet you incessantly stand on your head:
> Do you think, at your age, it is right?

My own judgment would place Conington first among competitors, with Sir Theodore Martin second (surpassing him in occasional brilliance but falling some way behind on the long run), De Vere third. But these preferences are idle; since, in the ordinary sense, Horace defies translation.

Secondly I shall ask your leave, this morning, to plant our Deus Terminus yet nearer—on this side of the *Satires* and *Epistles*. I do not deny that this fences off a deal of the genuine Horace, or pretend that we can either summarise or appreciate the total Horace if we leave the *Satires*, *Epistles* and *Ars Poetica* out of account. But I shall take little more than a glance at them because his magic secret does not hide anywhere in these, and as a fact their style, in all its essentials, has been caught and transferred into modern literature—certainly into French and English— by a number of writers. I am not talking of satire as we commonly understand it today. When we think of satire we think of Juvenal and of Swift, of Pope, of Churchill, who derive from Juvenal—not from Horace, save but occasionally and then at a remove. Satire has come to connote something of savagery, of castigation: and I am glad to be quit of it this morning because (to be frank) it is a form of art that appeals to me very faintly, especially in warm weather—and this not merely because bad temper is troublesome, but for the reason that anger—valuable, indeed, now and then—is a passion of which it behoves all men to be economical. To be indignant is better than to be cynical: to rage is manlier than to sneer. Yet to be constitutionally an angry man—to commence satirist and set up in business as a professionally angry man—has always seemed to me, humanly speaking (and therefore artistically), more than a trifle absurd. Few will deny Juvenal's force: yet after all as we open a volume entitled *Sixteen Satires of Juvenal*, what are we promised but this —'Go to! I, Decimus Junius Juvenalis, propose to lose my temper on sixteen several occasions'? In fact, when we have been scolded through eleven or so of these efforts, even such a genius as his is left laboriously flogging a dead horse; reduced to vituperating some obscure Egyptians for an alleged indulgence in cannibalism. Say, now, that you pick up tomorrow's newspaper and read that a missionary has been eaten in the Friendly Islands. You will pay his exit the tribute of a sigh: but the distance, and anthropology, will soften the blow. You will not fly into a passion. At the most you will write to *The Times* calling for a punitive visit by one of His Majesty's ships. More likely you will reckon your debt of humanity discharged by ingeminating, after Sir Isaac Newton, 'O Diamond, Diamond, thou little knowest what thou hast devoured!'

## II

But the *Satires* of Horace were not satires in this sense at all: no more satires than this week's *Punch* is the London Charivari. *Satura* literally translated, is a 'hotch potch': in letters it becomes (as we should say) a 'miscellany,' a familiar discourse upon this, that and the other. With a man of Horace's temperament such *sermones* could not miss to be urbane, gossipy, sententious a little, wise a great deal, smooth in address, pointed in wit; and I dare to say that these qualities have been achieved by his English and French descendants. To prove that the trick can be done even in a straight translation, let me quote you an example from Conington's version of Epistle 2, Book II.—*Luculli miles*, etc.:

> A soldier of Lucullus's, they say,
> Worn out at night by marching all the day,
> Lay down to sleep, and, while at ease he snored,
> Lost to a farthing all his little hoard.

This woke the wolf in him;—'tis strange how keen
The teeth will grow with but the tongue between;—
Mad with the foe and with himself, off-hand
He stormed a treasure-city, wall'd and manned,
Destroys the garrison, becomes renowned,
Gets decorations and two hundred pound.
Soon after this the general had in view
To take some fortress—*where*, I never knew;
He singles out our friend, and makes a speech
That e'en might drive a coward to the breach:
'Go, my fine fellow! go where valour calls!
There's fame and money too inside those walls.'
'I'm not your man,' returned the rustic wit:
'He makes a hero who has lost his kit.'

At Rome I had my schooling, and was taught
Achilles' wrath, and all the woes it brought;
At classic Athens, where I went erelong,
I learnt to draw the line 'twixt right and wrong,
And search for truth, if so she might be seen,
In academic groves of blissful green;
But soon the stress of civil strife removed
My adolescence from the scenes it loved,
And ranged me with a force that could not stand
Before the might of Caesar's conquering hand.
Then when Philippi turned me all adrift
A poor plucked fledgling, for myself to shift,
Bereft of property, impaired of purse,
Sheer penury drove me into scribbling verse:
But now, when times are altered, having got
Enough, thank Heaven, at least to boil my pot,
I were the veriest madman if I chose
To write a poem rather than to doze.

Now I would repeat here an observation of Newman's
which I have quoted before to you, that to invent a style is
in itself a triumph of genius—'It is like crossing a country

before roads are made between place and place' and the author who does this deserves to be a classic both because of what he does and because he can do it. But this originality being granted in the Horace of the *Satires* and *Epistles*, I do think that our English translator has caught the trick of the Latin, or very nearly. But he derives it, of course, through countless English imitators of Horace who repeat the model at short intervals, mile after mile, for two centuries and more. Here, for example, is Bishop Hall (1574–1656):

> Late travelling along in London way,
> We met—as seem'd by his disguised array—
> A lusty courtier, whose curlèd head
> With abron locks was fairly furnishèd.
> I him saluted in our lavis wise;
> He answers my untimely courtesies.
> His bonnet vail'd, or ever he could think,
> The unruly wind blows off his periwinke.
> He 'lights, and runs, and quickly hath him sped
> To overtake his overrunning head.

Here is the note in Cleiveland (1613–1658):

> Lord! what a goodly thing is want of shirts!

Here in Oldham (1653–1683):

> Some think themselves exalted to the Sky
> If they light in some noble Family:
> Diet, an Horse, and thirty Pounds a Year,
> Besides th' Advantage of his Lordship's ear.

Here it is in Dryden:

> Shimei, whose youth did early promise bring
> Of zeal to God and hatred to his King,
> Did wisely from expensive sins refrain,
> And never broke the Sabbath, but for gain.

Here in Pope (of Dr Bentley):

> Before them march'd that awful Aristarch:
> Plough'd was his front with many a deep remark.
> His hat, which never vail'd to human pride,
> Walker with reverence took, and laid aside.

Still mark it in Goldsmith:

> In arguing, too, the Parson own'd his skill,
> For e'en though vanquish'd, he could argue still;
> While words of learned length and thund'ring sound
> Amazed the gazing rustics all around,
> And still they gaz'd, and still the wonder grew
> That one small head could carry all he knew...

in Cowper:

> O barb'rous! wouldst thou with a Gothic hand
> Pull down the schools? What! all the schools i' th' land?
> Or throw them up to liv'ry nags and grooms,
> Or turn them into shops and auction rooms?...

even in Crabbe:

> We had a sprightly nymph. In every town
> Are some such sprights, who wander up and down.
> She had her useful arts, and could contrive,
> In time's despite, to stay at twenty-five;—
> 'Here will I rest; move on, thou lying year,
> This is my age, and I will rest me here.'

## III

But the truly magical secret of Horace lies nowhere in his *Satires* and *Epistles*. It lies in his *Odes*. *There* haunts that witchery of style which, the moment you lose grasp of it, is dissipated into thin air and eludes your concentrated pursuit—so that, like any booby schoolboy, you have your hands for certain over the butterfly, and, opening them ever so cautiously, find it gone. You know the man's story (he has told much of it in the lines of which I have read Conington's paraphrase)—born of parentage humble enough, but with gentle instincts; a University man, of Athens and (as Mr Verdant Green said) proud of the title —a brief spell of military campaigning, which he did not pretend to enjoy, and enjoyed all the less because his was the losing side—then Rome again with a brief experience of what in Rome corresponded to Grub Street—then a post in the Quaestor's office—put it at a Treasury Clerkship—then Maecenas, patronage, success, with a small Sabine farm to which he could retreat whenever his footsole tired of pavement—a small country house, frugal but with good wine in the cellar, and silver, well-rubbed, on the table:

> A bin of wine, a spice of wit,
> A home with lawns enclosing it,
> A living river by the door,
> A nightingale in the sycamore,

or their equivalents. Horace enjoyed these rural comforts the better that they were tinged with a delicate nostalgia for the Town. He would have said with Locker-Lampson

> Whatever my mood is, I love Piccadilly.

You know the man too. If you know him well, he is not a mere 'man-about-town' but so commonsensical at that as to seem a kind of glorified 'man-in-the-street,' with a touch of Browning's poet, in *How it strikes a Contemporary*:

> I only knew one poet in my life...
> He took such cognizance of men and things...
> Yet stared at nobody,—you stared at him,
> And found, less to your pleasure than surprise,
> He seemed to know you and expect as much...

an Epicurean, yet a patriot with firm views about patriotism;
a middle-aged man who had 'lived' (as we say) and made
no secret about it, yet by luck or good management had so
nursed his pleasures as to keep a steady supply for the
advance of age, calling in humour and earned wisdom to
amuse when appetite failed.

You know, too, what kind of poetry the man wrote, and
have had his characteristics labelled for you a score of
times—its clarity, its nicety, its felicity of phrase, its instinct
for the appropriate, its delicate blend of the scholar and
the gentleman. I suppose one must add 'its faultless taste'
since the one trick of Horace which offends me has somehow passed for permissible from his day to ours and apparently still delights the audiences of the late Sir William
Schwenck Gilbert—I mean the trick of gibing at a woman
because she is growing old and losing her beauty ('Little
Butter-cup,' 'There will be too much of me in the coming
by-and-by' and the like), a form of merriment which I
shall continue to regard as inhumane until Death reconciles
me with the majority and may be (but I wonder) with
enlightenment.

Critics there are, I find, who deny the title of 'poet,' or
at any rate of 'great poet,' to Horace, because they miss in
him certain qualities—moral earnestness, σπουδαιότης,
splendour of diction, intensity of imagination, and other
abstract virtues, with all of which, though necessary to *their*
notion of a poet, Horace rather deliberately had nothing
to do. I point to one or two of the odes, say the grand
Cleopatra towards the end of Book i, or the yet more celebrated Regulus in Book iii, and observe that if our critics'
notion of poetry do not include these, why then it had
better be enlarged to make room for them: and further
that I do not care one obol (as neither would he—yet he

knew—*exegi monumentum*) what is meant by 'great poet' or even 'poet' in the abstract, when here you have a man whose verses have such a diuturnity of charm that, as has been said, 'Men so wide apart in temperament and spirit as Newman and Gibbon, Bossuet and Voltaire, Pope and Wordsworth, Thackeray and Gladstone, Rabelais and Charles Lamb, seem all to have felt in Horace a like attraction and to have made of him an intimate friend.' And I solemnly subscribe to the sentence that follows. 'The magnetic attraction to which such names as these collectively testify is a phenomenon of sufficient rarity to invite some attempt to explain it.'

## IV

Whatever the secret be, our English poets have been chasing it these four hundred years. Start, if you will, with Sir Thomas Wyat's *Vixi puellis*:

> They flee from me that some time did me seek,
> With naked foot stalking within my chamber....

Take Campion's *Integer Vitae*:

> The man of life upright,
>     Whose guiltless heart is free
> From all dishonest deeds,
>     Or thought of vanity....

Take Wotton in a like strain:

> How happy is he born and taught
> That serveth not another's will;
> Whose armour is his honest thought,
> And simple truth his utmost skill.

Or, varying the strain, take Peele's *Farewell to Arms*:

> His golden locks Time hath to silver turn'd...
> His helmet now shall make a hive for bees.

Or Ben Jonson's

> Still to be neat, still to be drest,
> As you were going to a feast.

Take Herrick's

> Gather ye rosebuds while ye may.

Or Randolph's *Ode to Master Anthony Stafford, to hasten him into the country*.

Or—to leave quoting by fragments—let me read this one lyric of Campion's, in two stanzas:

> Now winter nights enlarge
>   The number of their hours,
> And clouds their storms discharge
>   Upon the airy towers.
> Let now the chimneys blaze
>   And cups o'erflow with wine;
> Let well-tuned words amaze
>   With harmony divine.
> Now yellow waxen lights
>   Shall wait on honey love,
> While youthful revels, masques, and courtly sights
>   Sleep's leaden spells remove.
>
> This time doth well dispense
>   With lovers' long discourse;
> Much speech hath some defence,
>   Though beauty no remorse.
> All do not all things well;
>   Some measures comely tread,
> Some knotted riddles tell,
>   Some poems smoothly read.
> The summer hath his joys,
>   And winter his delights;
> Though love and all his pleasures are but toys,
>   They shorten tedious nights.

The second stanza loses grip for a while; but the whole is right Horace.

## V

But let us come to more learned imitation—learned, that is to say in the matter of technique. It has been pointed out —first I believe by our present Poet Laureate—that Milton in his sonnets was deliberately adapting the sonnet-form to the Horatian ode; and the suggestion had only to be made, to convince.

> Lawrence, of vertuous Father vertuous Son,
>     Now that the Fields are dank, and ways are mire,
>     Where shall we sometimes meet, and by the fire
> Help waste a sullen day; what may be won
> From the hard season gaining? Time will run
>     On smoother till Favonius re-inspire
>     The frozen earth; and clothe in fresh attire
> The Lily and Rose, that neither sow'd nor spun.
> What neat repast shall feast us, light and choice,
>     Of Attick taste, with Wine, whence we may rise
> To hear the Lute well toucht, or artful voice
>     Warble immortal Notes and Tuscan Ayre?
>     He who of those delights can judge, and spare
>     To interpose them oft, is not unwise.

Consider that, or the sonnet to Cromwell, or that to Cyriack Skinner:

> To day deep thoughts resolve with me to drench
>     In mirth, that after no repenting draws;
>     Let Euclid rest and Archimedes pause,
>     And what the Swede intend, and what the French.
> To measure life, learn thou betimes, and know
>     Toward solid good what leads the nearest way;
>     For other things mild Heav'n a time ordains,
> And disapproves that care, though wise in show,
>     That with superfluous burden loads the day,
>     And when God sends a cheerful hour, refrains.

I shall discuss the technique later: but who can read that
without exclaiming *Aut Flaccus aut nullus*? Now I proceed to point out that just when Milton was endeavouring
to break up the old Petrarcan sonnet, and refit it to the
Horatian ode, he was Cromwell's Latin Secretary and, for
comrade in the Secretaryship, he had another poet, Andrew
Marvell, who was at the same time working upon the
Horatian model though in a different way: and I have
sometimes wondered what Cromwell would have said had
he happened in and caught his two secretaries at it, one at
either end of the table. Now Andrew Marvell's *Garden*
and *Coy Mistress* are Horatian enough, as are his later
satires written under Charles II. But his *Horatian Ode
upon Cromwell's Return from Ireland* has been praised as
the most Horatian thing not written by Horace. Therefore
I pause upon it, and will quote its two best-known stanzas,
those upon Charles I at his execution:

> He nothing common did, or mean,
> Upon that memorable scene,
>   But with his keener eye
>   The axe's edge did try;
>
> Nor called the gods with vulgar spite
> To vindicate his helpless right;
>   But bowed his comely head
>   Down, as upon a bed.

What falls short, here, of Horace's

> scilicet invidens
> privata deduci superbo
> non humilis mulier triumpho,

or of the conclusion of the great Regulus ode, where the
noble Roman, simply obedient to his honour, parts the
anguished crowd that would have stayed him at any price,

and goes back to certain death by torture, cheerful as though bound on a week-end release from business?

> Tendens Venafranos in agros
> Aut Lacedaemonium Tarentum.

I should consent—and no two words about it—with the general opinion that this 'falling close' is one of the noblest on which ever poem concluded, were it not that a critic whose judgment as a rule I respect—Dr Tyrrell of Dublin[1] —has twice at least and recently derided it for sheer bathos. I hardly know where to begin with such a pronouncement. Yet if Dr Tyrrell be somehow mixing up Venafrum or Tarentum with some reminiscences of cheap week-end tickets, I would remind him that Venafrum was a home of Samnite warriors (who were among the best), while the verse itself reminds him of Tarentum's origin; and the noble associations of both may not improbably have crossed Horace's mind as it usually crosses his reader's. A great deal depends in poetry on the dignity thus associated with a name: the 'busman's call 'Penny all the way—Shepherd's Bush to Marble Arch!' would (as Dr Tyrrell will allow) be enhanced in allurement if beneath that Arch sat Jove, father of gods and men, if that bush sheltered pastoral Apollo with the flock of Admetus. But take the verse alone, in its own beauty. Is it possible that Dr Tyrrell's ear has missed to hear the lovely tolling vowels of 'Venafranos in agros' or missed to note the even more lovely cadences of vowels on which it chimes a close—'*Au*t L*a*c*e*d*ae*m*o*n*iu*m T*a*r*e*nt*u*m'?

Gentlemen, listen to this—though you listen to nothing else this morning. You would write strongly and melodiously, so that out of the strong should come forth sweetness.

---

[1] Now *valde deflendus*.

Well, as the *strength* of style rests on the verb—*verbum*, the word; as your noun is but a name and your adjective but an adjunct to a name, while along your verb runs the nerve of life; so, if you would write melodiously, *through your vowels must the melody run*. What are the consonants, all of them? Why, as their name implies, they are assistant sounds, naught by themselves. Some of them are mute, and known as 'mutes.' With others you can make queer abortive noises. But take any phrase, of verse or prose, renowned for beauty:

> O passi graviora, dabit deus his quoque finem...
>
> Tuba mirum spargens sonum...
>
> In la sua volontade è nostra pace...
>
> Open the temple gates unto my love,
> Open them wide that she may enter in!...
>
> Bare ruin'd choirs, where late the sweet birds sang...
>
> Where the bright Seraphim in burning row
> Their loud-uplifted Angel trumpets blow...

Give unto the Lord the glory due unto his name: worship the Lord in the beauty of holiness.

The voice of the Lord is upon the waters; the God of glory thundereth: the Lord is upon many waters...

I say that after allowing all you can for the beautiful assistance of consonants you must recognise that the vowels carry the main music.

It amazes me therefore to find Stevenson—himself a melodious writer—in an Essay *On Some Technical Elements of Style* playing about with these secondary letters P, V, H, and the rest, while almost totally neglecting the great vowels, and that though he had this very Regulus ode in his thoughts at the time, for he quotes it with special approval. Yet what is approval worth when he talks of 'these thundering verses'? What?—'thundering'?—

> Aut Lacedaemonium Tarentum.

No: I will swear, not thundering; or if thundering, but as a storm rolling away southward beyond distant hills and muted into calm.

Now in Marvell's stanza

> Nor called the gods with vulgar spite
> To vindicate his helpless right;
> But bowed his comely head
> Down, as upon a bed...

with its shrill, spitting, 'spite'—the sharp *i* and *s* concentrating on the labial *p*—lowered at once and duplicated as by echo in the thinner *i* and softer sibilant *v* (spite—to vind)—followed by the quiet

> But bowed his comely head
> Down...

(mark the full *o*'s)

> Down, as upon a bed...

in Marvell's stanza we do in sense and sound get the Horatian falling close almost perfectly suggested. Yes: but not quite perfectly, I think. For why? Because the ear is all the while attending for the rhyme—'head,' 'bed.' That is the nuisance with rhyme: it can hardly help suggesting the epigram, the clinch, the verse 'brought off' with a little note of triumph. In rhyme you cannot quite 'cease upon the midnight with no pain.' Your ear expects the correspondent, and 'you are not quite happy until you get it.' Bearing this in mind, will you turn to a sonnet of Milton, whose sonnets (as everyone knows) are peculiarly constructed? Bearing this in mind, and that Milton was labouring to make the English sonnet a vehicle for the Horatian ode, you see, in a flash, two things:

(1) You see why Milton rejected the Shakespearean form, with its three quatrains and rhymed distich coming at the end as a *clou* of the whole: *e.g.*

> If this be error and upon me proved,
> I never writ, nor no man ever loved.

For this epigrammatic *clou*, of all things, Milton wished to avoid.

(2) You see why Milton, wisely preferring the Petrarcan form, yet made the curious innovation of running octave and sestet together into a continuous strain. He wanted to rid it of all clinches, to ease the ear of expectancy, to let the rhymes come unobtrusively—as if they just happened. That is why he cut, so to speak, through the cross-trench and let the verse run, on the Horatian model, like a brook.

## VI

Just here, Gentlemen, I find myself on the verge of preaching heresy, and shall break off for a minute or so to hazard some other reasons why our poets, though pursuing it by the pack, have never captured the whole of Horace's secret. You will find the Restoration men—Etherege, Dorset, Sedley and others in full chase. But all these men missed—as did Prior and his followers in the next age— the serious side of Horace; or, more likely perhaps, it did not interest them. Yet it is just his real concern in high affairs of state that gives Horace his Roman *gravitas*, a sense of which weights our understanding of the man even while he is telling of his banquets or his lights-of-love.

> The merchant, to secure his treasure,
> Conveys it in a borrowed name:
> Euphelia serves to grace my measure,
> But Chloe is my real flame.

This trifling is all very well: but, to arrive at Horace, you must ballast your light boat with such things as

> Delicta majorum immeritus lues....

Or,

> Divis orte bonis, optime Romulae
> Custos gentis....

You may demur: but I shall be ready, at some future occasion, to defend my firm belief that of all our poets the one who, but for a stroke of madness, would have become our English Horace, was William Cowper. He had the wit, with the underlying moral seriousness. You will find almost everywhere in his poetry hints of the Horatian touch. Moreover he had originality along with the Horatian sense of the appropriate. But darkness came down on him and he was lost. I am sure, at any rate, that if any one of you wish to rival Horace, he must not be afraid of serious politics, of saying—as his conviction moves him:

> Asquith, a name to resound for ages!...

Or,

> Asquith, thou most unhappy man of men!...

Or, when the assault was (or was not) intended upon the province of Ulster,

> Carson, our chief of men, who thro' a cloud
> Not of war only, but detractions rude....

Or,

> Carson, bound Jephthah to thy Covenant....

To employ a classical phrase, I will not presume to dictate.

## VII

Time presses, and we need not pursue this part of our enquiry to its end, because the moral of it—that the style is the man himself—may be easily applied. Praed has Horatian touches, but he again is light, sometimes light to flimsiness—*levitas cum levitate*. Landor has all the classical sense of form, and his best I dare almost aver to be as good as Horace:

> Tanagra! think not I forget
> Thy beautifully storied streets!

But he is heir rather to the Greek anthologists than to Augustan Rome. In our own day Mr Austin Dobson has chiselled out exquisite lyrics in the Horatian mode: but one feels that the poet's gaze all the while is retrospective, wistful of the past, a trifle *distrait* about current affairs; that its quiz is of a period, of a bygone age; that it follows the fair Gunnings along the Mall:

> The ladies of St James's
> Go swinging to the play...

in sedan chairs; whereas it is a part again of Horace's secret to be for all time, just because he belonged to his age and—curiously interested in it, perceiving it to be full of meaning and worth any man's interest—caught, fixed, the flying hour.

I revert, then, to what is more important. We can compass the Horatian manner; we can compass the Horatian phrase. The Horatian phrase is everywhere in our best literature—even in the Book of Common Prayer. See how it leaps out in the *Te Deum*, 'When thou hadst *overcome the sharpness of death*.' That is right Horace. But what of his metrical secret? If you examine Horace's work—what he did (which I shall ever preach to you as the first business of criticism)—one thing, quite ludicrously missed by a good half of his translators and imitators, leaps forthwith to the eye. *He chose the most tantalisingly difficult foreign metres and with consummate skill tamed them to the Latin tongue.* Once grasp this—once grasp that the secret of the odes cannot at any rate be dissociated from their metrical cunning —once perceive that in an Alcaic, major Sapphic, fourth Asclepiad, fifth Archilochian, Horace is weaving his graceful way through measures intricate as any minuet, gavotte, saraband—and you will start by laughing out of court all easy renderings (say) in flat-footed octosyllables such as Gladstone's

> What if our ancient love awoke
> And bound us with its golden yoke?
> If auburn Chloe I resign,
> And Lydia once again be mine.

> [They stopped the coach and all got out
> And in the street they walked about:
> But when the rain began to rain
> In haste they all got in again.]

In the common anapaestic measure I know of but one happy experiment, and that is Thackeray's gay little rendering of *Persicos odi*:

> But a plain leg of mutton, my Lucy,
>     I prithee get ready at three;
> Have it smoking, and tender and juicy,
>     And what better meat can there be?

But now listen to this, by Sir Theodore Martin:

> I myself, wooed by one that was truly a jewel,
>     In thraldom was held, which I cheerfully bore
> By that vulgar thing Myrtăle, tho' she was cruel—
>     But I reckon Sir Theodore Martin was more.

[The last line is conjectural.]

Shall we turn to such pretty measures as Tennyson employed in *The Daisy* and the Invitation to F. D. Maurice (noting by the way their delicate metrical differences, especially in the last line of the stanza: the one

> Of olive, aloe, and maize and vine,

the other

> Making the little one leap for joy)?

For a sample:

> You'll have no scandal while you dine,
> But honest talk and wholesome wine,
>     And only hear the magpie gossip
> Garrulous under a roof of pine.

That is better: and good, too, is our present laureate's *Invitation to the Country*:

> And country life I praise,
>     And lead, because I find
>     The philosophic mind
> Can take no middle ways;
>
> She will not leave her love
>     To mix with men, her art
>     Is all to strive above
> The crowd, or stand apart.

## VIII

But it is time to return on my steps and state, very briefly, my heresy; a heresy (you will say) killed long ago in Elizabethan times, when Spenser and Gabriel Harvey, Sidney, Campion and Daniel disputed the question of rhyme *v.* no-rhyme, and the honours happily rested with the rhymers. Yes, most happily; and yet—that the narrow gauge system on our railways has killed the broad gauge does not prove to every mind that the narrow gauge is the better. And moreover rhyme did not kill no-rhyme. On the contrary, were this demand suddenly and dreadfully sprung upon you, 'Of rhyme and no-rhyme in English Poetry you must today surrender one or the other—which shall it be?' You would find it a desperate choice. Could you abandon *Paradise Lost* with *Hamlet*, *Macbeth*, *Lear*—all the great Elizabethan drama?

Well, as everybody knows, Daniel had the better in the dialectic, and, we have to own, the better cause. At all events we have plenty of reason to congratulate ourselves that Campion's arguments were not convincing. But as a poet Campion none the less was a better man than Daniel and as it were casually, by an experiment, just by 'taking and doing the thing' as we say, he had really proved this much of his case—that, though we cannot afford to lose rhyme, there is plenty of room for the unrhymed lyric too. Listen to this:

> Rose cheek'd Laura, come;
>   Sing thou smoothly with thy beauty's
> Silent music, either other
>   Sweetly gracing.
>
> Lovely forms do flow
>   From concent divinely framèd:
> Heaven is music, and thy beauty's
>   Birth is heavenly.
>
> These dull notes we sing
>   Discords need for helps to grace them;
> Only beauty purely loving
>   Knows no discord;
>
> But still moves delight,
>   Like clear springs renew'd by flowing,
> Ever perfect, ever in them-
>   -selves eternal.

Campion never pretended that classical metres could be exactly transferred to our English use: nay he expressly denied it and was at pains to lay down lines on which they can be *adapted*. In this he was undoubtedly right. Attempts have been made *e.g.* to write pure Sapphics in English, the most successful being one by Doctor Watts who (though some of you may remember him as the author of 'Let dogs delight To bark and bite') was a considerable poet, and wrote excellent Sapphics on the unpromising subject (by which I mean, unpromising for Sapphics) of the Day of Judgment:

> When the fierce North-wind with his airy forces
> Rears up the Baltic to a foaming fury;
> And the red lightning with a storm of hail comes
> Rushing amain down.
>
> . . . . .
>
> Such shall the noise be, and the wild disorder
> (If things eternal may be like these earthly),
> Such the dire terror when the great Archangel
> Shakes the creation;
>
> Tears the strong pillars of the vault of Heaven,
> Breaks up old marble, the repose of princes,
> Sees the graves open, and the bones arising,
> Flames all about them.

He ends:

> O may I sit there when He comes triumphant,
> Dooming the nations! then ascend to glory,
> While our Hosannas all along the passage
> Shout the Redeemer.

This, in the polite language of its own generation, is monstrous fine: but I once spent time and pains on studying the English Sapphic and convinced myself that our language cannot be constrained to it naturally or without a necessary loss beyond all likely gain. Nevertheless I sometimes wonder that Milton—no lover of rhyme, as his preface to *Paradise Lost* tells you—having gone some way to efface the impression of rhyme in his Horatian sonnets, did not experiment farther and try working on the Horatian model without it.

That is my heresy. If any one in this room feels that he has at all the Horatian *genius* (I use the word in its Latin sense, not its modern) I would commend to him the experiment of rendering it in delicate metres divorced from rhyme, being convinced that Horace's secret, though it may never be captured in that way, will be captured in no other. Then if he ask 'But have you any one concrete example to encourage me?' I answer 'Yes, one: and it is Collins's *Ode to Evening*. There, if anywhere in English poetry, if he seek, he will find the secret of Horace's 'falling close':

> Then lead, calm votaress, where some sheety lake
> Cheers the lone heath, or some time-hallow'd pile,
>     Or upland fallows grey
>     Reflect its last cool gleam.
>
> Or if chill blustering winds, or driving rain,
> Prevent my willing feet, be mine the hut
>     That from the mountain's side
>     Views wilds and swelling floods,
>
> And hamlets brown, and dim-discover'd spires,
> And hears their simple bell, and marks o'er all
>     Thy dewy fingers draw
>     The gradual dusky veil.

You will not accept the suggestion, but I commend it to your thoughts; and so, for today, conclude.

# ON THE TERMS 'CLASSICAL'
# AND 'ROMANTIC'

## I

I PROPOSE to say a few words upon two terms—'Classical' and 'Romantic'—with which your handbooks to English Literature have doubtless by this time made you familiar, though you will not find them frequently mentioned in the masterpieces of which those handbooks are supposed to treat.

They are adjectives, epithets, assigning to this and that work of art either this or that of two qualities which (I shall not be wrong in saying) these handbooks suggest to you as opposed to one another, if not mutually exclusive. Further, I shall not be much amiss, perhaps, in suggesting that you have no very sharply defined idea of how exactly, or exactly why, or exactly how far, these qualities 'classical' and 'romantic' stand opposed one to another, or of how far exactly they exclude one another. You can say of this paper that it is white, of the print typed upon it that it is black: your sense accurately distinguishes and you can indicate with finger or pencil precisely where black impinges on white.

But we cannot draw any such line between 'classical' and 'romantic' work; since, to begin with, the difference between them is notional and vague (even if we admit a true difference, which at this point I do not). You have probably not defined the difference, even to yourselves.

You have (I dare to assert) a positive opinion that Pope is 'classical' and Blake 'romantic,' as you have (I dare to suggest) a notion that it means something like the difference between St Paul's Cathedral and Westminster Abbey. We may get to something a little more definite than that before we have done, this morning. But for the moment maybe I do few of you a grave injustice in assuming that you are more confident of 'knowing what you mean' by the epithets 'classical' and 'romantic' than of your ability to determinate their difference in words: and that if suddenly presented with some line or passage of literature, admittedly beautiful, and halted with the demand 'Is this classical? or is it romantic?' you might conceivably find yourself yet more diffident. Say, for example, you were thus held up to stand and deliver yourself upon Hamlet's dying speech to Horatio:

> If thou didst ever hold me in thy heart,
> Absent thee from felicity awhile
> And in this harsh world draw thy breath in pain
> To tell my story...

or upon this from *Lycidas*:

> Together both, ere the high lawns appeared
> Under the opening eyelids of the Morn,
> We drove a-field...

or upon the last words of Beatrice Cenci:

> Give yourself no unnecessary pain,
> My dear Lord Cardinal. Here, Mother, tie
> My girdle for me, and bind up this hair
> In any simple knot; ay, that does well.
> And yours I see is coming down. How often
> Have we done this for one another; now
> We shall not do it any more. My Lord,
> We are quite ready. Well, 'tis very well...

I say that I may do you no grave injustice in supposing that, confronted with those famous passages and having it suddenly demanded of you 'Is this classical? or romantic? —Under which king, Besonian? speak, or die!'—you would hesitate, might be inclined to temporise, might even save your life by admitting that, all things considered, there was a little bit of both about them.

Well, that is a useful admission! It concedes that the two epithets describe things which may be contraries, but are at any rate not contradictories, are not mutually exclusive, may meet in the same work, may blend in a line or phrase even, and so as to be hard to distinguish.

## II

But let us go a little further. These epithets—'romantic' and 'classical'—vague and indeterminate as we have found their frontiers to be, are still epithets, adjectives by which we qualify real things. We say, for example, of *The Faerie Queene*, that it is 'romantic,' of *Samson Agonistes* that it is 'classical' and, *The Faerie Queene* and *Samson Agonistes* being things, good nouns concrete and substantive, poems actually printed in ink upon paper, we can bring our epithets to the test. They are not epithets like 'blue' or 'wine-dark' (of the sea), like 'acid' (of the taste of lemon), like 'deafening' (of the explosion of a shell), like 'penetrating' (of the effect of a bullet). They are not epithets of sense, but of concept. They belong to the realm of opinion. If you say of a bullet that it is penetrating, you appeal to the evidence of sense, and the description cannot be denied. If you say of the German behaviour in Belgium that it has been beastly, you appeal to opinion: and a German will say it has been humane, not godlike.

Still your epithet—'romantic' or 'classical'—is, however indeterminate, referable to a real thing, and can be corrected by it.

But when we go a step further yet, and convert our epithets of opinion—'classical,' 'romantic'—into abstract nouns—'classicism,' 'romanticism'—I would point out to you with all the solemnity at my command that we are at once hopelessly lost: lost, because we have advanced a vague concept to the pretence of being a thing; hopelessly lost, because we have removed our concept out of range of the *thing*; which is not only what matters, but the one and single test of our secondary notions. 'The play's the *thing*.' *Hamlet, Lycidas* or *The Cenci* is the *thing*. Shakespeare, Milton, Shelley did not write 'classicism' or 'romanticism.' They wrote *Hamlet, Lycidas, The Cenci*.

## III

Gentlemen, I would I could persuade you to remember that you are English, and to go always for the thing, casting out of your vocabulary all such words as 'tendencies,' 'influences,' 'revivals,' 'revolts.' 'Tendencies' did not write *The Canterbury Tales*; Geoffrey Chaucer wrote them. 'Influences' did not make *The Faerie Queene*; Edmund Spenser made it: as a man called Ben Jonson wrote *The Alchemist*, a man called Sheridan wrote *The Rivals*, a man called Meredith wrote *The Egoist*.

Now it is the weakness of Germans in criticism that, not having a literature of their own to rank with the great, but being endowed as a race with an unusual talent for philosophising, they habitually think and talk of a literary masterpiece—which is a work of art achieved in the way of practice—as though it were a product, or at any rate a by-product, of philosophy, producible by the methods of philosophy. And the reason, I believe, why the Germans have never had, nor are likely to have, a literature comparable with the best does not lie in the uncouthness of their language. Our English tongue was uncouth enough until, in their varied ways Chaucer and Wyat and Spenser; the early translators and Tindale; Sidney, Hooker; Milton, Waller and Dryden; Browne and Clarendon and Berkeley; Pope, Addison, Swift, Gibbon, Johnson (to go no further) practised and polished it. But these men, and specially, of course, the earlier ones, saw the difficulty of their task as a condition of overcoming it. You can scarcely open a preface of the old translators, or of an early collection of Songs and Sonnets, but your eye falls on some passage of pathetic apology for our unmusical and barbarous tongue, in which nevertheless the poor fellow affirms that he has done his best

> To find out what you cannot do,
>     And then—to go and do it...

That was the way of the men who made English Literature exquisite.

Now the Germans would seem never, or rarely, to have felt that humility of mind before the great masterpieces, that prostration in worship, that questioning and almost hopeless self-distrust, out of which, by some divine desire of emulation yet persistent in him, the artist is raised to win the crown. Yes, I do assure you, Gentlemen, that George Herbert's loveliest lyric, though it speak of holier things, may be applied in parable, and scarcely with exaggeration, to the attitude of the true artist before his art. Let me remind you of it:

> Love bade me welcome; yet my soul drew back,
>     Guilty of dust and sin.
> But quick-eyed Love, observing me grow slack
>     From my first entrance in,
> Drew nearer to me, sweetly questioning
>     If I lack'd anything.

'A guest,' I answer'd, 'worthy to be here':
    Love said, 'You shall be he.'
'I, the unkind, ungrateful? Ah, my dear,
    I cannot look on thee.'
Love took my hand, and smiling did reply,
    'Who made the eyes but I?'

'Truth, Lord, but I have marr'd them: let my shame
    Go where it doth deserve.'
'And know you not,' says Love, 'Who bore the blame?'
    'My dear, then I will serve.'
'You must sit down,' says Love, 'and taste my meat.'
    So I did sit and eat.

## IV

Apparently (I say) the Germans feel no such humility
of soul before other peoples' great literature: and by consequence—it may seem a strange thing to assert of them—
they don't take pains enough; they don't take the trouble
because they don't see it. They are at ease in other peoples'
Sions: but they cannot build one, and moreover it is not
Sion. Literature being literature, and philosophy philosophy,
you can never understand or account for literature—still
less can you produce literature—by considering it in terms
of philosophy; that is, by being wise about it in a category
to which it does not happen to belong.

So when a German, cultivating his own bent, bemuses
himself with a theory that Wordsworth (we will say) wrote
naturalism, or that naturalism wrote Wordsworth, it
matters which even less than it matters to us what the
German thinks he means. For we know that what Wordsworth wrote was *Tintern Abbey*, while what naturalism
wrote was nothing at all: for it never existed but as a
concept in somebody's mind, an abstract notion. God

made man in His image. Germans make generalisations in theirs. That is all, and that is just the difference.

To men who really practise writing as an Art—to every true man of letters in France, in England, in Russia, in Belgium—to an Anatole France, to a Rostand, to a Rolland, to a Thomas Hardy, to a Maxim Gorky, to a Maurice Maeterlinck, these abstract notions are about as useful as the wind in the next street; and the more you practise good actual writing, the more composedly you will ignore them.

But they do confuse and nullify criticism all over Europe, even among men of strong mind who happen to be critics only, and have never undergone the discipline of creative writing. For example—yesterday I took down a volume by that man of really powerful mind, Dr George Brandes. I opened it quite at random, and read:

> The strongest tendency even of works like Byron's *Don Juan* and Shelley's *Cenci*...

Do you know any works 'like' these, by the way?

> The strongest tendency even of works like Byron's *Don Juan* and Shelley's *Cenci* is in reality Naturalism. In other words Naturalism is so powerful in England that it permeates Coleridge's Romantic supernaturalism, Wordsworth's Anglican orthodoxy, Shelley's atheistic spiritualism, Byron's revolutionary liberalism...

-ism, -ism, -ism! 'Omm-jective and summ-jective!' I open at another page, again at haphazard:

> Keats's poetry is the most fragrant flower of English Naturalism. Before he appeared, this Naturalism had had a long period of continuous growth. Its active principle had been evolved by Wordsworth....Coleridge provided it with the support of a philosophy of nature which had a strong resemblance

to Schelling's. In Scott it assumes the highly successful form of a study of men, manners and scenery, inspired by patriotism, by interest in history, and by a wonderful appreciation of the significance of race.

At this point I began to yearn for five minutes of Jane Austen, and wondered idly what sort of figure *she* could be made to cut in this galley. But, being too listless to search, I turned back to the Introduction and read:

> It is my intention to trace in the poetry of England of the first decades of this century the course of the strong, deep, pregnant current in the intellectual life of the country, which, sweeping away the classic forms and conventions, produces a Naturalism dominating the whole of literature, which from Naturalism leads to Radicalism, from revolt against traditional convention in literature to vigorous rebellion against religious and political reaction....Though the connection between these authors and schools is not self-evident, but only discernible to the understanding critical eye, yet the period has its unity, and the picture it presents, though a many-coloured restless one, is a coherent composition, the work of the great artist, history.

Is not that fine? Everything ending in 'ion' permeating everything that ends in 'ance' or 'ity' or 'ism,' fighting it out like queer aquatic monsters in a tank, all subdued finally to a coherent com-pos-it-ion by a wave of the pen in the hand of that great personi-fi-cat-ion history! Gentlemen, tell yourselves that these foolish abstractions never did any of these foolish things. 'The great artist, history!' Call up your courage and say with Betsey Prig that you 'don't believe there is no sich a person.' Cure yourselves, if you would be either artists or critics, of this trick of personifying inanities. 'My brethren,' said a clergyman addicted to this foible, 'as we feast and revel, catering for the inner man, Septuagesima creeps up to our elbow, and plucking us by the sleeve whispers "Lent is near!"' Beware, I beg you, of such personifying of what isn't there, whether it be of 'the great artist, history,' or of that minatory virgin, Septuagesima.

But you will find (thanks to the servility of English professors) this German trick of philosophising art and fobbing off abstractions for things at its most rampant, at its most dangerous, in your literary handbooks, which, for convenience' sake, obliterate all that is vital to the work you ought to be studying, to chatter about 'schools,' 'influences,' 'revivals,' 'revolts,' 'tendencies,' 'reactions.'

Come: shall we make such a Handbook of English Literature together? It can be done, and completed in five minutes or so: as thus—

### A Short History of English Literature

Roman occupation of Britain. 450 years. Reason why no results.

Extirpation of colonists by sturdy Anglo-Saxon race. *Beowulf*. 'Book of our origins': 'our *Genesis*': 'not one word about England in the poem.' No school of *Beowulf*. Surprise at this.

Story of Cædmon, a cowherd. No school of Cædmon. Surprise at this.

Rise of Anglo-Saxon Prose under Ælfred. Orosius. Boethius. Collapse of Anglo-Saxon Prose. Surprise at this. Conjectural explanation.

Norman Conquest. Consequent explicable invasion of Norman-French influence. Layamon's *Brut*. Wace. Geoffrey of Monmouth. Sturdy persistence of Anglo-Saxon. Significance of *Piers Plowman*.

Tendencies producing Chaucer's debt to Italian influences, to French influences, to other influences. Chaucer's inflexions, Chaucer's word-endings. Influence of Chaucer. Scottish

Chaucerians; English school of Chaucer. Decline of Chaucerian tradition. General tendency (shared by us) to look everywhere but in the right place. Lydgate and Hoccleve writing bad poetry, but improving Middle English endings. 'Transition period' (which means we haven't much to say just hereabout).

Italianate Revival: French Pleiad: Influence producing Wyat and Surrey: School of Wyat and Surrey. The Renaissance, The New Learning: Columbus discovers America. Surprise at this. Sir Thomas More at home in Chelsea. Simultaneous rise of the Drama. Evolution of the Miracle Play. The Miracle Play superseded by the Morality. Evolution of the Drama. Evolution of Blank Verse. Shakespeare—his Comedies —his Tragedies—his Historical plays—his indebtedness to his times—his many-sidedness—his Will—his second-best bed— his romanticism. Classicism of Ben Jonson. Reaction (metaphysical) led by Donne. The mystical school. The Platonical school. Milton's indebtedness to the Copernican system. Tendency of Waller, Dryden, Pope. Decline of metaphysical school. Rise of the classical school. Tyranny of the Pamphlet, rise of the Essay, rise of the Novel. Tendency to write like Gray, or Collins: tendency to admire Dr Johnson: tendency not to admire Dr Johnson so much—tendency to make up on the swings what you have lost on the roundabouts: tendency to be Cowper or Crabbe: all these tendencies culminating in Romantic revolt. Naturalism (*alias* Wordsworth), mysticism (*alias* Coleridge), deism (*alias* Shelley), the revolutionary spirit (*alias* Byron), and sensuous naturalism (*alias* Keats). Exhaustion of tendencies. Reform Act of 1832—its devastating influence on English Literature, and especially on its study in Cambridge. Albeit we have heard it rumoured that in a later generation Tennyson, Browning, Carlyle, Ruskin, Arnold, Morris and others made a spirited attempt to revive the interplay of those tendencies and reactions which we have been considering, at this point we down the curtain and count the takings.

## V

Now this method of considering literature as the product not of successive men of genius and talent, but of abstract 'influences' and 'tendencies' divisible in periods and capable of being studied in compartments, has various vices, mostly consequent upon its being untrue.

For one, it gets you into a habit of regarding literature as a compost of blocks or slabs laid down in segments with dabs of editorial cement to fill up the chinks: and concurrently (*this is the mischief*) you lose your sense of it as an organic living thing with delicate, often infinitesimal, roots, thrown out this way and that way and every way, feeding it all the while by suction from the brain and blood of living men: and so (last and worst) you arrive at losing faith, which is the substance of things hoped for. I do not believe in youth that is content to abide in the past: for I am very sure it prepares for itself a desert prospect against the day when it shall have children of its own.

For another vice, this method constantly throws the story for you into a false perspective; a perspective which belies now the order of time and anon the degrees of right importance. Doubtless there are, have been, always will be, fashions in writing as in most of man's activities; but in the minds and feelings of men—literature being ever personal—they so overlap, so interlace, so blend, dispart, reunite their forces, that if, copying the method of science and the manner of Euclid, you superimpose the compartment *ABC* upon the compartment *DEF*, you are bound to be misled, logically and even chronologically.

For an example, take these lines, upon a certain translator:

> That servile path thou nobly dost decline
> Of tracing word by word, and line by line.

Those are the laboured births of slavish brains,
Not the effects of poetry, but pains;
Cheap vulgar arts, whose narrowness affords
No flight for thoughts, but poorly sticks at words.
A new and nobler way thou dost pursue,
To make translations and translators too.
They but preserve the ashes, thou the flame,
True to his sense, but truer to his fame.

'Classicism,' I hear you say. 'Age of Pope: finished coup-
let, balanced antithesis—the whole armoury of tricks.' Sirs,
they were written by Sir John Denham, who was born in
1615, more than seventy years before Pope, and died
almost twenty years before Pope was born or thought of.

## VI

But come—What do you understand by the words
'classical' and 'classicism'? I gather from the essays you
bring me that they mean something you certainly dislike
(being children of your age, as we all are or alas! have
been), and that you incline to lay your grievance at the
door of Alexander Pope. You dislike it so much that when
we read Gray or Collins together and I pause say at these
lines *To Evening*:

O nymph reserved, while now the bright-hair'd sun
Sits in yon western tent, whose cloudy skirts,
    With brede ethereal wove,
    O'erhang his wavy bed...

there ensues some such dialogue as this:

The Tutor pauses on the verse and muses, half to himself,
    'Lovely! and lovelier every time.'
'Yes, isn't it?' the Pupil agrees ardently.
'And—classical?'

The Pupil hesitates. 'Well—no—I shouldn't say *that*. It seems to me that there's a feeling for Nature about it.' Pause.

*Tutor* (encouragingly). 'Yes. I seem to have observed that.'

*Pupil* (brightly). 'It seems to me just to illustrate what Mr So-and-So said the other day, that long before we come to the Romantic Revival—under Wordsworth and Coleridge and—yes, Scott of course—'

*Tutor*. 'Yes. Yes.'

*Pupil*. 'There were bound to be stirrings—"gropings," as he put it. Of course I know that Collins calls Evening a "nymph."'

*Tutor*. 'Let us look on the bright side of things. Browning—one of your romantics by the way—would have called her a "numph."'

*Pupil*. 'And then again he speaks of the "bright-hair'd sun" and—dolefully—I suppose *that's* classical: something out of Homer, no doubt. But'—with reviving courage—'But anyhow, Sir, you'll admit it's different from Pope?'

*Tutor*. 'With all my heart.'

Pupil's brow clears. He has established his point.


## VII

You, who have to listen, term in and term out, to all this talk about 'classicism' and 'classicality'—do you seriously suppose that Pope was a classical writer?

I am not going to define the term 'classical' for you, just at this moment. I prefer to oppose thing to thing. You will perhaps allow that Homer, at any rate, was a classical writer. As between him and Pope, Homer has—I am, perhaps, not extravagant in supposing—the first call on that title.

Well, when Homer, having to tell how Odysseus, ship-wrecked and far-spent with swimming, wins to shore and drags himself, naked, to hide in the bushes just as Nausicaa

—the king's daughter of the country—drives down to the beach with her maidens, to wash the court linen in a stream close by, he tells the business thus:

Then they took the clothes from the waggon, and carrying them to the dark water, trod them in pits briskly, in rivalry. Then, after they had washed and cleansed away all the stains, they spread everything out in order on the foreshore, even where the sea, beating on the coast, had washed the pebbles clean. Then, having bathed and anointed themselves with olive oil, they ate their mid-day meal on the river bank, waiting till the clothes should dry in the sun's rays. And anon, having finished their meal, the maidens and the Princess, they fell to playing at ball, casting away their veils, and among them white-armed Nausicaa sang the song which led the game.

Could anything be simpler, more direct, more *classical*? (We are approaching a definition.) But now turn to Pope's version—or rather, to Broome's, which Pope admired so much that he incorporated it in his rendering of the *Odyssey*:

> Then emulous the royal robes they lave,
> And plunge the vestures in the cleansing wave
> (The vestures cleansed o'erspread the shelly sand,
> Their snowy lustre whitens all the strand);
> Then with a short repast relieve their toil,
> And o'er their limbs diffuse ambrosial oil;
> And while the robes imbibe the solar ray,
> O'er the green mead the sporting virgins play
> (Their shining veils unbound). Along the skies,
> Toss'd and retoss'd, the ball incessant flies.
> They sport, they feast; Nausicaa lifts her voice,
> And, warbling sweet, makes earth and heaven rejoice.

Can you not see at once that if Homer's narrative be classical, Pope (or Broome) has induced something upon

it which changes its nature? something extraneous, orna-
mental, *fantastic*—

> And while the robes imbibe the solar ray—

something more alien from true classical than almost anything you can find in the wildest romanticist—as you will
call him?

## VIII

When you apply the word 'classical' or the word
'classicism' to such tawdry overlay as I have quoted, are
you not—are your professional instructors not—committing
the first of literary offences, that of perverting the sense of
words? Do you not—do not your professional instructors
—by this use of the word 'classical' mean in fact 'con-
ventional'—a word which contradicts almost every notion
that can be even remotely associated with the classics?
Your professors and compilers of little handbooks may not
go about like Théophile Gautier, wearing crimson waistcoats: but beneath whatever waistcoats they wear they carry
a stupidity which was never Gautier's, in his most intoxi-
cated moments.

Pope sealed a fashion. It was an artificial manner of
writing, as far removed from the practice of the men we
call classical authors as any manner of writing could well
be. Sophocles or Virgil or Dante would have shuddered
at it. Still he set up a fashion under which it became
unpoetical—that is, was esteemed unpoetical—to call the
moon the moon without adding 'sole regent of the night,'
or to talk of drying clothes: to be garments worthy of
poetry they had to 'imbibe the solar ray.'

But are we sure that our poets, having repudiated Pope,
are not practising very similar fooleries in our own year of
grace? The inventions of one age are always in process of

becoming the conventions, the tyrants, of the next. Listen to this, from Francis Thompson's *Essay on Shelley*; and mark you, it is written of *our own day*:

There is, in fact, a certain band of words, the Praetorian cohorts of poetry, whose prescriptive aid is invoked by every aspirant to the poetical purple, and without whose prescriptive aid none dares aspire to the poetical purple; against these it is time some banner should be raised.

And he goes on:

It is at any rate curious to note that the literary revolution against the despotic diction of Pope seems issuing, like political revolutions, in a despotism of its own making.

If our teachers persist in labelling Pope and his imitators as 'classical,' let us cheerfully claim the bulk of Greek and Roman literature as 'romantic' and have done with it. Why not? Do you postulate, for romantic writing, glamour and magic, adventures on 'perilous seas in faery lands forlorn'? Very well; then I exhibit this same *Odyssey* to you, with its isle of Circe,

> where that Æaean isle forgets the main,

its garden-court of Phæacia, its wonderlands of the Cyclops, the Sirens, the Lotus-eaters, its scene, a moment ago related, of the princess playing at ball with her maidens on the strand; or I exhibit the marvellous tale of *Cupid and Psyche*, parent of a hundred fairy-tales dispersed throughout the world (*Beauty and the Beast* for one).

Or is it passion you demand of romance? I exhibit the passionate verses of Sappho, preserved for us by Longinus, beginning

> φαίνεταί μοι κῆνος ἴσος θεοῖσιν
> ἔμμεν ὤνηρ...

or a speech of Phaedra, or Catullus's lyric of Acme and Septimius.

Is it pathos?—utter pathos? I exhibit to you Priam on his knees, kissing the hand that has murdered his son; Helen on the wall; Andromache bidding farewell to her husband at the gate, her boy kicking and crowing on her arm at sight of his father's nodding plume; and again that last glimpse Virgil gives of her, in slavery, returning from vows paid to the dead—of her that was 'Hectoris Andromache.'

Is it any sense of predestinate doom fulfilled? I refer you to the last stand of the Sicilian expedition in Thucydides. Or is it a general sense of the woe, the tears, the frailty, the transience inherent in all human things? A dozen passages from Virgil might be quoted.

I think, if you will look into 'classicism' and 'romanticism' for yourselves, with your own open eyes, you will find—though the whole pother about their difference amounts to nothing that need trouble a healthy man—it amounts to this: some men have naturally a sense of form stronger than their sense of colour: some men have a sense of colour stronger than their sense of form.

In proportion as they indulge their proclivities or neglect to discipline them, one man will be a classical, the other a romantic, writer. At their utmost, one will be a dull formalist, the other a frantic dauber. I truly believe there is not much more to be said.

I conclude by reciting to you two compositions by opposing which you may summarise for yourselves all that I have been saying today.

The first is a Table of Contents of a volume by Doctor George Brandes (*Main Currents in Nineteenth Century Literature*, Vol. IV).

Common Characteristics of the Period
National Characteristics
The Political Background
The Beginnings of Naturalism
Strength and Sincerity of the Love of Nature
Rural Life and its Poetry
Naturalistic Romanticism
The Lake School's Conception of Liberty
The Lake School's Oriental Romanticism
Historical Naturalism
All-embracing Sensuousness
The Poetry of Irish Opposition and Revolt
Erotic Lyric Poetry
The British Spirit of Freedom
Republican Humanism
Radical Naturalism
Byron: the Passionate Personality
Byron: the Passionate Personality (*continued*)
Byron: his Self-absorption
Byron: the Revolutionary Spirit
Comic and Tragic Realism
Culmination of Naturalism
Byron's Death
Conclusion

What shall I oppose to this? Something quite simple, something you all know by heart, yet something so lovely that it never can be hackneyed.

> Ah what avails the sceptered race,
>     Ah what the form divine!
> When every virtue, every grace!
>     Rose Aylmer, all were thine.
> Rose Aylmer, whom these wakeful eyes
>     May weep, but never see,
> A night of memories and of sighs
>     I consecrate to thee.

Is that classical? It is as classical as anything in Catullus. Is that romantic? Yes, I think it is also romantic.

But what matters either? It is the pure loveliness of it that alone should concern you.

All things considered, I advise that it may help our minds to earn an honest living if we dismiss the terms 'classical' and 'romantic' out of our vocabulary for a while.

# SOME SEVENTEENTH CENTURY POETS

## I. JOHN DONNE

### I

WHEN Izaak Walton first published that gem of biography, his *Life of Dr John Donne*—now one in a casket of five of his carving—it was to introduce a volume of his adored master's *Sermons*: and he prefaced it with a modest account of how he had first but collected materials for Sir Henry Wotton, betwixt whom and Donne 'there was so mutual a knowledge, and such friendship contracted in their youth, as nothing but death could force a separation.' But Wotton died, with the projected *Life* unwritten.

'When I heard that sad news,' Walton continues, 'and heard also that these Sermons were to be printed, and want the Author's life, which I thought to be very remarkable: indignation or grief (indeed I know not which) transported me so far, that I reviewed my forsaken collections....And if I shall now be demanded, as once Pompey's poor bondman was:—(the grateful wretch had been left alone on the sea-shore, with the forsaken dead body of his once glorious lord and master; and was then gathering the scattered pieces of an old broken boat, to make a funeral pile to burn it, which was the custom of the Romans)—"Who art thou that alone hast the honour to bury the body of Pompey the Great?" so, who am I that do thus officiously set the Author's memory on fire? I hope the question will prove to have in it more of wonder than disdain....

'And if the Author's glorious spirit, which now is in heaven, can have the leisure to look down and see me, the poorest, the meanest of all his friends, in the midst of his officious duty, confident I am that he will not disdain this well-meant sacrifice to his memory: for, whilst his conversation made me and many others happy below, I know his humility and gentleness were then eminent; and, I have heard divines say, those virtues which were but sparks upon earth, become great and glorious flames in heaven.'

Now of encomiums upon the dead, as of entries in hotel visitors' books, you may have (with me) found it observable that qualifications tend to disappear. But the poetical elegies upon Dr Donne do by their mass (they fill twenty-five pages in Dr Grierson's great edition) as by their writers' eminence in various stations of life (Bishop King, Browne of Tavistock, Edward Hyde—possibly the great Earl of Clarendon—Walton himself, Thomas Carew the poet and courtier, Lucius Cary, Endymion Porter, Sidney Godolphin, are among the signatory authors) convey that the men of his time who themselves counted accounted him a very great man indeed.

And truly he was a great man; yes, and is one of the greatest figures in English literature, albeit perhaps the worst understood: one of the tribe of strong generative giants in which—whether we like them or not, and whether or not we know why—we have to reckon (for examples) Ben Jonson, John Dryden, Samuel Johnson; giants whose stature we recognise albeit we cannot measure it by their writings, which sometimes disappoint and not seldom fatigue us; giants of whom we still feel, after reading *Sejanus* or *Absalom and Achitophel*, or *Rasselas*, that their worth is somehow known although their height be not taken.

Donne, I dare to say, if we range him up with that tall
three, stands an easy compeer. What is more, his work
does not disappoint—if we know where to look for it. He
wrote some of the most magnificent and astounding pages
in our literature, if we know where to look for them. We
may not call them, though unparalleled, absolutely beautiful: there is nothing absolute in Donne but his greatness
and his manhood. He is Demiourgos—a swart smith at
the forge, beating out things worthy of the heavenly city:
and he cares not what costly stuff he casts into the furnace
so that he hammer out a paving-stone, or it may be a
primrose for it: and, for the sake of a primrose great fiery
masses will hurtle up out of Etna. Also one has to peer
through the smoke to discern what the artificer, too intent
to help you, has there on the anvil. It may be just a primrose or it may be a whole length of celestial wall. He,
absorbed, sees only on the anvil a part of his vision.

## II

But first let me tell a little of this extraordinary man:
not enough to absolve you of the duty and delight of reading
about him in Walton: just enough to preface the remarks
I shall offer upon his work this morning, and thereafter
upon the work of his followers.

John Donne was born in London, in the parish of St
Olave, Bread Street, in the year 1573. His father, a prosperous ironmonger of the city of London, and well
descended, died when the boy was about three years old,
leaving a widow and six children. The mother was a devout
and uncompromising Roman Catholic; which explains
why the boy John, after tuition at home, went up at twelve
(with a younger brother, Henry, aged eleven) and was
entered at Hart Hall, now Hertford College, in Oxford:

for certain alleged proselytising activities of the Jesuits had hurried the government into making an order that all students admitted to Oxford must take the Oath of Supremacy, the crucial test of loyalty to the Crown and to the Reformed Church of England; an oath not enforced, however, upon boys under sixteen. So John and Henry dodged it by going up at twelve and eleven. In those days there were no Rhodes scholars: and I should imagine that, under this rule—which apparently did not apply to Cambridge, Cambridge would have had consistently the better of things in athletics—had there been any. But there were not.

Walton says that at fourteen or thereabouts he was 'transplanted'—which seems a good term—from Oxford to Cambridge, 'that he might receive nourishment from both soils.' I regret to tell you that no evidence for this, save Walton's, is discoverable, unless it be internal evidence. Walton says that at Oxford they avowed the age to have brought forth another Pico Mirandola: that at Cambridge he was a most laborious student, often changing his studies but endeavouring to take no degree. *Plus ça change, plus c'est la même chose.*

It is probable that, after leaving Oxford, he travelled for a while. At any rate we find him, at seventeen or so, admitted to Lincoln's Inn and living in London. His mother, anxious for his faith, surrounded him there with tutors who (according to Walton) under cover of the mathematics and other liberal sciences were advised to instil into him particular principles of the Romish Church. Donne, being of a detached mind—detached, but extraordinarily eager—set himself to read both sides of the question with all his might. The end was that he became a passionate, yet tolerant, Church of England man. Meantime his brother Henry—the same that had entered with him at

Hart Hall—had fallen under suspicion of disloyal commerce with the Jesuit fathers, and was thrown into the Clink for harbouring Harrington, a seminary priest, tracked to his chambers in Thavies' Inn and there arrested. Harrington was hurried to trial and hanged at Tyburn. Henry Donne contracted gaol fever and died, after a few weeks' imprisonment.

It may have been in prudence, being under suspicion, that in 1596, John cleared from London and joined in the Earl of Essex's famous expedition to Cadiz. Quite as likely it was to avoid the scandal of more worldly transgressions: for his poems (and Ben Jonson tells us that he wrote all his best pieces of verse before twenty-five) tell us autobiographically of wild living and licentious wooing:

> Th' expense of Spirit in a waste of shame...

and of shamelessness, we may add. They exhibit him as a genuine heir of the Renaissance, insatiable alike in carnal and intellectual curiosity: mad to possess, and, having possessed, violent in reaction, crueller even than Horace to his castaways, then even more cruelly, cynically, cold in analysing the ashes of disgust:

> Th' expense of Spirit in a waste of shame
> Is lust in action; and, till action, lust
> Is perjured, murderous, bloody, full of blame,
> Savage, extreme, rude, cruel, not to trust;
> Enjoy'd no sooner but despisèd straight;
> Past reason hunted; and, no sooner had,
> Past reason hated; as a swallow'd bait
> On purpose laid to make the taker mad:
> Mad in pursuit, and in possession so;
> Had, having, and in quest to have, extreme;
> A bliss in proof: and, proved, a very woe;
> Before, a joy proposed; behind, a dream....

Setting forth with Essex, the youth, already famous for gifts and learning, writes an Elegie of farewell to a lady with whom he had had an intrigue. This is the sort of thing:

> Was't not enough, that thou didst hazard us
> To paths in love so dark, so dangerous:
> And those so ambush'd round with household spies,
> And over all, thy husbands towring eyes...

and about the same time he was writing *The Curse* on his mistress and the man who succeeds him, which (as Andrew Lang said justly) 'far outdoes the *Epodes* of Horace in cold ferocity.' Or this:

> Love, any devile else but you,
> Would for a given soule give something too.

Or this:

> If thou beest borne to strange sights,
>     Things invisible to see,
> Ride ten thousand daies and nights,
>     Till age snow white haires on thee,
> Thou, when thou retorn'st, wilt tell mee
> All strange wonders that befell thee,
>         And sweare
>         No where
> Lives a woman true, and faire.
>
> If thou findst one, let mee know,
>     Such a Pilgrimage were sweet;
> Yet doe not, I would not goe,
>     Though at next doore wee might meet,
> Though shee were true, when you met her,
> And last, till you write your letter,
>         Yet shee
>         Will bee
> False, ere I come, to two, or three.

Now in two more short extracts watch the fierce contempt
withering down into worse cynicism:

> Now thou hast lov'd me one whole day,
> To morrow, when thou leav'st, what wilt thou say?
> Wilt thou then Antedate some new made vow?
>     And say that now
> We are not just those persons, which we were?
> Or, that oathes made in reverentiall feare
> Of Love, and his wrath, any may forswear?...
> Vaine lunatique, against these scapes I could
>     Dispute, and conquer, if I would,
>         Which I abstaine to doe,
> For by to morrow, I may thinke so too.

Last:

> Thus I reclaim'd my buzzard love, to flye
> At what, and when, and how and where I chuse;
>     Now negligent of sport I lye,
>     And now as other Falc'ners use,
> I spring a mistress, sweare, write, sigh and weepe:
> And the game kill'd, or lost, goe talke, and sleepe...

and there is worse—far worse—than that.

Donne shared the triumph of the Cadiz exploit with a
number of young gentlemen who had sailed with Essex as
volunteers. Its impudent success so enraged the king of
Spain that he started preparing a second Armada. To fore-
stall this, Elizabeth fitted out a grand fleet under Essex,
Howard and Ralegh; and Donne sailed with it. A storm
(described by him in a dull poem, praised by a modern
critic as 'most vivid' in pictures of nature and the sea;
actually as full of both, or of either, as this room) drove the
ships—it was real enough for that—back to Plymouth.
They weighed again, but in so damaged a condition that,
after a coasting raid, the larger foray was abandoned for a

dash on the Azores to intercept the Spanish plate-ships returning from America. This enterprise (known as the 'Islands Expedition') fell to pieces through bickerings between Essex and Ralegh, and the fleet trailed a broken wing home in the autumn of 1597. Walton tells us that, just after this, Donne visited Italy and Spain (presumably on minor errands of diplomacy) and that he designed to visit the Holy Land. 'But at his being in the furthest parts of Italy, the disappointment of company, or of a safe convoy, or the uncertainty of returns of money into those remote parts, denied him that happiness: which he did often occasionally mention with a deploration.' It is pretty certain he had wasted his patrimony in these wanderings.

We pursue with Walton:

Not long after his return into England, that exemplary pattern of gravity and wisdom, the Lord Elsemore [Ellesmere], then Keeper of the Great Seal, the Lord Chancellor of England, taking notice of his learning, languages, and other abilities, and much affecting his person and behaviour, took him to be his Chief Secretary; supposing and intending it to be an introduction to some more weighty employment in the State.

But here fate interposed. The Chancellor's wife had a niece, Anna, daughter of Sir George More, Lieutenant of the Tower, and kept her as frequent visitor and attendant. This young lady of sixteen and the handsome young secretary were thrown much together, read books together—

Galeotto fu il libro e chi lo scrisse.

The pair fell in love, secretly plighted troth, and were clandestinely married (1601). The father's wrath, when he discovered it, was fierce, even 'frenetical.' He not only procured the young husband's dismissal from the Chancellor's service, but had him committed to prison with two friends, Samuel and Christopher Brooke (both poets by the way, and Samuel destined to become Master of Trinity), who had abetted the love affair. Almost as quickly as in a comedy the choleric father relented, procured the bridegroom's enlargement, gave the young couple his blessing (with none of his money, however, to back it) and, not to do forgiveness by halves, begged the Chancellor to reconsider his dismissal of so commendable a young secretary. To which that exemplary pattern of gravity and wisdom replied 'that though he was unfeignedly sorry for what he had done, yet it was inconsistent with his place and credit, to discharge and re-admit servants at the request of passionate petitioners.'

## III

Thus Donne found himself cast on the world, with the obligation to provide for a wife he had dangerously won and passionately adored. After vicissitudes (and much fending for a fast-growing family), he found employ with Sir Robert Drury of Hawsted, Suffolk, one of the wealthiest men in England; whose only child, a daughter, had died at the age of sixteen. The rich poor parents applied to Donne to write her epitaph. Donne not only did so, but followed it up with that strangest of poems, *The Progresse of the Soule*. It was the first of his writings to see print. His earlier licentious poems he would gladly have suppressed, had it been possible. They were never published during his lifetime: but copies in MS—for his reputation was already the talk of the town—had blown everywhere, in court and throughout London.

He would gladly have suppressed them because his religious convictions were steadily deepening—or rather lifting him to a mystical exaltation—but more because the wandering bark of his love had found a polestar in his most adored wife. True and ten times true as are Burns's words of dissipated passion:

> I waive the quantum o' the sin,
> The hazard of concealing;
> But, och! it hardens a' within,
> And petrifies the feeling!...

Donne was one of the few who, out of that curse hold fire enough to revive the flame—

> I have been faithful to thee, Cynara, in my fashion—

and burn up past sins on the altar of a single devotion.

It was in Drury's employ, on an embassy to France, that Donne, in Paris, was visited by the apparition reported by Walton and always worthy to be mentioned because in this man it undoubtedly deepened the mysticism so important to the rest of our story: the vision of his wife passing twice by him 'with her hair hanging about her shoulders, and a dead child in her arms:...and am as sure,' said he, telling it to Drury, 'that at her second appearing she stopped, and looked me in the face, and vanished.' Sir Robert was so far shaken by Donne's earnestness that

he immediately sent a servant [home] to Drury House, with a charge to hasten back, and bring him word, whether Mrs Donne were alive: and, if alive, in what condition she was as to her health. The twelfth day the messenger returned with this account—That he found and left Mrs Donne very sad, and sick in her bed; and that, after a long and dangerous labour, she had been delivered of a dead child. And, upon examination, the abortion proved to be the same day, and about the very hour, that Mr Donne affirmed he saw her pass by him in his chamber.

Donne returned to England, where Drury housed him

with his rapidly increasing family. He became adviser to the Earl of Somerset; but yet lacked preferment proportionate to his merits, when in 1615, at the persuasion of King James himself, he took Holy Orders. Then preferment came, as it not seldom comes, to a man past enjoying it. Donne, at any rate, had but a short while to share the gratification with his wife. She died in 1617 and was buried in St Clement Danes. Here is a part of the epitaph:

*Annae.*

. . . . .

*Quod hoc saxum fari jussit*
*Ipse prae dolore infans*
*Maritus (miserrimum dictu) olim*
*Charae charus*
*Cineribus cineres spondet suos*
*Novo matrimonio (annuat Deus)*
*hoc loco sociandos*
*Joannes Donne*

In 1621 King James made him Dean of St Paul's. He was now forty-eight, the most famous preacher in London, and the most solitary, melancholy man.

## IV

*There* is where you shall seek for the great Donne, the real Donne: not in his verse, into which posterity is constantly betrayed, but in his *Sermons*, which contain (as I hold) the most magnificent prose ever uttered from an English pulpit, if not the most magnificent prose ever spoken in our tongue. I read you a passage this day fortnight: and I hope some day to speak to you of Donne and Andrewes, Hall, Fuller, Jeremy Taylor and others of the

Great Age of the Pulpit. Let me today stammer out to you, for evidence, two short passages; and ask you to imagine his wonderful voice (by all men's consent, wonderful) ringing them forth under the roof of St Paul's—the old St Paul's.

(1) First, for a specimen of his lighter controversial style, which I may call his *skirmishing* style. And here, by the way, if there be any present of the Catholic Church of Rome, let him not take offence at that which I present merely as a specimen. Donne's was an age of controversy: and if we pretend amiably there was no such thing, we emasculate our understanding of his time, and of the men who lived in it. And moreover I truly believe the passage will not bruise any man's ears; and—yet moreover—I engage me, when dealing with writers of 'the old profession' amply to redeem the balance.

Well, then, Donne is speaking of supplications addressed to saints. He quotes Justin Martyr's saying that it is a strange thing men should 'pray to Esculapius or to Apollo for health' when they may as easily pray to the masters who taught them all they know of physic; and he goes on:

Why should I pray to St George for victory, when I may go to the Lord of Hosts, Almighty God Himself; or consult with a serjeant, or corporal, when I may go to the general? Or to another saint for peace, when I may go to the Prince of Peace Christ Jesus? Why should I pray to Saint Nicholas for a fair passage at sea, when He that rebuked the storm is nearer me than St Nicholas? Why should I pray to St Antony for my hogs, when he that gave the devil leave to drown the Gergesens whole herd of hoggs, did not do that by St Antony's leave, nor by putting a *caveat* or *prae-non-obstante* in his monopoly of preserving hogs? I know not where to find St Petronilla when I have an ague, nor St Apollonia when I have the tooth-ache, nor St Liberius when I have the stone. I know not whether they can hear me in heaven, or no. Our adversaries will not say that all saints in heaven hear all that is said on earth. I know not whether they be in heaven or no: our adversaries will not say that the Pope may not err in a matter of fact, and so may canonise a traitor for a saint. I know not whether those saints were ever upon earth or no: our adversaries will not say that all their legends were really, historically true, but that many of them were holy, but yet symbolical inventions. ...I know my Redeemer liveth, and I know where he is; and no man knows where he is not.

(2) For a more solemn passage I choose this famous one on Jezebel:

The ashes of an oak in the chimney are no epitaph of that oak, to tell me how high or how large that was; it tells me not what flocks it sheltered while it stood, nor what men it hurt when it fell. The dust of great persons' graves is speechless, too: it says nothing, it distinguishes nothing. As soon the dust of a wretch whom thou wouldest not, as of a prince whom thou couldest not look upon, will trouble thine eyes, if the wind blow it thither; and when a whirlwind hath blown the dust of the Churchyard into the Church, and the man sweeps out the dust of the Church into the Churchyard, who will undertake to sift those dusts again and to pronounce, This is the Patrician, this is the noble flowre [flour], and this the yeomanly, this the Plebeian bran? So was the death of Jezabel (*Jezabel* was a Queen) expressed. They shall not say *This is Jezabel*; not only not wonder that it is, nor pity that it should be: but they shall not say, they shall not know, *This is Jezabel*.

## V

Thus in his *Sermons*, if you seek, you will find the Donne I maintain to be the greater Donne, master of well-knit argument, riding tumultuous emotion as with a bridle, thundering out fugue upon fugue of prose modulated with almost impeccable ear. Why do critics then go on judging him first and almost solely as a poet? And why do I, following them to do evil, speak of him today chiefly as a poet?

He had no architectonic gift in poetry: in poetry the skill that articulated, knit, compacted his *Sermons* and marched his arguments as warriors in battalion, completely forsook him. Through lack of it *The Progresse of the Soule* which might have been a triumph, is a wobbling fiasco. Of the art that constructs a *Divina Commedia*, an *Othello*, a *Samson Agonistes*, or even a *Beggar's Opera*, he had no inkling whatever. It was not that he strove for it and missed; it was that he either knew not or cared not a farthing about it.

He had (they say) a most peccable ear in verse. Critics so great as Dryden, Pope, Johnson, Coleridge, all agree on this point: so I suppose they must be right. They agree also in calling him difficult, crabbed, etc. Being so great men, therefore, let them be right.

I can only say that after trial, especially in reading him aloud to myself, I find him by nine-tenths less inharmonious, halting, crabbed, or difficult than these great critics take for granted that he is. Of course, if you choose a line of his and read it clumsily, if you accent

Blasted with sighs and surrounded with tears

as if you were ordering

Bacon and eggs and a half-pint of beer

you make little of it as a ten-syllable iambic; as if you choose to scan with your thumb instead of the organ God gave you:

Blastéd, with síghs, and súr-roundéd with teárs,

you will make less.  But if you read

Blásted with síghs, and surrounded with teárs,
    Hither I come to seek the spring,

letting the voice linger on 'sur-round,' the line becomes
exquisite.

But come, let us take a poem of his and test this alleged
harshness:

Little think'st thou, poore flower,
    Whom I have watch'd sixe or seaven dayes,
And seene thy birth, and seene what every houre
Gave to thy growth, thee to this height to raise,
And now dost laugh and triumph on this bough,
        Little think'st thou
That it will freeze anon, and that I shall
To morrow finde thee falne, or not at all.

Little think'st thou poore heart
    That labour'st yet to nestle thee,
And think'st by hovering here to get a part
In a forbidden or forbidding tree,
And hop'st her stiffenesse by long siege to bow:
        Little think'st thou,
That thou to morrow, ere that Sunne doth wake,
Must with this Sunne, and mee a journey take.

But thou which lov'st to bee
    Subtile to plague thy selfe, wilt say,
Alas, if you must goe, what's that to mee?
Here lyes my businesse, and here I will stay:
You goe to friends, whose love and meanes present
        Various content
To your eyes, eares, and tongue, and every part.
If then your body goe, what need you a heart?

Well then, stay here; but know,
　When thou hast stay'd and done thy most;
A naked thinking heart, that makes no show,
Is to a woman, but a kinde of Ghost;
How shall shee know my heart; or having none,
　　　Know thee for one?
Practise may make her know some other part,
But take my word, she doth not know a Heart.

Meet mee at London, then,
　Twenty dayes hence, and thou shalt see
Mee fresher, and more fat, by being with men,
Then if I had staid still with her and thee.
For Gods sake, if you can, be you so too:
　　　I would give you
There, to another friend, whom wee shall finde
As glad to have my body, as my minde.

None the less I grant you that Donne's ear for the beat
of verse is so wayward, its process often so recondite, that
the most of his poetry is a struggle rather than a success:
and I have already admitted that he could not plan a poem.

Why then does everyone insist on judging as a poet, and
a faulty one, this man who had a superlatively fine ear for
the rhythm of prose and could construct in prose? And
why am I following the multitude?

The first and most obvious answer is that nobody reads
sermons in these days, and few even trouble to attend them.
For reasons which we will examine on another occasion,
the once glorious art of preaching has perished out of our
midst. The tradition is there—laid up in Donne's *Sermons*:
'laid up, not lost!'

But the main reason is that his verse *did* smash up an
effete tradition of verse. It smashed up Petrarch-in-English,
and it was high time. It did so influence English verse for

at least half a century, that (as someone has said) like a glove of civet it scents every garment you take out of the wardrobe.

Gentlemen, never mind when someone smashes up a convention to make a new thing. That way—trust it—lies life: and literature may make almost any sacrifice to renew itself alive. What was it this man had to invent or to re-discover, that he broke up so much?

## VI

Most of you know Johnson's *Life of Cowley*, and the hay that great man made of the 'metaphysical' poets, tossing them on his horns. Why 'metaphysical' I don't know. Johnson had compiled a *Dictionary*, and therefore had no excuse for not knowing that 'metaphysical' was no accurate term for the thing he took so much joy in deriding. He probably meant something like 'fiddlesticks'; something contemptuous. He makes admirable play with a number of things that do not matter. But he never gets near what does matter.

What is Mysticism?

It is something, at any rate, which Johnson had small care or capacity to understand.

It is also something which even Shakespeare did not understand, though he unconsciously relied on it. You may choose your grandest passage from Shakespeare: choose Prospero's cloud-capped towers and gorgeous palaces; or choose Cleopatra's wail upon dead Antony:

> O! wither'd is the garland of the war,
> The soldier's pole is fall'n; young boys and girls
> Are level now with men; the odds is gone,
> And there is nothing left remarkable
> Beneath the visiting moon.

Then set beside it a line or two of Blake:

> When the stars threw down their spears,
> And water'd heaven with their tears...

or

> A Robin Redbreast in a cage
> Puts all heaven in a rage...

or Wordsworth's *Ode to Duty*:

> Thou dost preserve the stars from wrong;
> And the most ancient heavens, through Thee, are fresh
>     and strong...

and you will perceive that there are more things in heaven and earth than find their way into great Shakespeare's philosophy; and in particular a something which Plato had known, which Shakespeare did not know, which therefore had to be rediscovered by poets, wise men and children.

That something was Mysticism. And Mysticism is—well, Mysticism, Gentlemen, is something we will discuss in our next lecture; in which I shall also try to explain why Donne, who helped to rediscover it, was an imperfect mystic, as also to trace it in certain of his followers—Herbert, Vaughan, Traherne.

For the present be it enough to say that he was an imperfect poet, and mainly for two reasons: (1) he had no constant vision of beauty, (2) he had too busy an intellect, which ever tempted him (as Touchstone would say) to be breaking his shins on his own wit: or as an American friend used to put it, he suffered 'from a rush of brains to the head.' In lines and short passages he could be exquisite. Witness this:

> I long to talke with some old lovers ghost,
> Who dyed before the god of Love was borne...

or this, from his *Anatomie of the World*:

> Her pure, and eloquent blood
> Spoke in her cheekes, and so distinctly wrought,
> That one might almost say, her body thought.

But more than half his time we see the man sweating and straining at his forge and bellows. Obviously half the time he himself cannot see what he is working at, hammering at 'that is as it may turn out,' and then, suddenly, out of the smoke, shine verses like this, from *The Extasie*:

> As 'twixt two equall Armies, Fate
>   Suspends uncertaine victorie,
> Our soules, (which to advance their state,
>   Were gone out,) hung 'twixt her, and mee.
>
> And whil'st our soules negotiate there,
>   Wee like sepulchrall statues lay;
> All day, the same our postures were,
>   And wee said nothing, all the day.

## VII

In his last years, as disease, over-study and fasting broke up his body, his mind played more and more constantly upon death and its physical horrors, the charnel-house and the worm: yes, though he, always eloquent against the grave, had written this most holy sonnet defying it:

> Death be not proud, though some have called thee
> Mighty and dreadfull; for, thou art not soe,
> For, those, whom thou think'st, thou dost overthrow,
> Die not, poor death, nor yet canst thou kill mee.

From rest and sleepe, which but thy pictures bee,
Much pleasure, then from thee, much more must flow,
And soonest our best men with thee doe goe,
Rest of their bones, and soules deliverie.
Thou art slave to Fate, Chance, kings, and desperate men,
And dost with poyson, warre, and sicknesse dwell,
And poppie or charmes can make us sleepe as well,
And better then thy stroake; why swell'st thou then?
   One short sleepe past, wee wake eternally,
   And death shall be no more; death, thou shalt die.

This man lived his last days and slept for years with a full length portrait of himself (for which he stood on an urn, naked, clad in a winding-sheet) laid alongside his bed, 'where it continued and became his hourly object till his death.' You may see the horrible silly picture in many editions of the *Life*. It is kept among the archives of St Paul's. Reflex action, say I, of carnality *in exitu*. A very 'gloomy Dean' of St Paul's at any rate! First and last, Donne was always that man in Plato who, drawing near the city ditch and spying the rotten corpses of some malefactors that had been flung there, stood still between abhorrence and a filthy attraction; until at length, overcome, he ran to the spot opening his eyes wide with his fingers and crying, 'Take your fill, you wretches, since you must have it so.'

But a great man, indubitably a very great man: all the taller for standing in the mire of corruption and reaching up to grasp celestial doors. A great man: a very penitent man! He died on the 31st day of March 1631, and was buried in St Paul's. Let a simple admirer, a holy and humble man of heart—let Izaak Walton—say the last word on him, whom many apparently greater admired:

He was by nature highly passionate, but more apt to reluct

at the excesses of it. A great lover of the offices of humanity, and of so merciful a spirit, that he never beheld the miseries of mankind without pity and relief.

He was earnest and unwearied in the search of knowledge, with which his vigorous soul is now satisfied, and employed in a continual praise of that God that first breathed it into his active body: that body, which once was a Temple of the Holy Ghost, and is now become a small quantity of Christian dust:—

But I shall see it re-animated.

## II. HERBERT AND VAUGHAN

### I

ISHALL begin today, Gentlemen, by collecting from my previous lectures sundry scattered tenets which, if you remember them at all, you probably remember disconnectedly as things dropped disconnectedly, casually, on occasion: and I shall try (if you will allow the simile) to piece these scraps of glass together into a small window through which you may not only, as I hope, have a glimpse into the true meaning of 'Mysticism'—which was the question on which we parted, a fortnight ago—but even perhaps, into the last meaning of poetry. Oh yes!—a most presumptuous hope most presumptuously uttered. But we have to do our best in our little time: and my experience has been that while many things continue to lurk in a glass darkly, certain clear visions have come, and the clearest of these not seldom through the eyes of a friend. If that word, again, be presumptuous, you must forgive me.

*First*, then, I have preached to you over and over from this desk, and not seldom explicitly, that the function of all true art, and in particular of poetry (with which we are concerned) is to harmonise the soul of man with the immense Universe surrounding him, in which he divines a procession which is orderly, an order which is harmonious, a procession, an order, a harmony which obey, as law, a Will infinitely above him, infinitesimally careful of *him*— the many million-millionth part of a speck of dust, *yet sentient*.

Great thinkers (as you know) have all recognised this order. Indeed they *must*, for it conditions all their thinking. If the Universe were a chaos, which is anarchy—if the sun rose unpunctually and lay down when it felt inclined, if no moon commanded the tides, if the stars were peevish, running to and fro like spoilt children—any connected thought would be impossible and we no better but worse than blind men jostled about by a crowd. But as a fact we know that whatever it be, watching over Israel, it slumbers not nor sleeps. Begin where you will. Begin, if you choose, with the rebuke to Job:

Canst thou bind the sweet influences of Pleiades, or loose the bands of Orion?

Canst thou bring forth Mazzaroth in his season? or canst thou guide Arcturus with his sons?

Or with Ecclesiasticus:

The beauty of heaven, the glory of the stars, an ornament giving light in the highest places of the Lord.

At the commandment of the Holy One they will stand in their order, and never faint in their watches.

Come down to Wordsworth's *Ode to Duty*:

Thou dost preserve the stars from wrong,
And the most ancient heavens, through Thee, are fresh and
    strong.

Or to Meredith's *Lucifer in Starlight*:

On a starr'd night Prince Lucifer uprose.
    Tired of his dark dominion swung the fiend
    Above the rolling ball in cloud part screen'd.
Where sinners hugg'd their spectre of repose.
Poor prey in his hot fit of pride were those,
    And now upon his western wing he lean'd,
    Now his huge bulk o'er Afric's sands careen'd,
Now the black planet shadow'd Arctic snows.

Soaring through wider zones that prick'd his scars
  With memory of the old revolt from Awe,
He reach'd a middle height, and at the stars,
Which are the brain of heaven, he look'd, and sank.
Around the ancient track march'd, rank on rank,
  The army of unalterable law.

The poets, as you know, and philosophers (of whom
Plato is chief of course) with poetry in their souls, attempt
by many parables to convey their sense of this grand,
harmonious, universal orchestral movement. You recall the
supposed music of the spheres, inaudible to mortals:

Sit, Jessica, Look...
There's not the smallest orb which thou behold'st
But in his motion like an angel sings,
Still quiring to the young-eyed cherubins.

You remember in Plato the story of Er the Pamphylian,
whose relatives after ten days sought his dead body on
the battle-field, and found it without taint of corruption:
and how on the twelfth day, being laid on the pyre, he
came back to life and told them where he had wandered
in the other world, and what seen: but chiefly of the great
spindle on the knees of Necessity, reaching up to heaven
and turning in eight whorls of graduated speed—'and on
the rim of each sits a Siren, who revolves with it, hymning
a single note; the eight notes together forming one harmony.' Plato learned of Pythagoras, Dante of Plato, Chaucer of Dante, Milton of Plato again. Hearken to Milton:

                              Then listen I
To the celestial Sirens' harmony
That sit upon the nine infolded spheres
And sing to those that hold the vital shears,
And turn the adamantine spindle round
On which the fate of gods and men is wound.

> Such sweet compulsion doth in music lie,
> To lull the daughters of Necessity,
> And keep unsteady Nature to her law,
> And the low world in measured motion draw
> After the heavenly tune.

A commentator on this passage has informed the world in a footnote that 'Modern astronomy has exploded the singular notion of revolving hollow concentric spheres.' (By 'singular,' by the way, he probably meant 'curious' —the notion was never 'singular,' it was held by thousands.) But true, true! Not profoundly, perhaps, but how obviously true! Orpheus and Odysseus and Dante did not descend into Hell, really. There are no such places as Utopia or the Slough of Despond or the Delectable Mountains or Laputa or the Woods of Westermain or Hy Brazil —really. And the cow never jumped over the moon, really. But, poor thing, she might *try*! if she weren't suffering from the footnote and mouth disease. In short, there are such things as parables, and the greatest of teachers have not disdained them.

This parable presents a truth, and one of the two most important truths in the world:—*the Universe is not a Chaos but a Harmony.*

## II

Now the other and only equally important truth in the world is that this macrocosm of the Universe, with its harmony, cannot be apprehended at all except as it is focused upon the eye, intellect and soul of Man, the microcosm. All systems of philosophy—from the earliest analysed in 'Ritter and Preller' down to James and Bergson —inevitably work out to this, that the universal harmony is meaningless and nothing to man save in so far as he can apprehend it, and that he can apprehend it only by reference to some corresponding harmony in himself. He is, let us repeat the admission—You are, I am—but the million-millionth atom of a speck. None the less that atom, being sentient, is reflective: being reflective, draws and contracts the whole into its tiny ring. Impercipient, what were we but dead things?

> Rolled round in earth's diurnal course,
>     With rocks, and stones, and trees.

Percipient—solely by the grace of percipience, we are inheritors of it all, and kings. To quote one of the poets, Traherne, with whom I am to deal:

> But little did the infant dream
> That all the treasures of the world were by:
>     And that himself was so the cream
> And crown of all which round about did lie.
>         Yet thus it was: the Gem,
>             The Diadem,
>         The ring enclosing all
> That stand upon this earthly ball,
>         The Heavenly eye,
>     Much wider than the sky,
> Wherein they all included were,
>     The glorious Soul, that was the King
> Made to possess them, did appear
>     A small and little thing!

Hear another, Henry Vaughan:

> I saw Eternity, the other night,
> Like a great *Ring* of pure and endless light,
>     All calm, as it was bright;
> And round beneath it, Time, in hours, days, years,
>     Driv'n by the spheres,
> Like a vast shadow mov'd.

8—2

In that shadow he sees men of all sorts and conditions—the lover, the 'darksome statesman,' the 'fearful miser,' the 'downright epicure'—pursuing their particular cheats of shadow:

> Yet some, who all this while did weep and sing,
>     And sing and weep, soar'd up into the *Ring*;
>         But most would use no wing.
> 'O fools!'—said I—'thus to prefer dark night
>         Before true light!
> To live in grots and caves, and hate the day
>         Because it shews the way,
> The way which from this dead and dark abode
>         Leads up to God,
> A way where you might tread the Sun, and be
>         More bright than he!'
> But as I did their madnes so discusse,
>         One whisper'd thus,
> 'This Ring the Bride-groome did for none provide
>         But for his Bride.'

## III

So we have two rings—the immense orchestral ring of the Universe wheeling above and around us, and the tiny percipient ring which is the pupil of your eye or mine threaded to a brain infinitesimal and yet infinitely capable. But there is one thing more to be said—and a thing of first importance concerning this little soul of man. It instinctively aspires, yearns to know the greater harmony, if only to render it a more perfect obedience: and it aspires, yearns, through a sense of likeness, of oneness, of sonship. Man is, after all, a part of the Universe and just as surely as the Pleiades or Arcturus. Moreover he feels in himself a harmony correspondent with the greater harmony of his quest. His heart pumps his blood to a rhythm; like the plants by which he is fed, he comes to birth, grows, begets his kind, enjoys and adorns his day, dies, and returns to earth; and by seasons regulates his life, as summer and winter, seedtime and harvest sweep their circle over him, rhythmical and recurrent, to find him and his house standing, his garden a little better planted, his task a trifle advanced to completion. And then?—why then, of course, he is gone: another has his place, and digs his patch. But while his day lasts, the brain just behind his sweating brow is the percipient centre upon which the whole cosmic circle focuses itself as the sun through a burning-glass: and he is not shrivelled up by it. On the contrary, he feels that it is all for him. As Traherne writes:

The streets were mine, the temple was mine, the people were mine, their clothes and gold and silver were mine, as much as their sparkling eyes, fair skins and ruddy faces. The skies were mine, and so were the sun and moon and stars, and all the World was mine; and I the only spectator and enjoyer of it.

And again, magnificently:

You never enjoy the world aright, till the Sea itself floweth in your veins, till you are clothed with the heavens, and crowned with the stars.

Yes, and moreover man nurses a native impulse to merge himself in the greater harmony and be one with it; a spirit in his heart (as the Scripture puts it) 'of adoption, whereby we cry Abba, Father.' Open your Browning and read *Johannes Agricola*:

> There's heaven above, and night by night
>   I look right through its gorgeous roof;
> No suns and moons though e'er so bright
>   Avail to stop me; splendour-proof
>   I keep the broods of stars aloof,

For I intend to get to God,
　　For 'tis to God I speed so fast,
For in God's breast, my own abode,
　　Those shoals of dazzling glory, passed,
　　I lay my spirit down at last.
I lie where I have always lain,
　　God smiles as he has always smiled;
Ere suns and moons could wax and wane,
　　Ere stars were thunder-girt, or piled
　　The heavens, God thought on me his child.


IV

'All very well,' you may urge: 'but how is it *done*?'
Well it is not done by the way of philosophy. The quarrel
between philosophy and poetry is notorious and inveterate:
the patronage of poetry by philosophy as stupid as it is
solemnly recognisable. For philosophy attempts to comprehend God's purposes into some system or another: a way
which, if effectual, at once enables man to teach God his
business, or at least to nag him about it, playing Egeria to
his Numa. 'God,' says Heine, 'created man in his image
—and man made haste to return the compliment.' The
philosophers are always returning the compliment, stoking
the chimneys of Sion red-hot to run out the Almighty's
purposes into moulds of this or that system. But if by a
stretch of fancy we can conceive Hegel or Comte or Bergson or any of these constructives as knowing all about it,
why then Hegel or Comte or Bergson is theoretically as
good as God—and then, the Lord stiffen, for us all, the
last barrier between theory and practice!

The poet is more modest. He aspires, not to *comprehend*
but to *apprehend*: to pierce, by flashes, to some point or
other of the great wheeling circle. I have put it thus in an

earlier lecture—There are certain men, granted to dwell among us, of more delicate mental texture than their fellows; men (often in the rough-and-tumble unhappy therefore), whose minds have, as it were, exquisite filaments to intercept, *apprehend* and conduct stray messages between the outer mystery of the Universe and the inner mystery of the individual soul; even as telegraphy has learnt to snatch stray messages wandering over waste waters of ocean. And these men are poets.

## V

Still you may ask, 'How is this apprehending done? What is the process?'

Why, Gentlemen, last term, in a course of lectures 'On the Art of Reading'—a course which I hope to take up again after Christmas and to continue—I insisted almost to weariness on the trinity in Man: *What does, What knows, What is.* I insisted almost to weariness that through *What is* lies the way to spiritual understanding; that, all spirit attracting all spirit as surely as all matter attracts all matter, it is only by becoming like them, by being like them, that we apprehend a spiritual truth in Dante, Shakespeare or Tolstoy; as in that way and no other they brought the angel down. Paley's *Evidences?*—a folly of perversion! Any child has surer evidence within him; as any child, taking up *Hamlet*, feels that it was written for him, and in no condescension either—he *is* the Prince of Denmark. The Kingdom of Heaven is within us. A lost province? Maybe: but we know today, Gentlemen, how a lost province will remember its parent state, how hard a road the parent will travel to recover that which was lost.

You may not agree with me that here lies the deepest secret of poetry: but I present it to you as a historical fact that here lies the central tenet of the Mystics. Man and the Universe and God are in nature One: Unity (if we can find it) runs through all diversities and harmonises them. Therefore to know anything of God Himself we must be, to that extent, like God: therefore, too, the best part of revenge upon an enemy (think of it, in these days) is *not to be like him.*

## VI

But still you ask, 'What is the process?' Surely that lies implicit in what has been said. Man has in him—I will not say a 'subliminal self'—but a soul listening within for a message; so fain to hear that sometimes it must arise and tip-toe to the threshold:

> News from a foreign country came
> As if my treasure and my wealth lay there;
> So much it did my heart inflame,
> 'Twas wont to call my Soul into mine ear;
> Which thither went to meet
> The approaching sweet,
> And on the threshold stood
> To entertain the unknown Good.
> It hover'd there
> As if 'twould leave mine ear,
> And was so eager to embrace
> The joyful tidings as they came,
> 'Twould almost leave its dwelling-place
> To entertain that same.

But the news comes from without, in its own good time and often in guise totally surprising, like the Messiah:

> They all were looking for a king
> To slay their foes and lift them high:
> Thou cam'st, a little baby thing,
> That made a woman cry.

You must (says the mystic) await the hour and trust the invitation, neither of which you may command. The poets (say they) do not read the Word by vigorous striving and learning, as your philosophers do: neither, like the priests of Baal, do they cut themselves and yell. Nor do they wrestle with God like Jacob; but wait, prepare themselves with Mary, and say, 'Be it unto me according to thy word.' They wait, in what one of them called 'a wise passiveness':

> The eye—it cannot choose but see;
>   We cannot bid the ear be still;
> Our bodies feel, where'er they be,
>   Against or with our will.
>
> Not less I deem that there are Powers
>   Which of themselves our minds impress;
> That we can feed this mind of ours
>   In a wise passiveness.
>
> Think you, 'mid all this mighty sum
>   Of things for ever speaking,
> That nothing of itself will come,
>   But we must still be seeking?

And again this same Wordsworth, in his *Tintern Abbey*, tells of 'that serene and blessed mood' wherein

>         the breath of this corporeal frame
> And even the motion of our human blood,
> Almost suspended, we are laid asleep
> In body, and become a living soul:
> While with an eye made quiet by the power
> Of harmony, and the deep power of joy,
> We see into the life of things.

Let this, then, be said today about the mystical poets. Their way is not to strive and cry: it is enough for them to wait, receptacles of the divine passing breath. If you command, 'Strike and sing us a song of Sion,' they answer, 'How can we sing the songs of Sion in a strange land?' but the harp abandoned and hung on a willow by the waters of Babylon may catch at evening (say they) and hum a wind whispering from Israel. The poet merely by waiting and trusting arrives *per saltum* at truths to which the philosopher, pack-laden and varicose upon the military road of logic, can never reach.

There yet remain two things to be said about mysticism; and perhaps a third, at the end.

The first is that as a historical fact all mystics, however diverse their outlook or inlook, have been curiously gracious and yet more curiously happy men. They have found, if not contentment itself, the way of contentment and an anchorage for the soul. They possess it in patience. They are the pure in heart and blessed because they see, or believe they see, God.

The second is that, possessed with a sense of unity in all things, likeness in all things, every mystic has a propensity to deal in symbols, to catch at illustrations which to him seem natural enough, but to us far-fetched, 'conceited,' not *in pari materia*. You have, all the while, to lay account with this in dealing with these seventeenth century men, as I shall show.

## VII

Now to return to Donne on whom we discoursed last week. He is obviously an imperfect mystic, being too restlessly intellectual, having little or none of Wordsworth's 'wise passiveness.' He strives, he cries: and his wit is such that he will fetch an illustration from anywhere. I suppose his poem *The Flea* to be about the most merely disgusting

in our language.  He will ruin an exquisite poem (for us)
by comparing two lovers' souls with a pair of compasses:

> If they be two, they are two so
>     As stiffe twin compasses are two,
> Thy soule the fixt foot, makes no show
>     To move, but doth, if the' other doe.
> And though it in the center sit,
>     Yet when the other far doth rome,
> It leanes, and hearkens after it,
>     And growes erect, as that comes home.

Pass that: but what shall we say to this?

> As the sweet sweat of Roses in a Still,
> As that which from chaf'd muskats pores doth trill,
> As the Almighty Balme of th' early East,
> Such are the sweat drops of my Mistris breast.

## VIII

George Herbert——of the family of the great Earls of
Pembroke, though of a cadet branch——was born the 3rd of
April 1593 in the castle of Montgomery; the fifth of seven
sons of Sir Richard Herbert and his wife Magdalen, and
younger brother of Edward, Lord Herbert of Cherbury.
Sir Richard, whom George remembered as a black-avised,
well-knit, capable man, brave and somewhat stern, died in
the boy's fourth year and sleeps under an alabaster tomb
in Montgomery church. The widow thereafter consecrated
her life to her children.  She did 'often bless God, that
they were neither defective in their shapes, or in their
reason; and very often reprove them that they did not
praise God for so great a blessing.'  On her death George
lamented her in one of the most exquisite elegies ever
written in Latin by an Englishman:

Tota renident aede decus et suavitas
Animo renidentes prius.

With comeliness and kindness shone the whole
House, for they first were radiant in her soul.

The close friend and adviser of her widowhood (pray note) was Donne, Dean of St Paul's, and Donne eulogised her in a poem *The Autumnal*, and preached her funeral sermon. Donne was also a constant friend of George Herbert, and sent him a gift, a seal, from his death-bed.

This is not the place to speak of the eldest boy, Herbert of Cherbury, philosopher, duellist, diplomatist, poet and most remarkable fop of his age. All the Herberts have had 'blood'; from Charlemagne, to whom they seriously trace back their descent, to Sidney Herbert, War Minister and friend of Florence Nightingale—to carry it no farther.

But we speak of George. At twelve he was sent to Westminster School, where (says Walton) 'the beauties of his pretty behaviour and wit shined, and became so eminent and lovely...that he seemed to be marked out for piety, and to become the care of Heaven, and of a particular good angel to guard and guide him.' From Westminster he proceeded to Trinity here, where he stuck to his books and was in due time elected a Fellow, becoming Public Orator to the University in 1619.

As yet he had no intention to devote himself to the priesthood, though it seems that his mother desired it. On the contrary, King James's frequent visits to the University set the young Orator dreaming of Court preferment. With his high birth, his acknowledged talents, his engaging presence and manners always singularly attractive, there was nothing extravagant in the ambition, and we hear that he made himself master of Italian, Spanish and French with a view to qualifying himself for a Secretaryship of State. But the two great men on whose favour he counted died just then, and King James soon after. 'Nature,' said a not too friendly critic, 'intended him for a knight-errant, but disappointed ambition made him a saint.' Well, let us be thankful for saints, however they come.

With or without a sore heart Herbert withdrew from Cambridge and spent some years in retirement, the end of which was a resolve to take Holy Orders. As he puts it, in penitence:

> Whereas my birth and spirit rather took
>   The way that takes the town:
> Thou didst betray me to a lingering book,
>   And wrapt me in a gown.

In 1630 he accepted the living of Bemerton in Wiltshire, and was ordained priest. Meantime he had married Jane Danvers, the daughter of a Wiltshire squire—according to Walton, after a three days' courtship—and

The third day after he was made Rector of Bemerton, and had changed his sword and silk clothes into a canonical coat, he returned so habited…and immediately after he had seen and saluted his wife, he said to her—'You are now a Minister's wife, and must now so far forget your father's house, as not to claim a precedence of any of your parishioners: for you are to know, that a Priest's wife can claim no precedence or place, but that which she purchases by her obliging humility.'… And she was so meek a wife, as to assure him, 'it was no vexing news to her, and that he should see her observe it with a cheerful willingness.'

And this good wife was as good as her word—Walton adds, the love of her parishioners 'followed her in all places, as inseparably as shadows follow substances in sunshine.'

If ever two lives illustrated the beauty of holiness they were those lived by George and Jane Herbert at Bemerton; dull lives, intent mainly on parish work, or repairing church or chapel or rectory, over the mantel of the chimney of which he graved for his successor:

> If thou chance for to find
> A new house to thy mind,
> And built without thy cost;
>   Be good to the poor,
>   As God gives thee store,
> And then my labour's not lost.

It was a homely, homekeeping life, diversified only by trips into Salisbury—the Rector with a fiddle under his arm—to hear and join in music, of which he was passionately fond. But when the bell rang in the parsonage chapel, as it did twice daily, the labourers in the fields let their oxen rest and bowed over a prayer.

Let me read one short passage from Walton: for it ends on one of my favourite quotations, which you may recognise:

In another walk to Salisbury, he saw a poor man with a poorer horse, that was fallen under his load: they were both in distress, and needed present help; which Mr Herbert perceiving, put off his canonical coat, and helped the poor man to unload, and after to load, his horse. The poor man blessed him for it, and he blessed the poor man; and was so like the Good Samaritan, that he gave him money to refresh both himself and his horse; and told him, 'That if he loved himself he should be merciful to his beast.' Thus he left the poor man: and at his coming to his musical friends at Salisbury, they began to wonder that Mr George Herbert, which used to be so trim and clean, came into that company so soiled and discomposed: but he told them the occasion. And when one of the company told him 'He had disparaged himself by so dirty an employment,' his answer was, 'That the thought of what he had done would prove music to him at midnight; and that the omission of it would have upbraided and made discord in his conscience, whensoever he should pass by that place: for if I be bound to pray for all that be in distress, I am sure that I am bound, so far as it is in my power, to practice what I pray for. And though I do not wish for the like occasion every day, yet let me tell you, I would not willingly pass one day of my life without comforting a sad soul, or shewing mercy; and I praise God for this occasion. And now let's tune our instruments.'

A life—as you read of it in Walton—so delicately holy, so fragrant of the Wiltshire water meadows along which the biographer himself wandered with his rod, fishing for trout and 'studying to be quiet,' that it seemed made to tick on and on like a well-oiled clock! But Herbert had brought the seeds of consumption in him from the fens of Cambridge. He knew it, and, in Dr Grosart's words, 'he not merely *walked* down the "valley of the shadow of death"—knowing no "fear" and so making no "haste"—but sang.' A little before the end he withdrew from Bemerton to lodge with his friend Nicholas Ferrar at Little Gidding in Huntingdon, that famous religious house of retirement. There he died, and was buried on the 3rd day of March 1633. Upon a most touching, most eloquent description of the end, and, after it, upon a pause, 'Thus he lived, and thus he died, like a Saint, unspotted of the world, full of almsdeeds, full of humility,' Walton (sad to say) concludes with a bad misquotation of Shirley's

> Only the actions of the just
> Smell sweet and blossom in their dust.

Had he remembered even a little bit better, he might have quoted the same thought from a poem of Herbert's own, and nowadays his most famous. I mean the one beginning

> Sweet day, so cool, so calm, so bright!
> The bridal of the earth and sky.

But the close, being marred by conceits, is far inferior to Shirley's.

> Only a sweet and virtuous soul,
> Like season'd timber, never gives;
> But though the whole world turn to coal,
> Then chiefly lives...

which offends, even after we have reminded ourselves that 'coal,' in Herbert's day, meant charcoal. But that is always the trouble with Herbert. The example of Donne had infected him, who possessed scarcely a tithe of Donne's wit; so that he is always saying beautiful things and always spoiling (for us) his best lyrics. Very few are flawless. Now and then he can make a conceit lovely, as when of man's heavenly comfort he writes

> Not that he may not here
>     Taste of the cheer,
> But as birds drink, and straight lift up their head,
> So must he sip and think
>     Of better drink
> He may attain to, after he is dead.

And even a pun (you know) may be made lovely by emotion. Witness this little one in Hood's *Song of the Shirt*:

> Work—work—work,...
> While underneath the eaves
>     The brooding swallows cling
> As if to show me their sunny backs
>     And *twit* me with the spring.

But when, of man's declension from childish innocence,
Herbert says

> The growth of flesh is but a blister

we must demur.

It is the trouble with Herbert, among many beauties to
find any unflawed by this fault. I know three or four only.
Let me read you two:

### Discipline

Throw away Thy rod,
Throw away Thy wrath;
    O my God,
Take the gentle path!

For my heart's desire
Unto Thine is bent:
    I aspire
To a full consent.

Not a word or look
I affect to own,
    But by book,
And Thy Book alone.

Though I fail, I weep;
Though I halt in pace,
    Yet I creep
To the throne of grace.

Then let wrath remove;
Love will do the deed;
    For with love
Stony hearts will bleed.

Love is swift of foot;
Love's a man of war,
    And can shoot,
And can hit from far.

Who can 'scape his bow?
That which wrought on Thee,
    Brought Thee low,
Needs must work on me.

Throw away Thy rod;
Though man frailties hath,
    Thou art God:
Throw away Thy wrath!

### Love

Love bade me welcome; yet my soul drew back,
    Guilty of dust and sin.
But quick-eyed Love, observing me grow slack
    From my first entrance in,
Drew nearer to me, sweetly questioning
    If I lack'd anything.

'A guest,' I answer'd, 'worthy to be here':
    Love said, 'You shall be he.'
'I, the unkind, ungrateful? Ah, my dear,
    I cannot look on Thee.'
Love took my hand, and smiling did reply,
    'Who made the eyes but I?'

'Truth, Lord; but I have marr'd them: let my shame
    Go where it doth deserve.'
'And know you not,' says Love, 'Who bore the blame?'
    'My dear, then I will serve.'
'You must sit down,' says Love, 'and taste my meat.'
    So I did sit and eat.

It seems almost desecrating to draw your attention down to
the mere technique of so lovely, so apparently absolute a
thing. Yet I think you will admire it none the less for
noting the masterly use of monosyllables and the exquisite
sense of pause, hesitancy and finally command, produced
by it:

    Love said, 'You shall be he.'

'And know you not,' says Love, 'Who bore the blame?'
    'My dear, then I will serve.'
'You must sit down,' says Love, 'and taste my meat.'
    So I did sit and eat.

Monosyllables throughout.


## IX

The Herberts were a high family. But in Wales dwelt
another hardly less noble, the Vaughans: and the two had
preserved an ancient inveterate feud. Of the Vaughans in
1622 was born the poet Henry, in Brecknockshire at Llan-
saintffraed on the bank of the Usk.

He was a twin child. We know little of his parents,

though that old gossip Aubrey, who happened to be a relative, informs us with a relative's outspokenness that the father was 'a coxcomb and no honester than he should be —He cozened me out of 50s. once.'

The twin brothers Henry and Thomas received their schooling from a clergyman hard by; and in due course both went up to Jesus College, Oxford; then, as today, the resort of young Welshmen. Thomas took his degree, and entered Holy Orders; became rector of his native parish, but was ejected by the Parliamentary Commissioners; returned to Oxford; studied alchemy and wrote of it under the name Eugenius Philalethes; wrote some English and Latin verse too; and died in 1666. Henry left the university without taking a degree; studied law in London; got entangled in politics, on the royalist side: lost his money and hopes of a career at the bar; fell back upon medicine and retired to Brecknockshire, where among his native hills and beside his beloved Usk he won such present fame and awards as attend a benevolent medical practitioner in the country; and in the intervals of his practice translated some devotional prose works and left the poems we possess. He died in 1695 at the age of seventy-three —a fairly long life; but, as you see, quite a short story.

The first and most obvious remark upon Vaughan is that his genius was largely imitative; the next and almost as obvious, that it was curiously original.

For the imitation, his debt to Herbert is often patent, sometimes flagrant; and indeed here and there amounts to downright literary pilfering. For a couple of examples— in Herbert's poem *The Agonie* occurs this conceit—the beauty of which lifts it into a thought:

> Love is that liquor sweet and most divine
> Which my God feels as blood, but I, as wine.

Turn to Vaughan's poem *The Passion* and read

> Most blessed Vine!
> Whose juice so good
> I feel as Wine,
> But thy faire branches felt as blood.

The art of pilfering and spoiling could scarcely be better illustrated. The verse, as verse, is poorer: and the obtruded personification of the Vine robs Herbert's fancy of half his delicacy, converting a subtle metaphor into a flat simile. Take a second example.—Herbert in his *Providence* writes

> Rain, do not hurt my flowers; but *gently spend*
> *Your hony-drops.*

Vaughan in his *Rainbow* again conveys and spoils:

> When thou dost shine darkness looks white and fair,
> Forms turn to Musick, clouds to smiles and air:
> *Rain gently spends his honey-drops....*

But the sum of these direct borrowings by no means exhausts—does not begin to exhaust—Vaughan's debt to Herbert; as anyone may convince himself by half-an-hour's study of their poems side by side. (We must always remember however that plagiarism, in days when poets rarely printed their poems, but circulated them in MS among friends, was by no means the crime a later age has made it. It did the robbed one no commercial injury.) The influence of Herbert pervades and is felt everywhere. In the invention of 'conceits,' too, Vaughan the more certainly stamps himself the imitator the more audaciously he goes (as we should say) one better than his master. Herbert can be quaint: but Herbert must resign and lay down his arms before such a stanza as this describing daybreak:

But, as in nature, when the day
　　Breaks, night adjourns,
*Stars shut up shop*, mists pack away,
　　And the moon mourns.

Stars 'shut up shop'! *Et sunt commercia coeli* with a vengeance!

So much for the debit side; now for the credit. At first sight it seems a paradox to claim that a poet so imitative is actually more original and certainly of deeper insight as well as of ampler, more celestial range than the man he copied. And yet it is so, as I think almost anyone will confess after reading Vaughan's *Eternity* or *The Timber*:

Sure thou didst flourish once! and many springs,
　　Many bright mornings, much dew, many showers,
Pass'd o'er thy head; many light hearts and wings,
　　Which now are dead, lodged in thy living bowers.

And still a new succession sings and flies;
　　Fresh groves grow up, and their green branches shoot
Towards the old and still enduring skies,
　　While the low violet thrives at their root.

But thou beneath the sad and heavy line
　　Of death, doth waste all senseless, cold, and dark;
Where not so much as dreams of light may shine,
　　Nor any thought of greenness, leaf, or bark.

And yet—as if some deep hate and dissent,
　　Bred in thy growth betwixt high winds and thee,
Were still alive—thou dost great storms resent
　　Before they come, and know'st how near they be.

Else all at rest thou liest, and the fierce breath
　　Of tempests can no more disturb thy ease;
But this thy strange resentment after death
　　Means only those who broke—in life—thy peace.

Or this poem on *Friends Departed*, of which I will read some verses:

> They are all gone into the world of light!
>     And I alone sit ling'ring here;
> Their very memory is fair and bright,
>     And my sad thoughts doth clear.
>
> It glows and glitters in my cloudy breast,
>     Like stars upon some gloomy grove,
> Or those faint beams in which this hill is drest
>     After the sun's remove.
>
> I see them walking in an air of glory,
>     Whose light doth trample on my days:
> My days, which are at best but dull and hoary,
>     Mere glimmering and decays.
>
> O holy Hope! and high Humility,
>     High as the heavens above!
> These are your walks, and you have show'd them me,
>     To kindle my cold love.
>
> Dear, beauteous Death! the jewel of the Just,
>     Shining nowhere, but in the dark;
> What mysteries do lie beyond thy dust,
>     Could man outlook that mark!
>
> He that hath found some fledged bird's nest may know,
>     At first sight, if the bird be flown;
> But what fair well or grove he sings in now,
>     That is to him unknown.
>
> And yet as Angels in some brighter dreams
>     Call to the soul, when man doth sleep:
> So some strange thoughts transcend our wonted themes,
>     And into glory peep.
>
> If a star were confined into a tomb,
>     Her captive flames must needs burn there;
> But when the hand that lock'd her up gives room,
>     She'll shine through all the sphere.

> O Father of eternal life, and all
> Created glories under Thee!
> Resume Thy spirit from this world of thrall
> Into true liberty.
>
> Either disperse these mists, which blot and fill
> My perspective still as they pass:
> Or else remove me hence unto that hill,
> Where I shall need no glass.

The paradox is not so strange as it appears. Some most original men—Vaughan among them—want starting. They have the soluble genius within them, but it will not crystallise of itself; it must have a shape, a mould. And such men take the mould supplied by their age: it may not be the best for them, but it is what comes to hand. That Vaughan's 'conceits' are often abominably bad where Herbert's were good, does not prove him the lesser genius. Rather, the argument may lie the other way—that he executed them badly because he was naturally superior to such devices, whereas they fitted Herbert's cleverer talent like a glove. To prove how simple and direct Vaughan could be when he chose I will conclude this sketch of him with a short and well-known poem quite free of conceits. It is called *Peace*:

> My soul, there is a country
> Far beyond the stars,
> Where stands a wingèd sentry
> All skilful in the wars:
> There, above noise and danger,
> Sweet Peace sits crown'd with smiles,
> And One born in a manger
> Commands the beauteous files.
> He is thy gracious Friend,
> And—O my soul, awake!—
> Did in pure love descend
> To die here for thy sake.

If thou canst get but thither,
    There grows the flower of Peace,
The Rose that cannot wither,
    Thy fortress, and thy ease.
Leave then thy foolish ranges;
    For none can thee secure
But One who never changes—
    Thy God, thy life, thy cure.

I propose in my next lecture, Gentlemen, to start by examining one most important poem of Vaughan's, which will lead us on to deal expeditiously with Traherne, Quarles, the two Fletchers, Crashaw, and maybe one or two other poets on this line of spiritual ancestry.

Yet one last word, which I had almost forgotten. Can you not see that, while we have mystics among us, death for our literature is impossible? No schoolmaster, even, can kill an instinct which lifts the heads of all nobler young spirits to look past his herding, for they scent the high water-brooks. So mysticism too, in its turn, witnesses and guarantees that until the soul of man be dust, literature shall be alive.

# III. TRAHERNE, CRASHAW AND OTHERS

## I

EVERYONE knows Wordsworth's ode *Intimations of Immortality from Recollections of Early Childhood*: and the stanza

> Our birth is but a sleep and a forgetting;
> The Soul that rises with us, our life's Star,
> > Hath had elsewhere its setting,
> > And cometh from afar:
> > Not in entire forgetfulness,
> > And not in utter nakedness,
> But trailing clouds of glory do we come
> > From God, who is our home:
> Heaven lies about us in our infancy....

I need rehearse no more. And almost everyone knows—or, to speak accurately, has been told (which is a somewhat different thing)—that Wordsworth borrowed his thought from Vaughan's famous poem *The Retreat*:

> Happy those early days, when I
> Shined in my Angel-infancy!
> Before I understood this place
> Appointed for my second race,
> Or taught my soul to fancy aught
> But a white celestial thought:
> When yet I had not walk'd above
> A mile or two from my first Love...
> When on some gilded cloud, or flow'r
> My gazing soul would dwell an hour.
> And in those weaker glories spy
> Some shadows of Eternity.

Now very likely, indeed, Wordsworth took it from Vaughan: but quite as easily he might have taken it from any one of a score of the seventeenth century writers with whom we are dealing. With them man's fall from grace was a preoccupation. How does the greatest of them begin his greatest poem?

> Of Man's first disobedience, and the fruit
> Of that forbidden Tree, whose mortal taste
> Brought death into the World, and all our woe,
> With loss of Eden, till one greater Man
> Restore us, and regain the blissful seat,
> Sing, Heavenly Muse!

Please understand that I do no more here than assert a historical fact, expressing no opinion outside the province of this Chair as by Statute restricted; that I have not the authority, nor the leisure, nor (anyway) the inclination to re-start the Pelagian heresy in Cambridge. I simply affirm, without comment, that these theological poets and preachers of the seventeenth century—happy though they were in having no Darwinian hypothesis of man's descent to answer —were intrigued—almost, you may say, one and all—by man's lapse from a state of innocence. You may pursue their curiosity about this down (say) to Dr South, who was born in 1633 and died a Canon of Christchurch at eighty-three—so that, if actual experience or observation could attest man's depravity, he had, as men go, plenty of both. Take up a sermon of his, *Human Perfection: or Adam in Paradise*, and read

The image of God in man [he writes] is that universal rectitude of all the faculties of the soul, by which they stand apt and disposed to their respective duties and operations.

And first for its noblest faculty, the understanding: it was then [*i.e.*, in Paradise] sublime, clear and inspiring, and, as it

were, the soul's upper region, lofty and serene, free from the
vapours and disturbances of the inferior affections. It was the
leading controlling faculty; all the passions wore the colours of
reason; it did not so much persuade as command; it was not
counsel but dictator....It did not so properly apprehend as
irradiate the object; not so much find, as make things intel-
ligible. It did arbitrate upon the several reports of sense and
all varieties of imagination: not like a drowsy judge, only
hearing, but also directing their verdict. In sum, it was vegete,
quick and lively; open as the day, untainted as the morning,
full of the innocence and sprightliness of youth; it gave the
soul a bright and full view into all things.

South then divides this Understanding into Understanding Speculative, which gives the mind its general notions
and rules, and the Practical Understanding, 'that storehouse
of the soul in which are treasured up the rules of action and
the seeds of morality. Of the first, the Speculative Understanding with its notions, he goes on:

Now it was Adam's happiness in the State of Innocence to
have these clear and unsullied. He came into the world a
philosopher. He could see consequences yet dormant in their
principles, and effects yet unborn and in the womb of their
causes; his understanding could almost pierce into future contingents; his conjectures improving even to prophecy, or to
certainties of prediction: till his fall it was ignorant of nothing
but of sin; or at least it rested in the notion without the smart
of the experiment. Could any difficulty have been propounded,
the solution would have been as early as the proposal....Like a
better Archimedes, the issue of all his enquiries was an εὕρηκα.
An εὕρηκα, the offspring of his brain without the sweat of his
brow....An Aristotle was but the rubbish of an Adam, and
Athens but the rudiments of Paradise.

Now if you ask me, Gentlemen, what I think of that,
as prose, I answer that I find it not half as good as it looks.

If you ask me what I think of its doctrine, I answer that I don't believe a word of it: that the learned Dr South is dispensing positive information on a subject of which he is as ignorant as anyone else. Adam's 'understanding could almost pierce into future contingents.' Why 'almost'? Why, because there was, as King George III said of the dumpling, the apple to be accounted for. So when, of the practical understanding, South goes on to instance such maxims as 'That God is to be worshipped,' 'That parents are to be honoured,' 'That a man's word is to be kept,' I ask concerning the middle proposition, what Adam could possibly know about parents, or at that time even about children, having neither? As when South assures us, of Love, that 'this affection, in the state of innocence, was happily pitched upon its right object,' I cannot forgo the reflection that, after all, there was but one lady in the garden. Forgive me that I speak brusquely. In my belief the first three chapters of Genesis contain nothing to justify South; and in my belief no handling can well be too rough-and-ready for one who expands himself so pretentiously upon ground where an angel might be diffident.

But this is opinion: and I have quoted South's sermon, not for what it is worth as opinion, but for what it is worth as evidence of a historical fact—that the minds of the seventeenth century played more persistently than do ours with the picture of a state of innocence and the way of man's fall from it, and, by consequence, with the notion which Wordsworth afterwards elaborated—the notion of an ante-natal realm of bliss out of which the child descends (as the children you may remember in Maeterlinck's *Oiseau Bleu*, the little ones waiting to be born), to lose his ineffable aura as this world entraps him, encloses him in the shades of its prison-house.

Let us turn to a more delicate mind than South's, and consult the Platonist John Earle. These seventeenth century men, as you know, were much given to penning *Characters* more or less in imitation of the *Characters* of Theophrastus. It was a literary craze in its day; and not seldom, to my thinking, they achieved things far more philosophical, as well as far more poetical, than any in Theophrastus's range. Here is what John Earle, in his *Microcosmographie*, writes of 'A Child':

### A Child.

He is nature's fresh picture newly drawn in oil; which time, and much handling, dims and defaces. His soul is yet a white paper unscribbled with observations of the world, wherewith at length it becomes a blurred note-book. He is purely happy because he knows no evil, nor hath made means by sin to be acquainted with misery. He arrives not at the mischief of being wise, nor endures evils to come by foreseeing them. He kisses and loves all, and, when the smart of the rod is past, smiles on his beater....

We laugh at his foolish sports, but his game is our earnest: and his drums, rattles and hobby-horses but the emblems and mockings of men's business. His father hath writ him as his own little story, wherein he reads those days of his life that he cannot remember, and sighs to see what innocence he has outlived. The elder he grows he is a stair lower from God; and like his first father much worse in his breeches.

He is the Christian's example, and the old man's relapse; the one imitates his pureness, and the other falls into his simplicity. Could he put off his body with his little coat, he had got Eternity without a burthen, and exchanged but one heaven for another.

## II

But for faith in this notion which Earle treated so playfully, and for burning fervour in that faith we must go to a lowly follower of Herbert and Vaughan, to an exceedingly humble man of heart—Thomas Traherne.

Who was Traherne? Well, we know him now to have been a poor Welsh parson, born in 1636 or thereabouts, somewhere on the Welsh border (likeliest at Hereford), the son of a shoemaker; that somehow in 1652 he managed to enter at Brasenose College, Oxford, was made Bachelor of Arts in 1656, Master of Arts in 1661, Bachelor of Divinity in 1669; that he took Orders and became vicar of Credenhill, in Herefordshire, about 1661: where, he tells us, 'being seated among silent trees, and meads and hills' he made a resolve to cling to this childish felicity. Yes, 'I chose rather to live upon ten pounds a year, and to go in leather clothes, and feed upon bread and water, so that I might have all my time clearly to myself'; that after nine years or so he was removed to London to be chaplain to Sir Orlando Bridgman, Lord Keeper of the Seals, and that he died in Bridgman's house at Teddington in October, 1674, aged but thirty-eight.

For two hundred and fifty years his writings were lost, and his name was not even the shade of a name. When, in 1896 or 1897, a Mr Brooke picked up two innominate volumes in MS for a few pence at a street bookstall, and submitted them to Dr Grosart, that veteran at once and excusably pronounced them to be the work of Vaughan and set about including them in a new edition of Vaughan which, just before his death, he was endeavouring to find means to publish. On his death, his library being dispersed, the volumes again started wandering. It were a fascinating story—had I the time to tell it—how they came into the hands of the late Mr Bertram Dobell, most lovable of booksellers (which is saying a great deal), how Mr Dobell hit on a clue, followed it, and discovered the true author, and how later a third MS, not bearing Traherne's name, was found in the British Museum. I will only recount my own very small part in the affair. Seventeen years ago, when preparing the *Oxford Book of English Verse* I was sent by the late Professor York Powell, without comment, a bookseller's catalogue with a poem on its back page. It was the poem beginning 'News from a foreign country came,' part of which I read to you a fortnight ago. I made enquiries, and Mr Dobell very kindly copied out some other poems for me—none of which, however, seemed to me quite so good as *News*, which duly went into the *Oxford Book*—and with them some prose passages from the second MS volume entitled *Centuries of Meditations*. I wrote back that the prose seemed to me even finer stuff than the poems, and urged him to publish it. The poems appeared—that is, first saw print—in 1903, *Centuries of Meditations* in 1908, and I cannot forbear telling you what pleasure it was to open the volume, to find my own name on the editor's page of dedication, and to reflect (a little wistfully if not whimsically) that maybe this author, forgotten for two hundred and fifty years might, after another two hundred and fifty, rescue from complete oblivion the name of another who had admired him.

Well, let that be—we all have our little vanities. But of Traherne himself the first and last word is that he carries into a sustained ecstasy this adoration of the wisdom of childhood—*Regnum Scientiae ut regnum coeli non nisi sub persona infantis intratur*: and it is truly marvellous how the man can harp so long and elaborately on one string.

I have said that his verse, in my opinion, ranks lower than
his prose: but here is a specimen:

How like an Angel came I down!
How bright are all things here!
When first among His works I did appear
O how their Glory me did crown!
The world resembled his Eternity
In which my soul did walk;
And everything that I did see
Did with me talk.

. . . . .

The streets were paved with golden stones,
The boys and girls were mine,
O how did all their lovely faces shine!
The sons of men were holy ones,
In joy and beauty they appear'd to me:
And every thing which here I found,
(While like an angel I did see)
Adorn'd the ground

. . . . .

Proprieties [properties] themselves were mine,
And hedges ornaments;
Walls, boxes, coffers, and their rich contents
Did not divide my joys, but all combine.
Clothes, ribbons, jewels, laces, I esteem'd
My joys by others worn:
For me they all to wear them seem'd
When I was born.

So much for his verse: now for similar thinking in prose:

These pure and virgin apprehensions I had from the womb,
and that divine light wherewith I was born are the best unto
this day, wherein I can see the Universe. By the Gift of God
they attended me into the world, and by His special favour I
remember them till now....

The corn was orient and immortal wheat, which never should be reaped, nor was ever sown. I thought it had stood from everlasting to everlasting. The dust and stones of the street were as precious as gold: the gates were at first the end of the world. The green trees when I saw them first through one of the gates transported and ravished me, their...unusual beauty made my heart to leap, and almost mad with ecstasy, they were such strange and wonderful things. The Men! O what venerable and revered creatures did the aged seem! Immortal Cherubims.

At this point I break off to wonder, irreverently, what Traherne would have made of some of my own uncles and aunts; the Calvinistic ones. At that age I could have spared them to him or to anyone for experiment.

And young men glittering and sparkling Angels, and maids strange seraphic pieces of life and beauty! Boys and girls tumbling in the street, and playing, were moving jewels. I knew not that they were born or should die. But all things abided eternally as they were in their proper places....The city seemed to stand in Eden, or to be built in Heaven. The streets were mine, the temple was mine, the people were mine, their clothes and gold and silver were mine, as much as their sparkling eyes, fair skins and ruddy faces. The skies were mine, and so were the sun and moon and stars, and all the World was mine; and I the only spectator and enjoyer of it....So that with much ado I was corrupted, and made to learn the dirty devices of this world. Which now I unlearn, and become, as it were, a little child again that I may enter into the Kingdom of God.

So much then, again, for Traherne. But before leaving him I will ask you to note that Donne, Herbert, Vaughan and he—the four whose spiritual kinship we have been tracing, came all by ancestry, proud or poor, from the Welsh Marches. Donne's forefathers were of Wales and spelt their name 'Dwynne.' The Herberts were lords over

Pembroke, the Vaughans over Brecknockshire, Traherne a poor tradesman's son of Hereford. I distrust generalisations: but there would seem to be something here in 'the Celtic spirit.'

### III

Before taking up another line of mystics let me deal briefly with three or four who fall to be mentioned here.

Sir John Davies (1570 or thereabouts—1626—another Welshman) and Phineas Fletcher (1582–1650 or so) reduced this great order of the universe to harmony with man, its microcosm, in elaborate poems by quaint methods. Davies in his *Orchestra* set it all dancing, treading a measure much like his mistress Queen Elizabeth, 'high and disposedly.' For a taste:

> For loe the Sea that fleets about the Land,
> And like a girdle clips her solide waist,
> Musicke and measure both doth understand;
> For his great chrystall eye is alwayes cast
> Up to the Moone, and on her fixèd fast;
> And as she daunceth in her pallid spheere,
> So daunceth he about his Center heere.

To Phineas Fletcher and to his *Purple Island* (entrancing name) I hied as a boy after buried treasure, only to discover it a weary allegory of the human body and its functions. (His brother, Giles Fletcher, who died young, was an imitator of Spenser and does not come into this purview.)

Henry King, Bishop of Chichester (1592–1669), though little of a mystic, may come in as a friend of Donne's, one of his legal executors and withal a poet; of extraordinary charm, too, within the short range which he knew how to keep, so that you cannot make his acquaintance but you remember it with pleasure. He is best known, I suppose, by his lyric 'Tell me no more how fair she is.' But let me quote you a few lines from his lovely *Exequy on his Wife*:

Meantime thou hast her, earth: much good
May my harm do thee! Since it stood
With Heaven's will I might not call
Her longer mine, I give thee all
My short-lived right and interest
In her whom living I loved best.
Be kind to her, and prithee look
Thou write into thy Doomsday book
Each parcel of this rarity
Which in thy casket shrined doth lie,
As thou wilt answer Him that lent—
Not gave—thee my dear monument.
So close the ground, and 'bout her shade
Black curtains draw: my bride is laid.

Sleep on, my Love, in thy cold bed
Never to be disquietèd!
My last good-night! Thou wilt not wake
Till I thy fate shall overtake:
Till age, or grief, or sickness must
Marry my body to that dust
It so much loves; and fill the room
My heart keeps empty in thy tomb.
Stay for me there...
Each minute is a short degree
And every hour a step towards thee....

'Tis true—with shame and grief I yield—
Thou, like the van, first took'st the field;
And gotten hast the victory
In thus adventuring to die
Before me, whose more years might crave
A just precedence in the grave.

> But hark! my pulse, like a soft drum,
> Beats my approach, tells thee I come;
> And slow howe'er my marches be
> I shall at last sit down by thee.
>
> The thought of this bids me go on
> And wait my dissolution
> With hope and comfort. Dear! forgive
> The crime—I am content to live
> Divided, with but half a heart
> Till we shall meet and never part.

Nor is William Habington (1605–1654) quite a mystic. Though a Roman Catholic he might be ranked alongside Herbert, did he own even a measure of Herbert's capacity for rapture, for fine excess. His much admired *Nox Nocti Indicat Scientiam*

> When I survey the bright
> Celestial sphere...

says little more than Addison's hymn, 'The spacious firmament on high,' says later on: and that, to tell truth, does not amount to much. Its opening

> When I survey the bright
> Celestial sphere;
> So rich with jewels hung, that Night
> Doth like an Ethiop bride appear...

is good: or might be, did it not challenge the deadly comparison with Shakespeare's

> O, she doth teach the torches to burn bright!
> It seems she hangs upon the cheek of night
> Like a rich jewel in an Ethiope's ear.

Its close is better:

> For as yourselves your empires fall,
> And every kingdom hath a grave.

> Thus those celestial fires,
>   Though seeming mute,
> The fallacy of our desires
>   And all the pride of life confute:—
>
> For they have watch'd since first
>   The World had birth:
> And found sin in itself accurst,
>   And nothing permanent on Earth.

Quite good commonplace: but commonplace, nevertheless.

As for Christopher Harvey (1597–1663), friend of Walton—a Cheshire man who became rector of Whitney in Herefordshire (again we are on the Welsh Marches)—he was a mystic of the epigrammatic kind. He imitated Herbert and, what is more, didn't care who knew it. The title of his best known volume runs thus—*The Synagogue: or The Shadow of the Temple. Sacred Poems and Private Ejaculations in Imitation of Mr. George Herbert. Printed for Philemon Stephens at the Guilded Lyon in St. Paul's Churchyard.* The poem I like best in it is nothing mystical. It opens magnificently, thus

> The Bishop? Yes, why not?...

but cannot, of course, maintain that level. Two stanzas, however, may be worth quoting in these days:

> The Bishop? Yes, why not? What doth that name
>   Import which is unlawful or unfit?
> To say The Overseer is the same
>   In substance, and no hurt (I hope) in it:
>     But sure if men did not despise the thing,
>     Such scorn upon the name they would not fling.
>
> Some priests—some presbyters I mean—would be
>   Each Overseer of his sev'ral cure;
> But one Superiour, to oversee
>   Them altogether, they will not endure.
>     This the main difference is, that I can see,—
>     Bishops they would not have, but they would be.

## IV

Before speaking of a more important and more mystical mystic, Francis Quarles (1592–1644) I must say just a word upon a tenet of the mystical faith which naturally flows from the two principles we have discussed at some length. If the universe be an ordered harmony, and the soul of man a tiny lesser harmony, vibrating to it, yearning to it, seeking to be one with it: if, again, of recollection it knows itself to *have been* at some time one with it, though now astray upon earth, a lost province (as I put it, a fortnight ago) of the Kingdom of God; why, then, it follows that the King himself passionately seeks to recover, to retrieve, that which was lost. The idea of a Christ bruising his feet endlessly over stony places, insatiate in search of lost Man, his brother, or the lost Soul, his desired bride, haunts all our mystical poetry from that lovely fifteenth century poem *Quia Amore Langueo*, down to Francis Thompson's *Hound of Heaven*. In a former lecture I read *Quia Amore Langueo* to you almost *in extenso*. Suffer me today to recall but two verses of the wounded Christ chanting his bride:

> I crowned her with bliss and she me with thorn;
> I led her to chamber and she me to die;
> I brought her to worship and she me to scorn;
> I did her reverence and she me villany.
> To love that loveth is no maistry;
> Her hate made never my love her foe:
> Ask me then no question why—
> *Quia amore langueo.*

. . . . . . .

My love is in her chamber: hold your peace!
  Make ye no noise, but let her sleep.
My babe I would not were in dis-ease,
  I may not hear my dear child weep.
    With my pap I shall her keep;
    Ne marvel ye not that I tend her to:
    The wound in my side were ne'er so deep
      But *Quia amore langueo.*

That cry still haunts out of a small innominate poem of the
century with which we are dealing:

    My blood so red
      For thee was shed,
  Come home again, come home again;
  My own sweet heart, come home again!
    You've gone astray
      Out of your way,
  Come home again, come home again!

It haunts Quarles; but with Quarles it is rather the cry of
the soul, the Bride, seeking the Bridegroom:

I will rise now, and go about the city in the streets, and in
the broad ways I will seek him whom my soul loveth: I sought
him, but I found him not.

The watchmen that go about the city found me: to whom
I said, Saw ye him whom my soul loveth?

It was but a little that I passed from them, but I found him
whom my soul loveth. I held him and would not let him go,
until I had brought him into my mother's house, and into the
chamber of her that conceived me.

I charge you, O ye daughters of Jerusalem, by the roes and
by the hinds of the field, that ye stir not up, nor awake my
love, till he please.

'So I my best-Beloved's am: so he is mine.' That is a
refrain of Quarles, and his constant note. But in the one

poem I shall quote from him I am redeeming, in some fashion—or trying to redeem—a wrong. By an error into which no less a man than the late W. E. Henley fell along with me, an old book misled us into giving the lines to so unlikely a man as Rochester. And there they are, in the *Oxford Book of English Verse* ascribed to Rochester, and the ascription must be corrected though I find it will involve destroying about sixty pages of stereotyped plates. But they are Quarles's. They run:

> Why dost thou shade thy lovely face? O why
> Does that eclipsing hand of thine deny
> The sunshine of the Sun's enlivening eye?
>
> Without thy light what light remains in me?
> Thou art my life: my way, my light's in thee;
> I live, I move, and by thy beams I see.
>
> Thou art my life—If thou but turn away,
> My life's a thousand deaths. Thou art my way,—
> Without thee, Love, I travel not but stray.
>
> My light thou art: without thy glorious sight
> My eyes are darken'd with eternal night.
> My Love, thou art my way, my life, my light.
>
> Thou art my way; I wander if thou fly.
> Thou art my light; if hid, how blind am I!
> Thou art my life; if thou withdraw'st, I die.
>
> My eyes are dark and blind; I cannot see:
> To whom or whither should my darkness flee,
> But to that light?—and what's that light but thee?
>
> If I have lost my path, dear lover, say,
> Shall I still wander in a doubtful way?
> Love, shall a lamb of Israel's sheepfold stray?

. . . . . .

And yet thou turn'st away thy face and fly'st me!
And yet I sue for grace and thou deny'st me!
Speak, art thou angry, Love, or only try'st me?

.    .    .    .    .

Dissolve thy sunbeams, close thy wings and stay!
See, see how I am blind, and dead, and stray!
—O thou that art my life, my light, my way!

Then work thy will! If passion bid me flee,
My reason shall obey; my wings shall be
Stretch'd out no farther than from me to thee!

## V

Mention of wings reminds me to say a word—it shall be no more—on the quaint metrical and typographical devices in which these poets revelled; artificialities in far worse taste than mere puns and verbal conceits; very far worse than the rebuses and elaborate emblems around which Quarles, for example, as a symbolist, wrote so many of his poems. It was the day of such affectations; of ring-posies, acrostics, and the topiary art that designed mazes, trimmed yew trees and tortured them to the shapes of lions, camels, huntsmen with hounds. Its worst excess is seen, possibly, in the tricks (dear to Herbert, Harvey, and others) of writing verses to the shape of altars, pyramids, the wings of a bird. And my word upon these I shall borrow from Bacon's Essay *Of Gardens*:

As for the Making of Knots, or Figures, with Divers Coloured Earths, that they may lie under the Windowes of the House, on that Side, which the Garden stands, they be but Toyes: You may see as good Sights, many times, in Tarts.

## VI

Our last poet, Richard Crashaw (1613?–1649) ran to excesses of verbal conceit which anybody can arraign, albeit Johnson rather unaccountably overlooked their help, which had been priceless, for his indictment of the metaphysical poets. Everyone knows the flagrancies of *The Weeper* with the Magdalen's tearful eyes:

> Two walking baths, two weeping motions,
> Portable and compendious Oceans,

and the 'brisk Cherub' supposed to sip from them each morning,

> and his song
> Tastes of this breakfast all day long.

Yes, the flagrancies are flagrant: yet I think too much has been made of them. For (as I hold the business of an examiner is always to discover how much a student does know and never how much he does not), even so I hold that we may overlook a hundred flagrancies for such a stanza as this:

> The dew no more will weep
> The primrose's pale cheek to deck,
> The dew no more will sleep
> Nuzzled in the lily's neck:
> Much rather would it tremble here
> And leave them both to be thy tear.

Crashaw, one must admit, is often terribly at his ease in Sion: and if one must contrast him with Herbert—often so gently familiar, too, with his God—why, the difference is that Herbert had, with modesty, a breeding that made him at home in any company. But how Crashaw's tenderness

excuses all familiarity in his farewell to Saint Teresa, going
to martyrdom!

> Farewell then, all the world, adieu!
> Teresa is no more for you....
> Farewell whatever dear may be,
> Mother's arms or father's knee!
> Farewell house, and farewell home!
> She's for the Moors and Martyrdom.
> Sweet, not so fast....

For a last and longer taste of Crashaw let me read a few
verses of the *Hymn of the Shepherdmen* sung over the infant
Christ in his snow-bound cradle:

> *Tityrus* (*they are called Tityrus and Thyrsis*)
> I saw the curl'd drops, soft and slow,
>   Come hovering o'er the place's head;
> Off'ring their whitest sheets of snow
>   To furnish the fair infant's bed.
>     'Forbear,' said I; 'be not too bold,
>     Your fleece is white, but 'tis too cold.'

> *Thyrsis.*  I saw the obsequious seraphim
>   Their rosy fleece of fire bestow:
> For well they now can spare their wings
>   Since Heaven itself lies here below.
>     'Well done,' said I; 'but are you sure
>     Your down, so warm, will pass for pure?'

> *Both.*  No no; your King's not yet to seek
>   Where to repose his royal head:
> See, see, how soon his new-bloom'd cheek
>   'Twixt mother's breasts is gone to bed.
>     'Sweet choice,' said we; 'no way but so
>     Not to ly cold yet sleep in snow.'

*Chorus.*    She sings thy tears asleep, and dips
　　　　　Her kisses in thy weeping eye;
　　　　She spreads the red leaves of thy lips
　　　　　That in their buds yet blushing lie.
　　　　　　She 'gainst those mother diamonds tries
　　　　　　The points of her young eagle's eyes.

* * * * *

　　　　To thee, meek Majesty, soft King
　　　　　Of simple graces and sweet loves!
　　　　Each of us his lamb will bring,
　　　　　Each his pair of silver doves!
　　　　　　At last, in fire of thy fair eyes,
　　　　　　Ourselves become our own best sacrifice.


# VII

In conclusion,—you certainly will not charge me, Gentlemen, with having in these lectures withheld any due I could bring of admiration for our seventeenth century mystical poets. Yet—for a personal confession—I desire not to live very long at one stretch with them. You may put it, if you will, that he is blameworthy who finds them

　　　　　　too bright or good
　　　For human nature's daily food.

But I find their atmosphere too rare, and at the same time too nebulous, their manna too ambrosial, unsatisfying to my hunger. I turn from vapours, seeking back to the firm Greek outline, to the art which in Aristotle's phrase, exhibits men and women in action—πράττοντες—above all to the breathing, familiar, adorable bodies of my kind. I want Daphnis at the spring, Rebecca at the well, Ruth stretched at Boaz's feet, silent in the sleeping granary.

You promise heavens free from strife,
   Pure truth and perfect change of will;
But sweet, sweet, is this human life
   So sweet, I fain would breathe it still;
     Your chilly stars I can forgo;
     This warm kind world is all I know.

Forsooth the present we must give
   To that which cannot pass away;
All beauteous things for which we live
   By laws of time and space decay—
     But O the very reason why
     I clasp them, is because they die!

So even coming from the presence of Dante, with an old schoolmaster of mine I whisper, 'Ariosto, wait for me.' So from symposia of these mystics, rapturous but jejune, as from the vegetarian feast of Eugenists and of other men made perfect, I return to knock in at the old tavern with the cosy red blinds, where I may meet Don Quixote, Sancho Panza, Douglas and Percy, Mr Pickwick and Sam Weller, Romeo and the Three Musketeers—above all, Falstaff, with Mistress Quickly to serve me. I want the personal—Shakespeare, Johnson, Goldsmith, Lamb, among men: of women I need to worship no Saint Teresa, but Miranda the maid, Imogen the wife. For

  There vitality, there, there solely in song
    Resides, where earth and her uses to men, their needs
    Their forceful cravings the theme are: there it is strong.

That is the gospel of Meredith, and I subscribe to it. For we come out of earth and fall back to earth; and the spring of our craving soars—though it reach to God—on the homely jet of our geniture.

# THE POETRY OF
# GEORGE MEREDITH

## I

I HAVE chosen, Gentlemen, to speak of George Meredith's poetry, this morning, for two or three reasons; of which—to be honest—the foremost is that I delight in it. But, for a second, I think it time to hint at least that the Modern and Medieval Languages Board intend to justify by practice what they meant when, in framing the separate English Tripos, they so far ignored academic tradition and dared the rage of schoolmasters—which, like that of the sheep, is terrible—as to open the study of English down to our own times, declining to allow that any past date could be settled, even by university statute, as the one upon which English literature took to its bed, and expired, and was beatified. I have possibly as much reason as anyone in this room to know how faulty one's judgment may be about modern work, and specially about modern poetry. Still the task of appraising it has to be done, for the books of our time *are* the books of our time. They tell us in their various ways 'How it strikes a Contemporary': and we shall not intelligently prepare ourselves, here at Cambridge, by drawing an imaginary line somewhere between the past and the present and announcing, 'On this side are the certified dead, who are alive; on that, the living, who are non-existent.' Hazlitt's remark, 'I hate to read new books,' or somebody else's that, whenever a new book came out, he read an old one, is—well, just the sort of thing one does say at the beginning of a familiar essay or at the dinner-table; and to press it to absurdity were an easy waste of time. 'Ah, sir,' said the lady, 'this is a sad, degenerate age!' 'Ah, madam,' answered the philosopher, 'let us thank heaven that neither you nor I belong to it.'

And, after all, what does it matter to this large world in the long run if a tripos candidate should pronounce a mistaken judgment on the merits of Lascelles Abercrombie, John Masefield or John Drinkwater?

Moreover I have insisted, and shall go on insisting while I speak from this place, that upon a school of English here rests an obligation to teach the writing of good English as well as the reading of it: to teach the writing of it through the reading. I want the average educated Englishman to write English as deftly, as scrupulously, as the average educated Frenchman writes French; to have, as at present he has not, at least an equal respect for his language. Nay, our language being one of the glories of our birth and state, I want him to draw self-respect from his use of it, as men of good ancestry are careful not to derogate from their forefathers. I would have him sensible that a sloppy sentence is no more nearly 'good enough' than dirty linen is good enough. I want, indeed, *Prose* 'in widest commonalty spread.' I desire—to put it on merely practical grounds, using a fairly recent example—that among us we make it impossible to do again what our Admiralty did with the battle of Jutland, to win a victory at sea and lose it in a despatch. And I use this illustration because many who will hardly be convinced that a thing is worth doing well for its own sake, may yet listen when you show them that to do it ill, indifferently, laxly, means public damage.

There used to be a saying in the Fleet—and it should have reached the Admiralty—that 'Nighenough is the worst man in the ship.'

Now although our fathers—it must be confessed—tried harder than we to write prose; although to our age belongs that rampant substitute which I once denounced to you under the name of Jargon; nevertheless it were, as I hold, a folly to hedge off good writing of our day and bid you fasten your study upon remote masterpieces. Admire them, study them, by them improve your own style. But improve it also by studying how good writers today are adapting it to express what men and women think and do in our time. For we belong to it. We cannot, as Charles Lamb once threatened in a pet, say 'Damn the age! I will write for antiquity': and as little ought we to surrender to the baser fashions of the present. But we should, I contend, face the arena and make what best use we may of that present use,

Quem penes arbitrium est, et jus et norma loquendi.

## II

You are thinking perhaps that all this lies wide of any talk about George Meredith who, to begin with, is dead, and while alive was a doubtful exemplar of pellucid English.

Now, for the first point, you must forgive me that I, who had the honour to know him enough to hear him talk frankly, can scarcely think of him as dead, and certainly can never think of him as old.

'I suppose,' he admitted once, 'I should regard myself as getting old—I am seventy-four. But I do not feel to be growing old, either in heart or mind. I still look on life with a young man's eye. I have always hoped I should not grow

old as some do—with a palsied intellect, living backwards,
regarding other people as anachronisms because they themselves have lived on into other times and left their sympathies
behind them with the years.'

He never did. You must understand that while in conversation and bearing he played with innocent extrava-
gancies which, in a smaller man, might be mistaken for
affectations—in particular with a high Spanish courtesy
which was equally at the service of his cook and of his
king—you soon perceived all this to be genuine; the natural
manner of the man. It did not pretend a false sprightliness of

> Days, when the ball of our vision
>     Had eagles that flew unabash'd to sun;
> When the grasp on the bow was decision,
>     And arrow and hand and eye were one.

But he recognised that this had been, and was irrecover-
able; that while the time lasted it had been priceless. No
poet, no thinker, growing old, had ever a more fearless trust
in youth; none has ever had a truer sense of our duty to it:

> Keep the young generations in hail,
> And bequeath them no tumbled house.

None has ever been more scornful of the asserted wisdom
of our seniors, who,
>             on their last plank,
> Pass mumbling it as nature's final page...

and would petrify the young with rules of wisdom, lest—
as he says scornfully—

> Lest dreaded Change, long damm'd by dull decay,
> Should bring the world a vessel steer'd by brain,
> And ancients musical at close of day.

'Earth loves her young,' begins his next sonnet:

> Her gabbling grey she eyes askant, nor treads
> The ways they walk; by what they speak oppress'd.

## III

I have a more difficult defence to put up against his alleged and, in places, undeniable obscurity. Rather, it would be more difficult if I proposed to put up any. But I do not.

Let us separate obscurity from ugliness. Let us take, for example, Shakespeare's *King Lear*, which contains somewhat of both; and I put it to you that our sense of tremendous beauty as we read that play is twin with a sense of the bestial lurking in humankind. Or I ask you to consider Shakespeare's *Pericles* and say 'Is it or is it not the test of the brothel scenes that passes Marina for adorable?'—to consider *The Tempest* and answer 'Where would be Ariel or where even Miranda, or where the whole lovely magic, with Caliban left out?' But obscurity is failure. It may be a partial failure; it may be an entirely honourable failure, born of bravery to face truths for which, because they are difficult or rugged, the writer can hardly find expressive words, and smooth mellifluous words yet more hardly. Still it is a disability, albeit (let me add) with this compensation, that when the fuliginous clouds are rifted, when, as often with Donne, with Browning, with Meredith, we stand and gaze into a sudden vista of clear beauty, the surprise is strangely effective: it has an awe of its own and a reward not illegitimate. I might quote you from Meredith separate lines or very short passages by the score to illustrate this. Take one example only, summarising that love of Earth which, as we shall find, is the master secret he teaches:

> Until at last this love of Earth reveals
> A soul beside our own, to quicken, quell,
> Irradiate, and through ruinous floods uplift.

'Irradiate, and through ruinous floods uplift.' Milton taught that line: but for Milton it had never been written: and yet it could never have been written, after Milton, by any but an authentic poet.

## IV

Fortunately, however, Meredith has left some poems, unchallengeably beautiful, in which a reader impatient of obscurity will discover little or nothing to tease him. And since—and although my practice this morning may seem to contradict it—no small part of a teacher's duty consists in saving other people's time, let me indicate a few of Meredith's poems which, if you like them, will lead you to persevere with more difficult ones in which, if my experience be of use, you will find much delight: for there is a pleasure in critical pains as well as in poetic. If you like them not, why then you will be in a position to decide on saving further time, though you lose something else.

The first—*Phoebus with Admetus*—I will read in full. You know the legend: how Phoebus Apollo—lord of the sun, of music, of archery, of medicine—was exiled by his father Zeus for having slain the Cyclops, and condemned to serve a term on earth, tending the flocks of king Admetus of Thessaly. This is the tale of the shepherds and herdsmen who had known the divine guest and the wondrous great season of plenty he brought[1]:

> When by Zeus relenting the mandate was revoked,
>     Sentencing to exile the bright Sun-God,
> Mindful were the ploughmen of who the steer had yoked,
>     Who: and what a track show'd the upturn'd sod!

[1] Mark the triple hammer-beat, closing the 2nd, 4th, 6th, 8th stanzaic lines throughout. It is one of Meredith's master-tricks.

Mindful were the shepherds as now the noon severe
  Beat a burning eyebrow to brown evetide,
How the rustic flute drew the silver to the sphere,
  Sister of his own, till her rays fell wide.
            God! of whom music
            And song and blood are pure,
            The day is never darken'd
            That had thee here obscure.


Chirping none the scarlet cicalas crouch'd in ranks:
  Slack the thistle-head piled its down-silk grey:
Scarce the stony lizard suck'd hollows in his flanks;
  Thick on spots of umbrage our drowsed flocks lay.
Sudden bow'd the chestnuts beneath a wind unheard,
  Lengthen'd ran the grasses, the sky grew slate:
Then amid a swift flight of wing'd seed white as curd,
  Clear of limb a Youth smote the master's gate.


Water, first of singers, o'er rocky mount and mead,
  First of earthly singers, the sun-loved rill,
Sang of him, and flooded the ripples on the reed,
  Seeking whom to waken, and what ear fill.
Water, sweetest soother to kiss a wound and cool,
  Sweetest and divinest, the sky-born brook,
Chuckled, with a whimper, and made a mirror-pool
  Round the guest we welcomed, the strange hand shook.


Many swarms of wild bees descended on our fields:
  Stately stood the wheatstalk with head bent high:
Big of heart we labour'd at storing mighty yields,
  Wool and corn, and clusters to make men cry!
Hand-like rushed the vintage; we strung the bellied skins,
  Plump, and at the sealing the Youth's voice rose:
Maidens clung in circle, on little fists their chins;
  Gentle beasties through pushed a cold long nose.

Foot to fire in snowtime we trimm'd the slender shaft:
  Often down the pit spied the lean wolf's teeth
Grin against his will, trapp'd by masterstrokes of craft;
  Helpless in his froth-wrath as green logs seethe!
Safe the tender lambs tugg'd the teats, and winter sped
  Whirl'd before the crocus, the year's new gold.
Hung the hooky beak up aloft the arrowhead
  Redden'd through his feathers for our dear fold.

Tales we drank of giants at war with Gods above:
  Rocks were they to look on, and earth climb'd air!
Tales of search for simples, and those who sought of love
  Ease because the creature was all too fair.
Pleasant ran our thinking that while our work was good,
  Sure as fruits for sweat would the praise come fast.
He that wrestled stoutest and tamed the billow-brood
  Danced in rings with girls, like a sail-flapp'd mast.

Now of medicine and song, of both of which Apollo is
God. Song—good poetry is always linked with medicine
in Meredith's mind: twin restoratives of human sanity:

Lo, the herb of healing, when once the herb is known,
  Shines in shady woods bright as new-sprung flame.
Ere the string was tighten'd we heard the mellow tone,
  After he had taught how the sweet sounds came.
Stretch'd about his feet, labour done, 'twas as you see
  Red pomegranates tumble and burst hard rind.
So began contention to give delight and be
  Excellent in things aim'd to make life kind.

Last, the invocation to all beasts, leaves, trees, to join in
remembering him:

You with shelly horns, rams! and promontory goats,
  You whose browsing beards dip in coldest dew!
Bulls, that walk the pastures in kingly-flashing coats!
  Laurel, ivy, vine, wreath'd for feasts not few!

You that build the shade-roof, and you that court the rays,
    You that leap besprinkling the rock stream-rent:
He has been our fellow, the morning of our days!
    Us he chose for housemates, and this way went.
            God! of whom music
            And song and blood are pure,
            The day is never darken'd
            That had thee here obscure.

## V

Begin with that, or begin with its fellow, the exquisite
gentle tale of Melampus the good physician to whom the
woodland creatures in reward that he
                    loving them all,
    Among them walk'd, as a scholar who reads a book,
taught their love of medicine, and where to find the herbs
of healing: and from *Melampus* go on to the ringing ballad
*The Nuptials of Attila*, or that favourite of mine *The Day
of the Daughter of Hades* which tells how Persephone
(ravished wife of dark Hades, released by him on a day to
revisit earth and embrace her mother Demeter) takes with
her in the chariot her daughter Skiageneia, child of Shadow;
and how this girl-goddess, slipping from the car, confronts
a mortal youth, Callistes:
                    She did not fly,
            Nor started at his advance:...
for all the wonder and beauty of this upper earth were
running through her blood, quickening love and memories
half surmised in every drop from her mother inherited—
'the blood of her a lighted dew':
                    She did not fly,
            Nor started at his advance:

She looked, as when infinite thirst
Pants pausing to bless the springs,
Refreshed, unsated. Then first
He trembled with awe of the things
He had seen; and he did transfer,
Divining and doubting in turn,
His reverence unto her;
Nor asked what he crouched to learn:
The whence of her, whither, and why
Her presence there, and her name,
Her parentage: under which sky
Her birth, and how hither she came,
So young, a virgin, alone,
Unfriended, having no fear,
As Oreads have; no moan,
Like the lost upon earth; no tear;
Not a sign of the torch in the blood,
Though her stature had reached the height
When mantles a tender rud
In maids that of youths have sight,
If maids of our seed they be:
For he said: A glad vision art thou!
And she answered him: Thou to me!
    As men utter a vow.

Classical to me it seems; and classically radiant, as if painted
by Titian, the Sicilian day that followed for these two: she
grandly innocent in his company, recognising and naming
the fruits of earth:

Pear, apple, almond, plum...
And she touch'd them with finger and thumb,
As the vine-hook closes: she smiled,
Recounting again and again,
Corn, wine, fruit, oil! like a child,
With the meaning known to men.

Read this poem carefully (I dare to say), and you will read in this girl-goddess not only what is the secret of the heroines in many of Meredith's novels—Lucy Desborough, Sandra Belloni, Clara Middleton—but also the secret of Shakespeare's later heroines—Perdita, Imogen, Miranda: and will not wonder how the youth Callistes, when at evening her father's awful chariot rapt her from him, was left with no future but to crave for her until his life's end

> And to join her, or have her brought back,
> In his frenzy the singer would call,
> Till he followed where never was track,
> On the path trod of all.

There are those who would counsel you to begin your study of Meredith with *Modern Love* rather than with the poems I have chosen: and here their counsel may easily be wiser than mine, personal taste interfering to make me wayward. As a poetic form, the sonnet-sequence—even when turned as Meredith turns it, from quatorzain to seizain—is (unless handled by Shakespeare) about the last to allure me. I should add, however, that Meredith's use of the sixteen-line stanza in *Modern Love* is exceedingly strong and individual: and that in the past hundred years few quatorzains, or sonnets proper, will match his *Lucifer in Starlight*, which I read to you last term. As a subject, the relations of the husband, the wife and the other man, especially when rehearsed by the husband, have usually (I state it merely as a private confession) the same physical effect on me as a drawing-room recitation. I want to get under a table and howl. From the outset the recital makes me shy as a stranger pounced upon and called in to settle a delicate domestic difference; and as it goes on, I start protesting inwardly, 'My dear sir—delighted to do my best

...man of the world...quite understand...sympathetic, and all that sort of thing....But really, if you insist on all this getting into the newspapers....And where did I put my hat, by the way?' In short—take the confession—with the intricacies and self-scourgings of *Modern Love* I find myself less at home than with the franker temptations of St Anthony, and far less than with the larger, liberally careless amours of the early gods.

Nevertheless, and by all means, try both ways and choose which you will, provided it coax you on to search the real heart of Meredith's muse in *The Woods of Westermain*, *Earth and Man*, *A Faith on Trial*, *The Empty Purse*, *Night of Frost in May*, and the like. You will find many thorned thickets by the way; and some out of which, however hard you beat them, you will start no bird. The juvenile poems will but poorly reward you, until you come to be interested in them historically, as Pre-Raphaelite essays which Meredith outgrew. The later Odes celebrating French history —*The Revolution*; *Napoléon*; *France*, 1870; *Alsace-Lorraine*—should be deferred (I think) till you are fairly possessed by the Meredithian fervour. They have their splendid passages; but they are undeniably difficult. Moreover I hold you must acquire a thorough trust in a bard before trusting him at an ode, which is of all forms of poetry the most pontifical; before you compose your spirit to a proper humility while he indues his robes, strikes attitude and harp, and starts telling France what he thinks of her, or anything so great as France what he thinks of it, albeit he may sift out approval and end on a note of encouragement. After reading odes in this strain I, for one, always feel that I hear France—or whatever it is— murmuring politely at the close, 'Thank you—*so* much!'

## VI

But it is in the poems I named just now, and in others collected under the two general titles *A Reading of Earth* and *A Reading of Life*, that you will find the essential Meredith: and, as these titles hint, he is a teacher, an expositor. Now why many of our English poets should be teachers is a dark question—to be attempted perhaps though probably not resolved, in some later lecture: as why an expositor, of all men, should be obscure and even succeed in giving us enlightenment by means of obscurity, is an even darker question—although I make no doubt that the genius of this university, sometime adorned by the late and great Dr Westcott, can somehow provide it with an answer. But the philosophy of Meredith, when you come to it, cannot be denied for strong, for arresting, for athletic, lean, hard, wiry. It is not comfortable: Stoical, rather; even strongly Stoical, as we use the epithet. But it differs by the whole heaven from ancient Stoicism, being reared on two pillars of Faith and Love. And, yet again, the Faith differs utterly from the Faith which supports the most of our religions—it can and, as a fact does, consist with agnosticism, and the Love differs utterly from the Love which so often infects so much of saintliness with eroticism and even with slyness in daily life. Let me try to outline his belief, using his own words where I may.

The man is a modern man, lost in doubt, forlorn in a forest of doubt, but resolved to win through by help of the monitor, the lantern within him.

> I am in deep woods,
> Between the two twilights.

Whatever I am and may be,
Write it down to the light in me;
I am I, and it is my deed;
For I know that the paths are dark
　　Between the two twilights.

. . . . . .

I have made my choice to proceed
By the light I have within;
And the issue rests with me,
Who might sleep in a chrysalis,
In the fold of a simple prayer,
　　Between the two twilights.

. . . . . .

Having nought but the light in me,
Which I take for my soul in arms,
Resolv'd to go unto the wells
For water, rejecting spells,
And mouthings of magic for charms,
And the cup that does not flow.

　I am in deep woods
　　Between the two twilights:

Over valley and hill
I hear the woodland wave,
Like the voice of Time, as slow,
The voice of Life, as grave,
The voice of Death, as still.

He finds there is no true promise (I am but trying to interpret) in religious promises of a compensating life beyond this one. *Those* are the

　　　　　　　　　　　　　　spells,
And mouthings of magic for charms.

He is not appalled by the prospect of sinking back and dissolving into the earth of which we all are created:

　　Into the breast that gave the rose
　　Shall I with shuddering fall?

More and more deeply as he contemplates Earth he feels that—from her as we spring, to her as we return—so man is only strong by constantly reading her lesson, falling back to refresh himself from her mother-springs, her mother-milk. Even of prayer he writes in one of his last novels, *Lord Ormont and His Aminta*:

> Prayer is power within us to communicate with the desired beyond our thirsts....And let the prayer be as a little fountain. Rising on a spout, from dread of the hollow below, the prayer may be prolonged in words begetting words, and have pulse of fervour: the spirit of it has fallen after the first jet. *That* is the delirious energy of our craving, which has no life in our souls. We do not get to any heaven by renouncing the Mother we spring from; and when there is an eternal secret for us, it is best to believe that Earth knows, to keep near her, even in our utmost aspirations.

To be true sons of Earth, our Mother: to learn of our dependence on her, her lesson: to be frugal of self-consciousness and of all other forms of selfishness; to live near the bare ground, and finally to return to it without whining: that is the first article of his creed. Earth never whines, and looks for no son of hers to whine:

> For love we Earth, then serve we all;
>     Her mystic secret then is ours:
> We fall, or view our treasures fall,
>     Unclouded, as beholds her flowers
>
> Earth, from a night of frosty wreck,
>     Enrobed in morning's mounted fire,
> When lowly, with a broken neck,
>     The crocus lays her cheek to mire.

To set up your hope on a world beyond this one is (according to Meredith) but lust for life prolonged—'a

bloodthirsty clinging to life' in Matthew Arnold's phrase
—demanding a passport beyond our natural term:

> The lover of life knows his labour divine,
>   And therein is at peace.
> The lust after life craves a touch and a sign
>   That the life shall increase.
>
> The lust after life, in the chills of its lust,
>   Claims a passport of death.
> The lover of life sees the flame in the dust
>   And a gift in our breath.

Transience?—yes, and to be gratefully accepted, like
human love, for transience! Earth, the Stoic mother, looks
on while her son learns the lesson; she will not coddle:

> He may entreat, aspire,
> He may despair, and she has never heed:
> She, drinking his warm sweat, will soothe his need,
>   Not his desire.

To this extent, then, he is one with the beasts that perish.
To this extent he is like Walt Whitman's animals. Says
Whitman:

> I think I could turn and live with animals...
> They do not sweat and whine about their condition,
> They do not lie awake in the dark and weep for their sins,
> They do not make me sick discussing their duty to God.

But the difference is that man *understands*: understands
that as in his mother Earth,

>           deepest at her springs,
>   Most filial, is an eye to love her young...

so he, seeing how in life the love of boy and maid leads to
the nourishing and love of children, must see further that
his first duty in life is to love and care for the young. For
himself, he must curb our 'distempered devil of self,'

gluttonous of its own enjoyments. Meredith promises
nothing—nothing beyond the grave, nothing on this side
of it but love sweetening hard fare:

> The sense of large charity over the land,
> Earth's wheaten of wisdom dispensed in the rough,
> And a bell giving thanks for a sustenance meal.

## VII

Well, there it is, Gentlemen, for you to take or to leave.
I am here to talk about literature to you, not about doctrine.
But I think that, after the mystics we discussed last term,
you may find the herb of Meredith medicinal, invigorating:
a philosophy austere though suffused with love; mistaken,
if you will, but certainly not less than high, stern, noble,
meet for men.

I have indicated some of his poems through which you
may arrive at it. But he wrote one poem which stands
apart from these and might (you may say) conceivably
have been written by another man. If I allowed this, which
I cannot, I should still hold that no one short of a genius
could have invented it; as I hold that, with Spenser's
*Epithalamion*, it shares claim to be the greatest song of
human love in our language, as it is certainly the topmost
of its age: all that Swinburne or Rossetti ever wrote fading
out like fireworks or sick tapers before its sunshine. I mean
*Love in the Valley*, with a number of stanzas from which
I shall this morning conclude, feeling all the while that I
have no gift to read them as they deserve.

### Love in the Valley

> Under yonder beech-tree single on the green-sward,
>   Couched with her arms behind her golden head,
> Knees and tresses folded to slip and ripple idly,
>   Lies my young love sleeping in the shade.

Had I the heart to slide an arm beneath her,
  Press her parting lips as her waist I gather slow,
Waking in amazement she could not but embrace me:
  Then would she hold me and never let me go?

Shy as the squirrel and wayward as the swallow,
  Swift as the swallow along the river's light
Circleting the surface to meet his mirrored winglets,
  Fleeter she seems in her stay than in her flight.
Shy as the squirrel that leaps among the pine-tops,
  Wayward as the swallow overhead at set of sun,
She whom I love is hard to catch and conquer,
  Hard, but O the glory of the winning were she won!

When her mother tends her before the laughing mirror,
  Tying up her laces, looping up her hair,
Often she thinks, were this wild thing wedded,
  More love should I have, and much less care.
When her mother tends her before the lighted mirror,
  Loosening her laces, combing down her curls,
Often she thinks, were this wild thing wedded,
  I should miss but one for the many boys and girls.

Heartless she is as the shadow in the meadows
  Flying to the hills on a blue and breezy noon.
No, she is athirst and drinking up her wonder:
  Earth to her is young as the slip of the new moon.
Deals she an unkindness, 'tis but her rapid measure,
  Even as in a dance; and her smile can heal no less:
Like the swinging May-cloud that pelts the flowers
    with hailstones
  Off a sunny border, she was made to bruise and bless.

Lovely are the curves of the white owl sweeping
  Wavy in the dusk lit by one large star.
Lone on the fir-branch, his rattle-note unvaried,
  Brooding o'er the gloom, spins the brown eve-jar.

Darker grows the valley, more and more forgetting:
  So were it with me if forgetting could be willed.
Tell the grassy hollow that holds the bubbling well-spring,
  Tell it to forget the source that keeps it filled.

Stepping down the hill with her fair companions,
  Arm in arm, all against the raying West,
Boldly she sings, to the merry tune she marches,
  Brave in her shape, and sweeter unpossessed.
Sweeter, for she is what my heart first awaking
  Whispered the world was; morning light is she.
Love that so desires would fain keep her changeless;
  Fain would fling the net, and fain have her free.

Happy happy time, when the white star hovers
  Low over dim fields fresh with bloomy dew,
Near the face of dawn, that draws athwart the darkness,
  Threading it with colour, like yewberries the yew.
Thicker crowd the shades as the grave East deepens
  Glowing, and with crimson a long cloud swells.
Maiden still the morn is; and strange she is, and secret;
  Strange her eyes; her cheeks are cold as cold sea-shells.

. . . . . . .

Prim little scholars are the flowers of her garden,
  Trained to stand in rows, and asking if they please.
I might love them well but for loving more the wild ones:
  O my wild ones! they tell me more than these.
You, my wild one, you tell of honied field-rose,
  Violet, blushing eglantine in life; and even as they,
They by the wayside are earnest of your goodness,
  You are of life's, on the banks that line the way.

Peering at her chamber the white crowns the red rose,
  Jasmine winds the porch with stars two and three.
Parted is the window; she sleeps; the starry jasmine
  Breathes a falling breath that carries thoughts of me.

Sweeter unpossessed, have I said of her my sweetest?
   Not while she sleeps: while she sleeps the jasmine breathes,
Luring her to love; she sleeps; the starry jasmine
   Bears me to her pillow under white rose-wreaths.

. . . . . . . . .

Gossips count her faults; they scour a narrow chamber
   Where there is no window, read not heaven or her.
'When she was a tiny,' one aged woman quavers,
   Plucks at my heart and leads me by the ear.
Faults she had once as she learnt to run and tumbled:
   Faults of feature some see, beauty not complete.
Yet, good gossips, beauty that makes holy
   Earth and air, may have faults from head to feet.

Hither she comes; she comes to me; she lingers,
   Deepens her brown eyebrows, while in new surprise
High rise the lashes in wonder of a stranger;
   Yet am I the light and living of her eyes.
Something friends have told her fills her heart to brimming,
   Nets her in her blushes, and wounds her, and tames.—
Sure of her haven, O like a dove alighting,
   Arms up, she dropped: our souls were in our names.

A Song of Songs, which is Meredith's!

# THE POETRY
# OF THOMAS HARDY

## I

IN speaking to you, the other day, Gentlemen, on the poetry of George Meredith, I admitted how faulty one's judgment may be—nay almost must needs be—upon all modern work. 'Still,' I went on, 'the task of appraising it has to be done, for the books of our time *are* the books of our time. They tell us in their various ways "How it strikes a Contemporary."'

Yes: but I deferred a qualification of this—a somewhat important qualification—to which I shall begin today by asking your assent.

My qualification is this:—We elders—from among whom, for various reasons, your professors are chosen as a rule—may hope to help you in understanding poets long since dead. For Chaucer, Shakespeare, Milton, Dryden, Wordsworth, Byron, Shelley, are removed almost as far from us as from you. They have passed definitely into the ward of Time. What was corrupt or corruptible in them is now dust, though we embalm it in myrrh, sandal-wood, cassia: dust equally for us and for you: what was incorruptible flowers as freshly for you as for us. We have but the sad advantage of having studied it a little longer.

Now when we come to poets of the time of Tennyson, Browning, Matthew Arnold, our difference of age asserts itself; middle-aged men of the 'sixties, young men of the

'nineties, children of this century, read them at correspondent removes, perceptible removes. And, though you
may like it not, it is (I believe) good that we seniors should
testify to you concerning these men who were our seniors,
yet alive when we were young, and gave us in youth,
believe me, even such thrills, such awed surmises, such
wonders and wild desires as you catch in your turn from
their successors. Nay, it is salutary, I believe; for the reason
that it appears to be the rule for each new generation to
turn iconoclast on its father's poetic gods. You will
scarcely deny that on some of you the term 'Victorian'
acts as a red rag upon a young bull of the pasture: that, to
some of you, Tennyson is 'that sort of stuff your uncle
read.' Well, bethink you that the children of yet another
generation will deal so and not otherwise with your heroes:
that it is all a part of the continuous process of criticism
through which our roseate raptures and our lurid anti-
pathies pass, if not into the light of common day, into that
of serener judgment. Blame not your uncle that at the
age of fourteen or earlier, in the walled garden screened
from the windows of the house, he charged among the
vegetables chanting

> A bow-shot from her bower-eaves,
> He rode between the barley-sheaves...

or

> Strew no more red roses, maidens,
>   Leave the lilies in their dew:
> Pluck, pluck cypress, O pale maidens!
>   Dusk, O dusk the hall with yew!...

or

> I forgot, thou comest from thy voyage—
>   Yes, the spray is on thy cloak and hair.
> But thy dark eyes are not dimm'd, proud Iseult!
>   And thy beauty never was more fair...

12—2

or

And the tent shook, for mighty Saul shuddered: and sparkles
   'gan dart
From the jewels that woke in his turban, at once with a start,
All its lordly male-sapphires, and rubies courageous at heart.

For to dream of these things, and to awake and find one-
self an uncle—that is the common lot. Nor blame him
that he continues loyal to them. It keeps him human: it
may set you pondering, reconsidering a little; and so may
help to advance the true business of criticism. I come down
a little further; past Morris and Swinburne to Yeats (say)
or Francis Thompson. We admired and admire them as
generously as, I hope, you admire them; but I think not
quite in the same way. To us, their almost exact contemporaries, their first poems appealed as youth to youth;
with none of the authority they exercise, I dare to say,
upon you. To us they carried no authority at all. They
carried hope, they bred ardour: but we criticised them
freely as poems written by the best of *us*. They have to
wait a few years for the race to deify them. You and we
possess them by a different line of approach.

Now take the young poets who are your contemporaries.
Of them I say sadly, resignedly, that a man even of my
years has no right to speak, or very little power to speak
usefully. Young poets write not for antiquity, nor for
middle-age. They write for *you*: their appeal is to *you*. All
that *we* can do is to keep our hearts as fresh as we may; to
bear ever in mind that a father can guide a son but some
distance on the road, and the more wisely he guides the
sooner (alas!) must he lose the fair companionship and
watch the boy run on. It may sound a hard saying, but we
can only keep him admiring the things we admire at the

cost of pauperising his mind. It may sound another hard saying, that the younger poets do not write for us old men; yet it is the right course of nature. I hope William Cory's apophthegm is not strictly true:

> One's feelings lose poetic flow
> Soon after twenty-seven or so;
> Professionising modern men
> Thenceforth admire what pleased them then.

But if it be (though I plead for some rise in the age-limit), then poetry but consents with the rule of Nature whose highest interpreter she is. Deepest in her too—in Meredith's phrase—

> Deepest at *her* springs
> Most filial, is an eye to love her young.

## II

After this somewhat wistful opening, let me claim an exception for my subject this morning. Thomas Hardy— I cannot call him Doctor Hardy even in a university which not long ago did itself honour in complimenting him— Thomas Hardy (long may he live!) is my elder, and so much my elder that for thirty years I have reverenced him as a master: that is, as a master of the Novel. His first novel *Desperate Remedies* dates back to 1871: his first artistic triumph *Under the Greenwood Tree*, to 1872. Pass intervening years and come to the grand close in *Tess of the D'Urbervilles* (1891), *Jude the Obscure* (1895): on that last date his career as a novelist ceases, and at the age of fifty-five. Three years later, in 1898, he publishes his first book of verse. Now any pettifogging fellow can point out that this volume, entitled *Wessex Poems*, contains many poems composed long before 1898—some so far back as

1865; and the more easily because Hardy is careful to print the dates[1]. So for that matter do some of Hardy's later volumes contain early poems, either printed as first written, or as revised. But no petty fog can obscure the plain fact that in 1895, or a little later, Hardy definitely turned his back on prose fiction and started to appeal to a new generation in verse; as a writer of high poetical verse if the gods should allow. To this purpose he has held. A second volume, *Poems of the Past and the Present* followed in 1901; *The Dynasts*, Part I in 1903, Part II in 1906, Part III in 1908, *Time's Laughing Stocks* in 1909. *Satires of Circumstance* were collected in 1914. His latest volume *Moments of Vision* appeared but the other day, and bears 1917 on its title-page. So, seeing that all this, including that great epical drama, *The Dynasts*, falls within the ken of the last twenty years, and not without it, you may allow perhaps that it concerns men of your age and mine, equally if not similarly.

## III

Ah, but you may answer, 'By all means let it concern you. The point is, can a man of Thomas Hardy's age write what appeals to *us*?' Well, yes, I think his poetry may appeal to you, as it certainly concerns you. That his Muse is predominantly melancholy I brush aside as no bar at all. If youth do not understand melancholy, why then the most of Shelley, the most of Byron, a great part of Keats, or—to come to later instances—a great, if not the greater, part of Francis Thompson and Yeats and most of

[1] So that, as Whistler said of an art-critic who judged a water-colour for an oil-painting, 'it was accurately described in the catalogue and he had not even to rely on his sense of smell.'

the young poets of the Irish school, is closed to it: which is absurd. 'No, no! go not to Lethe' for Melancholy. She dwells neither there nor with middle-age:

> She dwells with Beauty—Beauty that must die;
>     And Joy, whose hand is ever at his lips
> Bidding adieu; and aching Pleasure nigh,
>     Turning to poison while the bee-mouth sips:
> Ay, in the very temple of Delight
>     Veil'd Melancholy has her sovran shrine,
>         Though seen of none save him whose strenuous tongue
> Can burst Joy's grape against his palate fine;
>     His soul shall taste the sadness of her might,
>         And be among her cloudy trophies hung.

No, no: it is proper to youth to know melancholy as it is to have raptures. But only to middle-age is it granted to be properly cheerful. Yes, there are compensations! Let us assure you that only towards middle-age will you burst upon a palate fine the true juice of Chaucer's *Prologue*, written in *his* middle-age, or of Montaigne, or of Molière: as in youth you will choose Rossetti, but later transfer your choice to William Morris, least sick or sorry, best of cheer among the poets of his time.

As for Hardy's pessimism, that, to be sure, does not consort well with youth. But, as I shall hope to show, it always challenges youth; it is never faded, jejune, effete; it never plays—or, to be accurate, it seldom plays—with old mere sentimentalities. Even when it plays with commonplaces it never leaves them conventions. In his depths the man is always thinking, and his perplexities, being all-important and yet unsolved, are by your generation to be faced, whether you solve them or not.

## IV

For another point, close beside and yet more important, we have talked of insensibility to poetry and how with the years it may steal upon the reader. Now most of you remember, I daresay, Matthew Arnold's late and mournful lines on the drying up of poesy in the writer:

> Youth rambles on life's arid mount,
>     And strikes the rock, and finds the vein,
> And brings the water from the fount,
>     The fount which shall not flow again.
>
> The man mature with labour chops
>     For the bright stream a channel grand,
> And sees not that the sacred drops
>     Ran off and vanish'd out of hand.
>
> And then the old man totters nigh
>     And feebly rakes among the stones.
> The mount is mute, the channel dry;
>     And down he lays his weary bones.

Well, at any rate Thomas Hardy contradicts, and in practice, *that* rather cheap kind of pessimism. (There was always, I think, in Matthew Arnold a tendency to be Wordsworth's widow, and to fall rather exasperatingly 'a-thinking of the old 'un,' who undoubtedly did in later life, for some thirty years 'rake among the stones' and died in the end, as the country practitioner put it, 'of nothing serious.')

I am aware that to support this theory of desiccation in poets many startling instances may be cited. But without saying yea or nay, or supposing it symptomatic of our age, I cannot think it quite accidental that out of the small number of poets I have been privileged to know personally,

two should have tapped, quite late in life, a well of poetry
abundant, fresh, pure; of *lyrical* poetry, too, fresher, purer
and far more abundant than ever they found as young men.
It happened so, at all events, with an old schoolmaster of
mine, the late T. E. Brown, whose quality and whose
performance are now generally admitted. It has happened
so with Thomas Hardy. His first poems—or, to say it
more accurately, the poems in his first-published volume
—were stiff, awkward. They often achieved a curious,
haunting, countrified lilt; they worked always true to
pattern: you felt about them, too, that the verses held the
daemon of poetry, constricted, struggling for expression.
But in form they resembled the drawings with which the
author illustrated that first volume. They were architectural
draughts (Hardy had been an architect). When they told
a story, you wondered why he, so well able to do it, had
not written this particular story in prose. The poetic thought
was there: but the words were hard and precise, sometimes
scientifically pedantic. For instance, in the last poem I shall
read today he drags in the word 'stillicide,' which means
the drip of water in a cavern, or from eaves. Stevenson has
recorded his mingled feelings on discovering, in the process
of his scientific studies, that 'stillicide' was not a crime.
The early poems faceted no rays, they melted into none of
those magical, chemical combinations out of which words
became poetry and a new thing, 'half angel and half bird.'

Years pass, with their efforts; and then in his latest
volume, published by this man at the age of seventy-seven,
he discovers a lyrical note which I shall quote to you, not
at all because its theme is characteristic—for it is not—as
not at all because it is deep and wonted—for it is not. It
is, if you will, 'silly sooth, and dallies with the innocence
of love.' Yes, just for that reason I quote it, and because

in a poet of ordinary evolution it would fall naturally among the *Juvenilia*:

> Lalage's coming:
> Where is she now, O?
> Turning to bow, O,
> And smile, is she,
> Just at parting,
> Parting, parting,
> As she is starting
> To come to me?
>
> Lalage's coming,
> Nearer is she now, O,
> End anyhow, O,
> Today's husbandry!
> Would a gilt chair were mine,
> Slippers of vair were mine,
> Brushes for hair were mine
> 　Of ivory!
>
> What will she think, O,
> She who's so comely,
> Viewing how homely
> A sort are we!
> Nought here's enough for her,
> All is too rough for her,
> Even my love for her
> 　Poor in degree.
>
> 　　.　　.　　.　　.
>
> Lalage's come; aye,
> Come is she now, O!
> Does Heaven allow, O,
> A meeting to be?
> Yes, she is here now,
> Here now, here now,
> Nothing to fear now,
> 　Here's Lalage!

If that be too trivial, take another—remembering that I give them only as metrical specimens, merely to show how this poet, whose metrical muscles were stiff and hard at fifty-odd has at seventy-odd (the date is 1913) worked them supple, so that now the verse cadences to the feeling:

> Out of the past there rises a week—
>   Who shall read the years O!
> In that week there was heard a singing—
>   Who shall spell the years O!—
> In that week there was heard a singing,
>   And the white owl wondered why.
> In that week there was heard a singing,
>   And forth from the casement were candles flinging
> Radiance that fell on the deodar and lit up the path thereby.

Or take him on a lower note:

> I need not go
> Through sleet and snow
> To where I know
> She waits for me;
> She will wait me there
> Till I find it fair,
> And have time to spare
> From company...
>
> .      .      .
>
> What—not upbraid me
> That I delayed me,
> Nor ask what stayed me
> So long? Ah, no!—
> New cares may claim me,
> New loves inflame me,
> She will not blame me,
> But suffer it so.

I reserve for the while the most individual quality in

Hardy's versifying (to me an individual excellence) which has given it character from the first—I mean his country lilt; because I must approach it, and the man, and his philosophy of life, all three by one path.

## V

First of all, and last of all, he is a countryman. And the first meaning of this is that his mind works like most country minds in this great little island. They are introspective *because* insular: and their soil is cumbered, piled with history and local tradition: a land of arable inveterately and deeply ploughed; of pastures close-webbed at the root by rain and sun persistently reviving the blade which the teeth of sheep and cattle persistently crop; of its heaths—such as Newmarket—where racehorses in training gallops beat their hoofs in the very footprints of Boadicea's mares and stallions; of mines, working yet, that paid their first-fruits to Sidon and Carthage, choked harbours, dead empires. In this land of ours, I say, the mind of a native must dig vertically down through strata. Though it be the mind of a farm labourer, it knows its acres intimately; not only their rotation of crops, and slant to wind or sun, but their several humours, caprices, obstinacies of soil; and, always with an eye to windward, hopes for the weather it knows likeliest to profit them. So when, as with Hardy, a countryman has the further knowledge that comes of book-learning, and acquires with it the historical sense, that sense still feels vertically downwards, through soil and subsoil, through the mould of Norman, Dane, Saxon, Celt, Iber, and of tribes beyond history, to the geological formations layered over by this accumulated dust.

Further, you know that the tales of old time which haunt a true countryman's imagination are tales of violence, of lonely houses where suppressed passions inhabit to flame out in murder or suicide, to make a legend, to haunt a cross-road or a mile-post: fierce, primitive deeds breaking up through the slow crust of custom: unaccountable, but not unnatural. Along the king's highway, a gibbet where sheepstealers used to swing: in such and such a copse a tree, on that tree such and such a branch where a poor girl hanged herself for love: at the three roads by the blacksmith's a triangle of turf still called 'Betsy Beneath' because there they buried her uncoffined and drove a stake through her.

Further, if you know your rural England, you will know that every village in it is a small shop of gossip. 'Have you heard? Young Peter Hodge is at upsides with his wife? yes, already, and her only expectin'.' 'They tell me Farmer So-and-so have a mortgage, if you'll believe, on the Lower Barton Farm.' 'So, that girl Jenny is in trouble as I always foretold.' Vengeance o' Jenny's case!

Well as I interpret this most genuine, most autochthonous of living writers, I see him leaning over the gate of a field with a wood's edge bordering it. He knows the wood so intimately that his ear detects and separates the notes of the wind as it soughs in oak, hornbeam, pine (see the opening of *Under the Greenwood Tree*, or *The Woodlanders*, *passim*). Of the sheep on the pasture he knows when their lambs will fall. He judges the grass, if it be sufficient. He knows that breast-shaped knob on the knap of the hill and how many centuries have worn to this what was the high burial mound of a British chieftain: he knows the lias beneath the chief's grave, and the layered rock still deeper—that is, he knows as near as geologists can tell. He knows, having a boy's eye for this, where a nest is likeliest to be, and of what bird. But what more intrigues him than any of these things—still as he follows the line of the hedge—is that under one innocent-looking thorn such and such a parish tragedy was enacted. Just here, they tell, two brothers quarrelled and one smote the other with a reaping-hook; just there was lovers' bliss and just there, a brief while later, the woman's heart broke.

For (you must know) though a gossip's, this country-man's heart is strangely tender. Let me pause for proof, by one short poem, that even Blake's heart was not tenderer than Hardy's. It is called

### The Blinded Bird

So zestfully canst thou sing?
And all this indignity,
With God's consent, on thee!
Blinded ere yet a-wing
By the red-hot needle thou,
I stand and wonder how
So zestfully thou canst sing...

.     .     .     .     .

Resenting not such wrong,
Thy grievous pain forgot,
Eternal dark thy lot,
Groping thy whole life long,
After that stab of fire;
Enjailed in pitiless wire;
Resenting not such wrong!

Who hath charity? This bird.
Who suffereth long and is kind,
Is not provoked, though blind
And alive ensepulchred?
Who hopeth, endureth all things?
Who thinketh no evil, but sings?
Who is divine? This bird.

Above all, his pity is for women, partly for the fate that condemns their bloom to be brief and evanescent (unless written in time on a man's heart where it never grows old) —so brief the chance, with no term to the after-pain! But he pities them more because he sees the increase of our race to rest on an unfair game, in which, nine throws out of ten, the dice are loaded against the woman; a duel of sex, almost at times an internecine duel, which his soul grows to abhor: for

> Victrix causa deis placuit, sed victa Catoni,

and, looking up, he sees God, or whatever gods may be, deriding the victim. We are all flies to these gods who tease us for their sport. Even if man labour and profit his fellows with an idea, yet, in Milton's phrase (as quoted by Hardy)

> Truth like a bastard comes into the world
> Never without ill-fame to him who gives her birth.

But, for women, who, nine times out of ten, pay the price of the great jest, Hardy feels most acutely. 'Poor wounded name,' he quotes and inscribes on the title-page of *Tess*

> Poor wounded name! my bosom as a bed
> Shall lodge thee...

and in the last sentence of his most sorrowful tale he flings his now famous taunt up at 'the President of the Immortals,' even as passionately as did Cleopatra for her own loss:

*Iras.*                              Madam!
*Charmian.*    O madam, madam, madam!
*Iras.*                              Royal Egypt!
         Empress!
*Charmian.*           Peace, peace, Iras!

*Cleopatra.*    No more but e'en a woman, and commanded
      By such poor passion as the maid that milks

(Tess was a dairy-maid)

      And does the meanest chares. It were for me
      To throw my sceptre at the injurious gods;
      To tell them that this world did equal theirs
      Till they had stol'n our jewel.

## VI

Say what you will, this indignation in Hardy is noble, is chivalrous, and, as the world is worked, it has much reason at the back of its furious 'Why?—Why?—Why?' It has great excuse when it sours down to bitterest irony, as in this early ditty of two country-bred girls meeting in London—and you will note how the old market-jog of rhythm and rhyme *ache* themselves into the irony:

'O 'Melia, my dear, this does everything crown!
Who could have supposed I should meet you in Town?
And whence such fair garments, such prosperi-ty?'—
'O didn't you know I'd been ruined?' said she.

—'You left us in tatters, without shoes or socks,
Tired of digging potatoes, and spudding up docks;
And now you've gay bracelets and bright feathers three!'—
'Yes: that's how we dress when we're ruined,' said she...

   .    .    .    .    .    .    .

—'I wish I had feathers, a fine sweeping gown,
And a delicate face, and could strut about Town!'—
'My dear—a raw country girl, such as you be,
Isn't equal to that. You ain't ruined,' said she.

Women (I think) are more impatient of irony than men: and when Hardy turns his irony upon them—as he often does in his novels—I have observed that they eye it suspiciously, restively; they would be undetected in their devices, hate instinctively that which shows their secret ways of power at work under show of servility. Hardy, their champion, would break down the servility: and they distrust him for it.

Well—and though they be ungrateful—perhaps their instinct is true and his is a childless creed: and for men, though it be manly to face it out and test it, an unhopeful creed. For women it must be certainly unpromising to read the doctrine of *Jude the Obscure*, which works out to this, that man's aspirations to make the world better are chiefly clogged by the flesh, and that flesh is woman. To man it can scarcely be less heartening to be barred with the question

> Has some Vast Imbecility,
>   Mighty to build and blend,
>   But impotent to tend,
> Framed us in jest, and left us now to hazardry?
>
> Or come we of an Automaton
>   Unconscious of our pains?
>   Or are we live remains
> Of Godhead dying downwards, brain and eye
>   now gone?

Well, when it comes to this, I for one can only answer that, if it were, we must yet carry on somehow, sing a song on the raft we cannot steer, keep a heart of sorts, and share out the rations to the women and children. But that word recalls me. It is a *childless* creed. It has no more evidence than Meredith's: intellectually viewed, I find them equal: but Meredith has hope, hope for the young: and I must put my money on hope.

## VII

Further, when I consider, these poems—as those novels —crowd the sardonic laughter of the gods too thickly. There is irony enough in life, God wot: but here is a man possessed with it. All men, all stories, tramp with him to his titles *Life's Little Ironies, Satires of Circumstance, Time's Laughing Stocks*[1]. So one hesitates and asks: Is life, after all, a parish full of bad practical jokes? *Is* catholic man like *this*? No: as we take up poem after poem in which human loves and aspirations find themselves thwarted, set astray, or butting against some door that, having opened a glimpse of paradise, shuts by some power idiotically mischievous if not malignant—shuts with a click of the latch and a chuckle of mocking laughter—we tell ourselves, 'These things happen: but in any such crowd they never and in no life happen.' And while we debate this, Hardy confounds us, spreading out his irony upon one grand ironic drama, *The Dynasts*.

I suppose *The Dynasts* to be—and I shall not allow for

[1] Why, O why will authors choose loose, woolly, undescriptive titles? To take another writer of genius, why *Traffics and Discoveries, Life's Handicap, Many Inventions, The Day's Work*? And, to return to Hardy, what differentiates an Irony of Life from a Satire of Circumstance, and do not both equally make the victim a Laughing Stock of Time? And if there be a difference, are the poems divided by the titles based on any *fundamentum divisionis*? And, anyhow, what is wrong with *The Iliad, King Lear, Don Quixote, John Gilpin, Tom Jones, David Copperfield*? What is right with *The Eternal Mystery, Some Emotions and a Moral*, and so on? Are they not all too loose for their contents? And what is wrong again with a house—*The House with the Seven Gables, Bleak House, The House with the Green Shutters, The House of Usher, A Doll's House, The House that Jack Built*?

rival Doughty's noble but remote, morose, almost Chinese, epic, *The Dawn in Britain* (this, too, a product of a man well past meridian)—I suppose *The Dynasts* to be the grandest poetic structure planned and raised in England in our time. In the soar and sweep of that drama the poet—whom, a moment ago, we were on the point of accusing for provincial, lays Europe beneath us 'flat, as to an eagle's eye'—a map with little things in multitudes, ants in armies, scurrying along the threads which are roads, violently agitated in nodules which are cities. But let me quote one or two of Hardy's own stage directions and thereby not only save myself the vain effort to do what has been perfectly done for me, but send you, if you would practise the art of condensed and vivid description, to models as good as can be found in English prose. Imagine yourselves, then, an audience aloft and listening to the talk of such Spirits as watch over human destinies.

The nether sky opens, and Europe is disclosed as a prone and emaciated figure, the Alps shaping like a backbone, and the branching mountain-chains like ribs, the peninsular plateau of Spain forming a head. Broad and lengthy lowlands stretch from the north of France across Russia like a grey-green garment hemmed by the Ural mountains and the glistening Arctic Ocean.

The point of view then sinks downward through space, and draws near to the surface of the perturbed countries, where the people,...are seen writhing, crawling, heaving, and vibrating, in their various cities and nationalities.

(A picture of Europe today.) Then

A new and penetrating light descends on the spectacle, enduing men and things with a seeming transparency, and exhibiting as one organism the anatomy of life and movement in all humanity and vitalized matter included in the display.

So the focus slides down and up and again down: it narrows on the British House of Commons, or on a village green, or on a bedroom in a palace: it expands to sweep the field of Austerlitz. I ask you to turn for yourselves to one marvellous scene of a cellar, full of drunken deserters, looking out on the snow-tormented road along which straggles the army of Sir John Moore and struggles for Coruña....But here is a passage in the retreat from Moscow:

What has floated down from the sky upon the Army is a flake of snow. Then come another and another, till natural features, hitherto varied with the tints of autumn, are confounded, and all is phantasmal grey and white.

The caterpillar shape still creeps laboriously nearer: but instead of increasing in size by the rules of perspective, it gets more attenuated, and there are left upon the ground behind it minute parts of itself, which are speedily flaked over, and remain as white pimples by the wayside.

Pines rise mournfully on each side of the nearing object.... Endowed with enlarged powers of audition as of vision, we are struck by the mournful taciturnity that prevails. Nature is mute. Save for the incessant flogging of the wind-broken and lacerated horses there are no sounds.

The diction of the poem itself seldom rises to match its conception. In the rustic scenes we get that incomparable prose, nervous, and vernacular, yet Biblical, which Hardy has made out of his native dialect: but the major human characters talk in verse which is often too prosy, and the watching Spirits attain but spasmodically to the height of their high argument. Their lips are not touched by any such flame as kindles (for example) the lips of the watching Spirits in *Prometheus Unbound*. But we must not judge a poem of *The Dynasts'* range and scope apart from its total impression: and *that*, in *The Dynasts* is tremendous. And

I at this moment am committing a deadly artistic sin against proportion in attempting to talk of it in a part of a lecture. It should have two lectures to itself.

As for its philosophy, one naturally compares it with that of Tolstoy's great novel *War and Peace*. But whereas Tolstoy and Hardy both see Napoleon as a puppet under Heaven—as Plato pronounces Man to be 'at his best a noble plaything for the gods'—the one, being Russian and an idealist, sees the little great man's ends shaped by a Divinity, watching over Sion, having purpose: the other, a most honest pessimist, can detect no purpose, or no beneficent one. For all he can see, God works—if He work —a magnipotent Will, but

> Like a knitter drowsed,
> Whose fingers play in skilled unmindfulness,
> The will has woven with an absent heed
> Since life first was; and ever will so weave.

And there for today we must leave it.


## VIII

I fall back, to conclude, upon Wessex; appropriately, I think, upon a churchyard in a corner there, where kinsmen, friends, neighbours, mingle their dust; where, as Hardy's friend and homelier predecessor put it,

> The zummer aïr o' theäs green hill
> 'V a-heav'd in bosoms now all still.

Faithful to this dust, to ancestry, old associations, the

> Nescio quâ natale solum dulcedine cunctos
> Ducit, et immemores non sinit esse sui...

the native returns: and the dead whisper, and this is what
they tell:

> William Dewy, Tranter Reuben, Farmer Ledlow late at
>         plough,
>     Robert's kin, and John's, and Ned's,
> And the Squire, and Lady Susan, lie in Mellstock church-
>         yard now!

> 'Gone,' I call them, gone for good, that group of local
>         hearts and heads;
>     Yet at mothy curfew-tide,
> And at midnight when the noon-heat breathes it back
>         from walls and leads,

> They've a way of whispering to me—fellow-wight who
>         yet abide—
>     In the muted measured note
> Of a ripple under archways, or a lone cave's stillicide:

> 'We have triumphed: this achievement turns the bane to
>         antidote,
>     Unsuccesses to success,
> Many thought-worn eves and morrows to a morrow free
>         of thought.

> 'No more need we corn and clothing, feel of old terrestrial
>         stress;
>     Chill detraction stirs no sigh;
> Fear of death has even bygone us: death gave all that we
>         possess.'

*W. D.* 'Ye mid burn the wold bass-viol that I set such vallie
>         by.'

*Squire.* 'You may hold the manse in fee,
>     You may wed my spouse, my children's memory of me
>         may decry.'

*Lady*. 'You may have my rich brocades, my laces; take each
   household key;
  Ransack coffer, desk, bureau;
 Quiz the few poor treasures hid there, con the letters kept
  by me.'

*Far*. 'Ye mid zell my favourite heifer, ye mid let the charlock
   grow,
  Foul the grinterns, give up thrift.'

*Wife*. 'If ye break my best blue china, children, I shan't care
  or ho.'

*All*. 'We've no wish to hear the tidings, how the people's
   fortunes shift;
  What your daily doings are;
 Who are wedded, born, divided; if your lives beat slow
  or swift.

'Curious not the least are we if our intents you make or
   mar,
  If you quire to our old tune,
 If the City stage still passes, if the weirs still roar afar.'

—Thus, with very gods' composure, freed those crosses
   late and soon
  Which, in life, the Trine allow
(Why, none witteth), and ignoring all that haps beneath
  the moon,

William Dewy, Tranter Reuben, Farmer Ledlow late at
   plough,
  Robert's kin, and John's, and Ned's,
And the Squire, and Lady Susan, murmur mildly to me
  now.

# COLERIDGE

THE story of Coleridge's life is hard to write and, in a sense, even harder to read: hard to write because the innumerable lapses, infirmities, defections of the will, all claiming—as facts—to be chronicled, cannot but obscure that lovable living presence to which all his contemporaries bore witness and to which the biographer must hold fast or his portrait misses most that is true and essential; and hard to read because the reader, at the hundredth instance of Coleridge's taking the wrong coach, or forgetting to write to his wife and family, or accepting money and neglecting the conditions on which it was bestowed, is apt to let Christian charity go to the winds, and so on his part, too, to miss, nor care that he misses, the better Coleridge which is the real Coleridge, the affectionate forgiving Coleridge, so anxious to cure his faults, so eager to make people *see*, so childlike and yet condemned to sit

> obscure
> In the exceeding lustre and the pure
> Intense irradiation of a mind.

The story not only exasperates the temper; it dodges the understanding, and leaves even the patient reader in such bewilderment as, no doubt, afflicted the much-enduring Odysseus after a third attempt to embrace his mother in the Shades. For Providence (as De Quincey put it) set 'perpetual relays' along Coleridge's path through life. We pursue the man and come up with group after group of his friends: and each, as we demand, 'What have you done with Coleridge?' answers, 'Coleridge? That wonderful fellow?...He was here just now, and we helped him forward a little way.'

The late James Dykes Campbell (to whose *Life of Coleridge* the reader is referred) took up his task with enthusiasm and performed it with astonishing success. He honoured the poet's memory a little 'on this side idolatry.' Yet as we follow his condensed narrative we feel the growth of misgivings in the writer's mind, and at the close he has to make a clean breast of them. 'If,' says he, 'my present-ment of what I believe to be the truth be not found to tend, on the whole, to raise Coleridge in the eyes of men, I shall, I confess, feel both surprised and disappointed.'

I am sure that the temple, with all the rubble which blended with its marble, must have been a grander whole than any we are able to reconstruct for ourselves from the stones which lie about the field. The living Coleridge was ever his own apology —men and women who neither shared nor ignored his short-comings, not only loved him but honoured and followed him. This power of attraction, which might almost be called uni-versal, so diverse were the minds and natures attracted, is itself conclusive proof of very rare qualities. We may read and re-read his life, but we cannot know him as the Lambs, or the Wordsworths, or Poole, or Hookham Frere, or the Gillmans, or Green knew him. Hatred as well as love may be blind, but friendship has eyes, and their testimony may wisely be used in correcting our own impressions.

Samuel Taylor Coleridge was born on October 21, 1772, at the vicarage of Ottery St Mary in Devonshire, the youngest of nine sons by a second marriage. His father, the Reverend John Coleridge, was an amiable, absent-minded scholar, and apparently somewhat unpractical. We are told that he printed several books by subscription, and he tried to improve the Latin grammars in use by calling the ablative case the 'quale-quare-quidditive.' He died in 1781, and a few months later young Samuel obtained a presentation to Christ's Hospital.

The school and the Coleridge of those days were afterwards depicted in imperishable colours by Charles Lamb, who, though Coleridge's junior by two years, had become a Blue-coat boy some months earlier. In *Christ's Hospital Five-and-Thirty Years Ago,* by one of those tricks which were dear to him and endear him to us, Lamb professedly supplements his own *Recollections of Christ's Hospital* with the recollections of a lad not fortunate like him in having a home and parents near.

I was a poor friendless boy. My parents, and those who should care for me, were far away. Those few acquaintances of theirs, which they could reckon upon being kind to me in the great city, after a little forced notice, which they had the grace to take of me on my first arrival in town, soon grew tired of my holiday visits. They seemed to them to recur too often, though I found them few enough; and, one after another, they all failed me, and I felt myself alone among six hundred playmates.

O the cruelty of separating a poor lad from his early homestead! The yearnings which I used to have towards it in those unfledged years! How, in my dreams, would my native town (far in the west) come back, with its church, and trees, and faces! How I would wake weeping, and in the anguish of my heart exclaim upon sweet Calne in Wiltshire!

The child is Coleridge, of course, and sweet Calne in Wiltshire is sweet Ottery in Devon, disguised. Of course Coleridge felt this loneliness: a nature so sensitive could not help feeling it; and sixteen years later in *Frost at Midnight* he feelingly recalled it, and promised his own child a

happier fate. But, equally of course, he did not feel it all
the time. His earliest letters contain allusions to half-crowns
and 'a plumb cake,' and in due course, as he grows up, the
theme changes naturally to raiment. 'You will excuse me
for reminding you that, as our holidays commence next
week, and I shall go out a good deal, a good pair of breeches
will be no inconsiderable accession to my appearance,' the
pair in use being 'not altogether well adapted for a female
eye.'

In due course, too, he became a Grecian, fell in love
and wrote boyish poetry: and both the love-making and
the versifying, though no great matters at the time, were
destined to have more formidable consequences than usually
attach themselves to youthful experiments. The young lady
who inspired them was a Miss Mary Evans, a widow's
daughter, and sister of a small Blue-coat boy whom
Coleridge had protected.

And oh! from sixteen to nineteen what hours of paradise
had Allen [a schoolfellow] and I in escorting the Miss Evanses
home on a Saturday, who were then at a milliner's...and we
used to carry thither, of a summer morning, the pillage of the
flower-gardens within six miles of town, with sonnet or love-
rhyme wrapped round the nosegay.

But not all the inspiration came from Miss Evans. That
of the love-making she shared, if a Christ's Hospital
tradition be true, with the daughter of the school 'nurse';
to whom the poem *Genevieve* was addressed. ('For the
head boys to be in love with these young persons was an
institution of long standing,' says Mr Dykes Campbell.)
That of Coleridge's poetic awakening she undoubtedly
shared with the Rev. William Lisle Bowles, as we learn
from Chapter I of *Biographia Literaria*. Critic after critic
has found occasion for wonder in this; though in truth

there is none at all. To begin with, Bowles's sonnets are by no means bad; and, moreover, even today they are perceptibly, if palely, tinged with the dawn that was breaking over English poetry. Doubtless, had the book which fell into his hands as he was entering his seventeenth year been a volume of Blake, or of Cowper, or of Burns, his young conversion would have been more striking; would, at any rate, have made a better story. But by 1790 or thereabouts the new poetic movement was 'in the air,' as we say: a youth might take infection from any one, nor did it greatly matter from whom. Had Coleridge derived it from a stronger source the results might have been more precipitate, more violent. As it was, the blameless *Sonnets* —these and the equally blameless society of the Evans girls—weaned him from metaphysics and theology, on which he was immaturely feeding, and weaned him gently. He swore assent to Bowles: Bowles 'did his heart more good' than all other books 'excepting the Bible': but in his own attempts at versifying he still observed, even timidly, the conventions.

In January, 1791, the Committee of Almoners of Christ's Hospital emancipated him, with an Exhibition, to Jesus College, Cambridge. He started well. In 1792 he gained the Browne Gold Medal for a Sapphic Ode on the Slave Trade, and barely missed (on Porson's selection) the Craven Scholarship. In November, 1793, he bolted from Cambridge, in a fright of his college debts, or in a wild fit following on Mary Evans's rejection of his addresses. Both causes are suspected, and the two may have acted in combination. At all events he found his way to London, and on the second of December enlisted in the 15th or King's Light Dragoons, sinking all but his initials and his unlikeness to other men in the alias of Silas Tomkyn

Comberbacke. Probably a worse light dragoon—he was short of stature, fat, and unwieldy—never occupied, or failed to occupy, a saddle. In April, 1794, his relatives procured his discharge, and Jesus College readmitted him. In June he visited his old schoolfellow Allen at Oxford, and there became acquainted with Robert Southey of Balliol. Mr Robert Southey was then a youth of 'violent principles,' out of which—his friends and Coleridge aiding —the famous scheme of Pantisocracy was hastily incubated. Mr Campbell summarises it thus:

'Twelve gentlemen of good education and liberal principles are to embark with twelve ladies in April next,' fixing themselves in some 'delightful part of the new back settlements of America.' The labour of each man for two or three hours a day, it was imagined, would suffice to support the colony. The produce was to be common property, there was to be a good library, and ample leisure was to be devoted to study, discussion, and the education of the children on a settled system. The women were to be employed in taking care of the infant children and in other suitable occupations, not neglecting the cultivation of their minds. Among other matters not yet determined was 'whether the marriage contract shall be dissolved, if agreeable to one or both parties.' Every one was 'to enjoy his own religious and political opinions, provided they do not encroach on the rules previously made.' 'They calculate that every gentleman providing £125 will be sufficient to carry the scheme into execution.'

While Pantisocracy was hatching, Coleridge had departed on a walking-tour in Wales. On the thirteenth of July he reached Wrexham, and there, standing at the inn-window, he spied Mary Evans coming down the street with her sister, 'I sickened,' he writes, 'and well-nigh fainted, but instantly retired.' The two sisters, it appears, had caught sight of him. They 'walked by the window four or five times, as if anxiously.' But the meeting, the possible reconcilement, were not to be. Coleridge fled to Bristol, joined his friend Southey there, with other Pantisocrats, including a family of young ladies named Fricker. Southey married Edith Fricker. Coleridge—such things happen in the revulsion of disappointed passion—married Sara Fricker. The marriage, says Mr Campbell, was not made in Heaven. It was in great measure brought about by Southey.

Heaven alone knows—but no one who loves Coleridge can help wistfully guessing—what Dorothy Wordsworth might have made of him, as his wife. We have, perhaps, no right to guess at these things, but we cannot help it. He met her too late, by a little while, as it was all but too late that he met William Wordsworth. The Coleridges, after a brief experience of house-keeping at Clevedon and Bristol—interrupted by a tour to collect subscriptions for a projected newspaper, *The Watchman*—hied them down with their first-born to Nether Stowey in Somerset, to be neighbours of Thomas Poole, an admiring friend and a good fellow. To Nether Stowey, in July, 1797, came Wordsworth with his 'exquisite sister,' and were joined by Charles Lamb—all three as the Coleridges' guests. (The visit is commemorated in *This Lime-Tree Bower my Prison*.) At the end of his week's holiday Lamb returned to London; the Wordsworths, charmed by Coleridge's society, removed themselves but three miles away, to Alfoxden, and set up house.

Then the miracle happened. Coleridge had already published a volume of verse and brought it to a second edition: but it contained no promise of what was to come. Wordsworth was meditating the Muse, if the word 'meditating' can be used of a composition so frantic as *The Borderers*; but that he (the slower to take fire) would within a year be writing *Tintern Abbey* was a thing impossible, which nevertheless befell. Brother, sister, and friend— these three, as Coleridge has testified—became one soul. 'They saw as much of one another as if the width of a street, and not a pair of coombes, had separated their several abodes'; and in the soul of that intimacy, under the influence of Dorothy—herself the silent one, content to encourage, criticise, admire—wrapped around by the lovely solitudes of the Quantocks—Coleridge and Wordsworth found themselves poets, speaking with new voices in a new dawn. On the thirteenth of November, at half-past four in the afternoon, the three friends set off to walk to Watchet, on their way to the Exmoor country, intending to defray their expenses by the sale of a poem which the two men were to compose by the way. Before the first eight miles had been covered, the plan of joint authorship had broken down, and Coleridge took the poem into his sole hands. He wrought at it until the following March. On the twenty-third of that month, writes Dorothy, 'Coleridge dined with us. He brought his ballad [*The Ancient Mariner*] finished. We walked with him to the Miner's house. A beautiful evening, very starry, the horned moon.' We feel that the stars were out with excuse, to celebrate the birth of a star.

*The Ancient Mariner* sets one reflecting that, after all, the men of the Middle Ages had much to say for themselves, who connected poetry with magic, and thought of Virgil as a wizard. As we said just now, by taking small pains we can understand that the sonnets of Bowles—pale, faded essays as they appear to us—wore a different complexion in the sunrise of 1790. But we can ignore the time and circumstance of its birth, ignore the theorisings out of which it sprang, ignore Wordsworth and his prefaces and the taste on which they made war; and still, after more than a hundred years, *The Ancient Mariner* is the wild thing of wonder, the captured star, which Coleridge brought in his hands to Alfoxden and showed to Dorothy and William Wordsworth. Not in the whole range of English poetry— not in Shakespeare himself—has the lyrical genius of our language spoken with such a note.

> A voice so thrilling ne'er was heard...
> Breaking the silence of the seas
> Among the farthest Hebrides.

Its music is as effortless as its imagery. Its words do not cumber it: exquisite words come to it, but it uses and straightway forgets them. Not Shakespeare himself, unless by snatches, so sublimated the lyrical tongue, or obtained effects so magical by the barest necessary means. Take

> The many men, so beautiful!
> And they all dead did lie.

Or

> The moving Moon went up the sky,
> And nowhere did abide;
> Softly she was going up,
> And a star or two beside.

Or

> The body of my brother's son
> Stood by me, knee to knee:
> The body and I pull'd at one rope,
> But he said nought to me.

Here, and throughout, from the picture of the bride entering the hall to that of the home-coming in the moon-lit harbour, every scene in the procession belongs to high romance, yet each is conjured up with that economy of touch we are wont to call classical. We forget almost, listening to the voice, that there are such things as words.

> And now 'twas like all instruments,
> Now like a lonely flute;
> And now it is an angel's song,
> That makes the Heavens be mute.

If, in criticism, such an epithet be pardonable, we would call that voice seraphic; if such a simile, we would liken it to a seraph's, musing, talking before the gate of Paradise in the dawn.

Critics, allowing the magic of the poem, proceed to stultify the admission by enquiring why Coleridge did not follow it up and write others like it. The question, when foolishness has put it, can in terms of foolishness be readily answered. Coleridge yielded his will to opium. He had already begun to contract the habit, and he soon became a man capable (in Hazlitt's phrase) of doing anything which did not present itself as a duty. Once or twice, in *Christabel* and in *Kubla Khan*, he found new and divine openings, but his will could not sustain the flight, and the rest of the story of him as a poet resolves itself into repeated futile efforts to carry *Christabel* to a conclusion.

All this is true enough, or at least can be made convincing by any one who sets forth the story of Coleridge's subsequent aberrations. But before we blame his weakness let us ask ourselves if it be conceivably within one man's measure to produce a succession of poems on the plane of *The Ancient Mariner*; and, next, if—the magic granted, as it must be granted—it would not almost necessarily exhaust a man. In other words, let us enquire if, in a man who performed that miracle, his failure to perform others may not be more charitably set down to a divine exhaustion

than charged upon his frailties. Surely by *Christabel* itself
that question is answered; and almost as indisputably by
*Kubla Khan*. Coleridge himself tells us that he began
*Christabel* in 1797; that is, either before or during the
composition of *The Ancient Mariner*. Between the conception of the two poems there was no interval of opium-
taking. Yet who, studying *Christabel*, can, after the first
two or three pages have been turned, believe that the poem
could ever and by any possibility have been finished?
Coleridge, no doubt, believed that it could: but in his
struggles to finish it he was fighting against stronger adversaries than opium; against fate and a providence under
which, things being what they are, their consequences will
be what they will be.

The metre of *Christabel*, perfectly handled by its in-
ventor, probably suffers in our ears by association with the
jingle of Scott, and the vastly worse jingle of Byron, who
borrowed it in turn. It has since been utterly vulgarised,
and the very lilt of it nowadays suggests *The Mistletoe
Bough*, melodrama, and the balladry of *Bow Bells*. Yet,
and although the suspicion may be unworthy, one cannot
help tracing something of *Bow Bells* back to an origin in
such lines as

> Why waxed Sir Leoline so pale,
> Murmuring o'er the name again,
> 'Lord Roland de Vaux of Tryermaine'?

In short, there are some to whom *Christabel* rings false,
painfully false, here and there, in spite of its witchery. Yet,
where it rings true, we ask, Was there ever such pure
romantic music?

> Is the night chilly and dark?
> The night is chilly, but not dark.
> The thin gray cloud is spread on high,
> It covers but not hides the sky.

The moon is behind, and at the full:
And yet she looks both small and dull.
The night is chill, the cloud is gray:
'Tis a month before the month of May,
And the Spring comes slowly up this way.

Of *Kubla Khan*, even if 'a person...from Porlock' had not interrupted it, who will contend that it could ever have been finished, or even continued to any length? It abides the most entrancing magical fragment in English poetry; more than this it never could have been or have hoped to be.

Some three weeks after that starry evening on which Coleridge, his immortal ballad finished, walked with his friends, reciting it, we find Wordsworth writing to a friend that he, too, has been 'very rapidly adding to his stock of poetry,' and that the season is advancing with strides, 'and the country becomes almost every day more lovely.' The splendour of that summer in the Quantocks has passed into the history of our literature. Coleridge's best harvest was done; Wordsworth's—longer of continuance, yet brief in comparison with its almost insufferably long aftermath— on the point of ripening. The brother and sister quitted Alfoxden at Midsummer. In September Coleridge met them in London and voyaged with them on a happy, almost rollicking, jaunt to Hamburg. The *Lyrical Ballads* had been published a few days before, Coleridge contributing *The Ancient Mariner* (or, to spell it accurately, *The Rime of the Ancyent Marinere*), *The Nightingale*, *The Foster-Mother's Tale*, and *The Dungeon*. The two friends had launched their thunderbolt, and went off gaily. It was a real thunderbolt, too; a book to which the over-worked epithet 'epoch-making' may for once in a way be applied without strain on the truth; but for the moment

England took it with her habitual phlegm. Mrs Coleridge sent news that 'the *Lyrical Ballads* are not liked at all by any.'

At Hamburg, after a few crowded days, the travellers separated—Coleridge for Ratzeburg, intent on acquiring a thorough knowledge of German. He returned to Nether Stowey in July, 1799, and towards the close of the year met the Wordsworths again and toured with them through the Lake Country. Thither in June, 1800, he wandered back to them from London and Stowey. They had installed themselves at Dove Cottage, Grasmere, and in July the Coleridges settled at Greta Hall, Keswick, twelve miles away. Wordsworth was now working at the height of his powers: but to Coleridge the renewed intimacy brought no secondary spring. For him there was never to be another Stowey. And here, both fortunately and unfortunately, the story may break off: unfortunately, because his poetic period had come to an end (he had, he writes to Thelwall, 'for ever renounced poetry for metaphysics,' and moreover was beginning his long slavery to opium); fortunately, because its end releases us from following him to Malta and Bristol, through quarrels and patchings-up of friendship, through wanderings, returns, vows and defections, partial recoveries, relapses and despairs, to the long-drawn sunset of his life in the home of the Gillmans at Highgate.

Let two things be noted, however, before we give assent to those who write contemptuously of Coleridge and his infirmity. The first is, that even in the lowest depths he still fought, and in the end he *did* emerge with the victory. He had won it at a terrible cost; the fight had killed a hundred splendid potentialities; but though scarred, battered, enfeebled, the man emerged, and with his manhood still in his hands, though they trembled on the prize. Next let us, reading of quarrels and misunderstandings between him and his friends, note how, as time effaces the petty circumstance of each, so the essential goodness of the man shines through, more and more clearly; how, in almost any given quarrel, as the years go on, we see that after all Coleridge was in the right. He knew his weakness: but at least it taught him to be tender towards the weaknesses of his fellows, and no man had a better reason to ask of his sufferings

> But wherefore, wherefore fall on me?
> To be beloved is all I need,
> And whom I love, I love indeed.

As this affectionate disposition made him all but unintelligible to the Southeys and Hazlitts of his time, and lay somewhat outside the range of self-centred Wordsworth, whose fault in friendship was that of the Dutch in matters of commerce[1], so the very brilliance of his intellect too often isolated him within the circle of its own light. But on this Shelley has said the last word:

> You will see Coleridge—he who sits obscure
> In the exceeding lustre and the pure
> Intense irradiation of a mind
> Which, with its own internal lightning blind,
> Flags wearily through darkness and despair—
> A cloud-encircled meteor of the air,
> A hooded eagle among blinking owls.

---

[1] 'But this, my dear sir, is a mistake to which affectionate natures are too liable, though I do not remember to have ever seen it noticed—the mistaking *those who are desirous and well pleased to be loved by you, for those who love you.*'—Coleridge to Allsop, December 2, 1818. (The reference is to Wordsworth.)

In justice and in decency we should strive to imagine
Coleridge as he impressed those who loved him and listened
to him in his great days of promise; not the Coleridge of
later Highgate days, the spent giant with whose portrait
Carlyle made brutal play to his own ineffaceable discredit;
nor even the Coleridge of 1816, the 'archangel a little
damaged'—as Lamb, using a friend's privilege, might be
allowed to describe him in a letter to Wordsworth, a friend
of almost equal standing; not these, but the Coleridge of
whom the remembrance was the abiding thought in Lamb's
mind and on his lips during the brief while he survived
him—'Coleridge is dead.' 'His great and dear spirit haunts
me....Never saw I his likeness, nor probably the world
can see again. I seem to love the house he died at more
passionately than when he lived....What was his mansion
is consecrated to me a chapel.' If we must dwell at all on
the later Coleridge, let it be in the spirit of his own most
beautiful epitaph:

> Stop, Christian passer-by!—Stop, child of God,
> And read with gentle breast. Beneath this sod
> A poet lies, or that which once seem'd he.
> O, lift one thought in prayer for S. T. C.;
> That he who many a year with toil of breath
> Found death in life, may here find life in death!
> Mercy for praise—to be forgiven for fame
> He ask'd, and hoped, through Christ. Do thou the same!

None the less, in a world ever loath to admit that omelets
involve the breaking of eggs, men will go on surmising
what might have been, what full treasures of poetry Coleridge might have left, had he never drunk opium, had he
eschewed metaphysics, had he married Dorothy Wordsworth, had he taken a deal of advice his friends gave him
in good intent to rescue the Coleridge which God made

(with their approval) and the creature marred. 'He lived until 1834,' wrote the late Dr Garnett. 'If every year of his life had yielded such a harvest as 1797, he would have produced a greater amount of high poetry than all his contemporaries put together.' Yes, indeed! and *Kubla Khan* has this in common with a cow's tail—that it only lacks length to reach the moon. And yet, vain though these speculations are, we do wrong to laugh at them, for their protest goes deeper than their reasoning; and while fate tramples on things of beauty the indignant human heart will utter it. *Quis desiderio sit pudor aut modus*, when a poet—and such a poet—is broken in his prime?

On the other hand, the question sometimes raised— whether, in the Quantock time, when the pair learnt to be poets, Coleridge owed more to Wordsworth, or Words-worth to Coleridge—is, as Sir Thomas Browne would say, puzzling, but not beyond all conjecture: and we raise it again because we think it usually receives the wrong answer. It is usually argued that Coleridge received more than he gave, because he was the more impressionable. We might oppose this with the argument that Coleridge probably gave more than he received, as his presence and talk were the more inspiring. But let us look at a date or two. In June, 1797, Coleridge wrote *This Lime-Tree Bower my Prison*, and it contains such lines as these:

> Yet still the solitary humble-bee
> Sings in the bean-flower! Henceforth I shall know
> That Nature ne'er deserts the wise and pure...

and

> No sound is dissonant which tells of Life.

*Frost at Midnight* is dated February, 1798, and it contains the passage beginning

> Therefore all seasons shall be sweet to thee....

The exquisite *Nightingale* belongs to the summer of 1798, and it contains the images of the 'night-wandering man,' of the nightingale

> That crowds, and hurries, and precipitates
> With fast thick warble his delicious notes...

of the other birds awake in the bushes with

> Their bright, bright eyes, their eyes both bright and full...

and that most lovely picture of the infant hushing his woe as he gazes up at the moon through the orchard boughs:

> While his fair eyes, that swam with undropped tears,
> Did glitter in the yellow moonbeam! Well!—
> It is a father's tale. But if that Heaven
> Should give me life, his childhood shall grow up
> Familiar with these songs, that with the night
> He may associate joy.

Now the first thing to be noted of these lines, these images, is that they are what we now call Wordsworthian; some, the very best Wordsworthian; but all Wordsworthian with an intensity to which (if we study his verse chronologically) we find that in 1798 Wordsworth had never once attained —or once only, in a couple of lines of *The Thorn*. When Coleridge wrote these things, Wordsworth was writing *We are Seven, Goody Blake, Simon Lee*, and the rest. It was only after, though soon after, Coleridge had written them that Wordsworth is seen capable of such lines as

> The still sad music of humanity...

or of

> The stars of midnight shall be dear
> To her; and she shall lean her ear
> In many a secret place.

This note Coleridge might teach to Wordsworth, as Wordsworth might improve on it and make it his own. But that other note—the lyrical note of *The Ancient Mariner*—was incommunicable. He bequeathed it to none, and before him no poet had approached it; hardly even Shakespeare, on the harp of Ariel.

# MATTHEW ARNOLD

I do not hold up Joubert as a very astonishing and powerful genius, but rather as a delightful and edifying genius....He is the most prepossessing and convincing of witnesses to the good of loving light. Because he sincerely loved light, and did not prefer to it any little private darkness of his own, he found light. ...And because he was full of light he was also full of happiness. ...His life was as charming as his thoughts. For certainly it is natural that the love of light, which is already in some measure the possession of light, should irradiate and beatify the whole life of him who has it.

MANY a reader of *Essays in Criticism* must have paused and in thought transferred to Matthew Arnold these words of his in praise of Joubert, as well as the fine passage in which he goes on to ask What, in literature, we mean by fame? Only two kinds of authors (he tells us) are secure of fame: the first being the Homers, Dantes, Shakespeares, 'the great abiding fountains of truth,' whose praise is for ever and ever. But beside these sacred personages stand certain elect ones, less majestic, yet to be recognised as of the same family and character with the greatest, 'exercising like them an immortal function, and like them inspiring a permanent interest.' The fame of these also is assured. 'They will never, like the Shakespeares, command the homage of the multitude; but they are safe; the multitude will not trample them down.'

To this company Matthew Arnold belongs. We all feel it, and some of us can give reasons for our confidence; but perhaps, if all our reasons were collected, the feeling would be found to reach deeper into certainty than any of them. He was never popular, and never will be. Yet no one can say that, although at one time he seemed to vie with the public in distrusting it, his poetry missed its mark. On the other hand, while his critical writings had swift and almost instantaneous effect for good, the repute they brought him was moderate and largely made up of misconception. For the mass of his countrymen he came somehow to personify a number of things which their minds vaguely associated with kid gloves, and by his ironical way of playing with the misconception he did more than a little to confirm it. But in truth Arnold was a serious man who saw life as a serious business and chiefly relied, for making the best of it, upon a serene common-sense. He had elegance, to be sure, and was inclined—at any rate, in controversy— to be conscious of it; but it was elegance of that plain Attic order to which common-sense gives the law and almost the inspiration. The man and the style were one. Alike in his life and his writings he observed and preached the golden mean, with a mind which was none the less English and practical if, in expressing it, he deliberately and almost defiantly avoided that emphasis which Englishmen love to a fault.

Matthew Arnold, eldest son of Dr Thomas Arnold, the famous Head Master of Rugby, was born on Christmas Eve, 1822, at Laleham on the Thames, where his father at that time taught private pupils. The child was barely six years old when the family removed to Rugby, and at seven he returned to Laleham to be taught by his uncle, the Rev. John Buckland. In August, 1836, he proceeded to Winchester, but was removed at the end of a year and entered Rugby, where he remained until he went up to

Balliol College, Oxford, in 1841, with an open scholarship. He had written a prize poem at Rugby—the subject, *Alaric at Rome*; and on this performance he improved by taking the Newdigate in 1843—the subject, *Cromwell*. But we need waste no time on these exercises, which are of interest only to people interested in such things. It is better worth noting that the boy had been used to spending his holidays, and now spent a great part of his vacations, at Fox How, near Grasmere, a house which Dr Arnold had taken to refresh his eyes and his spirits after the monotonous ridge and furrow, field and hedgerow, around Rugby; and that, as Mr Herbert Paul puts it, young Matthew 'thus grew up under the shadow of Wordsworth, whose brilliant and penetrating interpreter he was destined to become.' Genius collects early, and afterwards distils from recollection; and if its spirit, like that of the licentiate Pedro Garcias, is to be disinterred, he who would find Matthew Arnold's must dig in and around Fox How and Oxford.

At Oxford, which he loved passionately, he 'missed his first,' but atoned for this, three months later, by winning a fellowship at Oriel. (This was in 1844–5. His father had died in 1842.) He stayed up, however, but a short while after taking his degree: went back to Rugby as an assistant master; relinquished this in 1847 to become private secretary to Lord Lansdowne, then President of the Council; and was by him appointed in 1851 to an Inspectorship of Schools, which he retained for five-and-thirty years. In 1851, too, he married Frances Lucy Wightman, daughter of a Judge of the Queen's Bench; and so settled down at the same time to domestic happiness and to daily work which, if dull sometimes, was not altogether ungrateful as it was never less than conscientiously performed.

Meanwhile, in 1849, he had put forth a thin volume,

*The Strayed Reveller, and other Poems, by A*; which was followed in 1852 by *Empedocles on Etna, and other Poems, by A*. In 1853 he dropped anonymity and under the title *Poems, by Matthew Arnold* republished the contents of these two volumes, omitting *Empedocles*, with a few minor pieces, and adding some priceless things, such as *Sohrab and Rustum*, *The Church of Brou*, *Requiescat*, and *The Scholar-Gipsy*.

'It was received, we believe, with general indifference,' wrote Mr Froude of the first volume, in *The Westminster Review*, 1854. We need not trouble to explain the fact, beyond saying that English criticism was just then at about the lowest ebb it reached in the last century, and that the few capable ears were occupied by the far more confident voice of Tennyson and the far more disconcerting one of Browning: but the fact—surprising when all allowance has been made—must be noted, for it is important to remember that the most and best of Arnold's poetry was written before he gained the world's ear, and that he gained it not as a poet but as a critic. In 1855 appeared *Poems by Matthew Arnold, Second Series*, of which only *Balder Dead* and *Separation* were new; and in 1858 *Merope* with its Preface: but in the interval between them he had been elected Professor of Poetry at Oxford (May 1857).

The steps by which a reputation grows, the precise moment at which it becomes established, are often difficult to trace and fix. The poems, negligently though they had been received at first, must have helped: and, since men who improve an office are themselves usually improved by it, assuredly the professorship helped too. The lectures on Homer which adorned Arnold's first tenure of the Chair strike a new note of criticism, speak with a growing undertone of authority beneath their modest professions, and would suffice to explain—if mere custom did not even more easily explain—why in 1862 he was re-elected for another five years. But before 1865, no doubt, the judicious who knew him had tested him by more than his lectures, and were prepared for *Essays in Criticism*.

Although we are mainly concerned here with the poems, a word must be said on *Essays in Criticism*, which Mr Paul pronounces to be 'Mr Arnold's most important work in prose, the central book, so to speak, of his life.' Mr Saintsbury calls it 'the first full and varied, and perhaps always the best, expression and illustration of the author's critical attitude, the detailed manifesto and exemplar of the new critical method, and so one of the epoch-making books of the later nineteenth century in English'—and on this subject Mr Saintsbury has a peculiar right to be heard.

Now for a book to be 'epoch-making' it must bring to its age something which its age conspicuously lacks: and *Essays in Criticism* did this. No one remembering what Dryden did, and Johnson, and Coleridge, and Lamb, and Hazlitt, will pretend that Arnold invented English criticism, or that he did well what these men had done ill. What he did, and they missed doing, was to treat criticism as a deliberate disinterested art, with laws and methods of its own, a proper temper, and certain standards or touchstones of right taste by which the quality of any writing, as literature, could be tested. In other words he introduced authority and, with authority, responsibility, into a business which had hitherto been practised at the best by brilliant nonconformists and at the worst by Quarterly Reviewers, who, taking for their motto *Judex damnatur cum nocens absolvitur*, either forgot or never surmised that to punish the guilty can be but a corollary of a higher obligation—to discover the truth. Nor can any one now read the

literature of that period without a sense that Arnold's teaching was indispensably needed just then. A page of Macaulay
or of Carlyle dazzles us with its rhetoric; strikes, arrests,
excites us with a number of things tellingly put and in
ways we had scarcely guessed to be possible; but it no
longer convinces. It does not even dispose us to be convinced, since (to put it vulgarly) we feel that the author
'is not out after' truth; that Macaulay's William III is a
figure dressed up and adjusted to prove Macaulay's thesis,
and that the France of Carlyle's *French Revolution* not only
never existed but, had it ever existed, would not be France.
Arnold helping us, we see these failures—for surely that
history is a failure which, like Cremorne, will not bear the
daylight—to be inevitable in a republic of letters where
laws are not and wherein each author writes at the top of
his own bent, indulging and exploiting his personal eccen-
tricity to the fullest. It has probably been the salvation of
our literature that in the fourteenth century the Latin pre-
vailed over the Anglo-Saxon line of its descent, and that in
the forming of our verse as well as of our prose we had, at
the critical moments, the literatures of Latin races, Italian
or French, for models and correctives; as it was the misfortune of the Victorian period before 1865 that its men
of genius wrote with eyes turned inward upon themselves
or, if outward, upon that German literature which, for all
its great qualities, must ever be dangerous to Englishmen
because it flatters and encourages their special faults[1].

Of Arnold from 1865 onward—of the books in which
he enforced rather than developed his critical method (for
all the gist of it may be found in *Essays in Criticism*)—of
his incursions into the fields of politics and theology—

---

[1] That Matthew Arnold himself over-valued contemporary
German literature does not really affect our argument.

much might be written, but it would not be germane to our purpose. *New Poems*, including *Bacchanalia, or the New Age*, *Dover Beach*, and the beautiful *Thyrsis*, appeared in 1867; and thereafter for the last twenty years of his life he wrote very little in verse, though the fine *Westminster Abbey* proved that the Muse had not died in him. He used his hold upon the public ear to preach some sermons which, as a good citizen, he thought the nation needed. In his hard-working official life he rendered services which those of us who engage in the work of English education are constantly and gratefully recognising in their effects; and we still toil in the wake of his ideals. He retired in November, 1886. He died on April 15th, 1888, of heart-failure: he had gone to Liverpool to meet his eldest daughter on her return from the United States, and there, in running to catch a tram-car, he fell and died in a moment. He was sixty-five, but in appearance carried his years lightly. He looked, and was, a distinguished and agreeable man. Of good presence and fine manners; perfect in his domestic relations, genial in company and radiating cheerfulness; setting a high aim to his official work yet ever conscientious in details; he stands (apart from his literary achievement) as an example of the Englishman at his best. He cultivated this best deliberately. His daily note-books were filled with quotations, high thoughts characteristically chosen and jotted down to be borne in mind; and some of these—such as *Semper aliquid certi proponendum est* and *Ecce labora et noli contristari!*—recur again and again. But the result owed its amiability also to that 'timely relaxation' counselled by Milton:

> To measure life, learn thou betimes, and know
>   Toward solid good what leads the nearest way;
>     For other things mild Heav'n a time ordains,

And disapproves that care, though wise in show,
    That with superfluous burden loads the day,
        And when God sends a cheerful hour, refrains.

To those, then, who tell us that Arnold's poetic period
was brief, and imply that it was therefore disappointing,
we might answer that this is but testimony to the perfect
development of a life which in due season used poetry and
at the due hour cast it away, to proceed to things more
practical. But this would be to err almost as deeply as those
who tell us that Arnold, as he himself said of Gray, 'never
spoke out'—whereas Arnold habitually spoke out, and
now and then even too insistently. Again it would be a
mistake for us to apply to him *au pied de la lettre* the over-
sad verses:

Youth rambles on life's arid mount,
    And strikes the rock, and finds the vein,
And brings the water from the fount,
    The fount which shall not flow again.

The man mature with labour chops
    For the bright stream a channel grand,
And sees not that the sacred drops
    Ran off and vanish'd out of hand.

And then the old man totters nigh,
    And feebly rakes among the stones.
The mount is mute, the channel dry;
    And down he lays his weary bones.

Yet it were stupid not to recognise that here is contained
a certain amount of general truth and of truth particularly
applicable to Arnold. 'The poet,' Mr Saintsbury writes
of him (and it sums up the matter), 'has in him a vein, or,
if the metaphor be preferred, a spring, of the most real and
rarest poetry. But the vein is constantly broken by faults,

and never very thick; the spring is intermittent, and runs at times by drops only.' Elsewhere Mr Saintsbury speaks of his 'elaborate assumption of the singing-robe,' a phrase very happily critical. Arnold felt—no man more deeply —the majesty of the poet's function: he solemnly attired himself to perform it: but the singing-robe was not his daily wear. The ample pall in which Tennyson swept, his life through, as to the manner born; the stiffer skirts in which Wordsworth walked so complacently; these would have intolerably cumbered the man who protested that even the title of Professor made him uneasy. Wordsworth and Tennyson were bards, authentic and unashamed; whereas in Arnold, as Sir William Watson has noted,

> Something of worldling mingled still
> With bard and sage.

There was never a finer worldling than Matthew Arnold: but the criticism is just.

The critics, while noting this, have missed something which to us seems to explain much in Arnold's verse. We said just now that English literature has been fortunate in what it owes to the Latin races; we may add that it has been most fortunate in going to Italy for instruction in its verse, to France for instruction in its prose. This will be denied by no one who has studied Elizabethan poetry or the prose of the 'Augustan' age: and as little will any one who has studied the structure of poetry deny that Italy is the natural, France the unnatural, school for an English poet. The reason is not that we understand Italian better than French history and with more sympathy—though this, too, scarcely admits of dispute; nor again that the past of Italy appeals to emotions of which poetry is the consecrated language. It lies in the very structure and play of the language; so

that an Englishman who has but learnt how to pronounce
the Italian vowels can read Italian poetry passably. The
accent comes to him at once; the lack of accent in French
remains foreign after many months of study. Now although
Arnold was no great admirer of French poetry (and indeed
had a particular dislike for the Alexandrine), France was,
to him, among modern nations, the heir of those classical
qualities which differentiate the Greek from the barbarian,
and his poetry seems ever to be striving to reproduce the
Greek note through verse subdued to a French flatness of
tone, as though (to borrow a metaphor from another art)
its secret lay in low relief. But an English poet fighting
against emphasis is as a man fighting water with a broom:
and an English poet, striving to be unemphatic, must yet
contrive to be various, or he is naught. Successfully as he
managed his prose, when he desired it to be emphatic
Arnold had, in default of our native methods of emphasis,
to fall back upon that simple repetition which irritates so
many readers. In his poetry the devices are yet more
clumsy. We suppose that no English poet before or since
has so cruelly overworked the interjection 'Ah!' But far
worse than any number of 'ah!'s' is Arnold's trick of italic
type:

> How *I* bewail you!...
>
> We mortal millions live *alone*...
>
> In the rustling night-air comes the answer:
> 'Wouldst thou *be* as these are? *Live* as they!'...

a device almost unpardonable in poetry. So when he
would give us variety, as in *Tristram and Iseult*, Arnold
has no better resource than frequent change of metre: and
although every reader must have felt the effect of that
sudden fine outburst

What voices are these on the clear night-air?
What lights in the court—what steps on the stair?...

yet some must also have reflected that the great masters, having to tell a story, choose their one metre and, having chosen, so adapt and handle it that it tells all. *Sohrab and Rustum* indeed tells itself perfectly, from its first line to its noble close. But *Sohrab and Rustum* is, and professes to be, an episode. *Balder* is little more, and most readers find *Balder*, in spite of its fine passages and general dignity, long enough. Arnold—let it be repeated—was not a bard; not a Muse-intoxicated man. He had not the bardic, the architectonic, gift. 'Something of the worldling' in him forbade any such fervour as, sustained day after day for years, gave the world *Paradise Lost*, and incidentally, no doubt, made Milton's daughters regret at times that their father was not as ordinary men.

Nor had Arnold an impeccable ear for rhyme (in *The New Sirens*, for instance, he rhymes 'dawning' with 'morning'): and if we hesitate to follow the many who have doubted his ear for rhythm, it is not for lack of apparently good evidence, but because some of his rhythms which used to give us pause have come, upon longer acquaintance, to fascinate us: and the explanation may be, as we have hinted, that they follow the French rather than the Italian use of accent, and are strange to us rather than in themselves unmusical. Certainly the critics who would have us believe that *The Strayed Reveller* is an unmusical poem will not at this time of day persuade us by the process of taking a stanza or two and writing them down in the form of prose. We could do the same with a dozen lines of *The Tempest* or *Antony and Cleopatra*, were it worth doing; and prove just as much, or as little.

Something of Arnold's own theory of poetry may be

extracted from the prefaces of 1853 and 1854. They contain, like the prefaces of Dryden and of Wordsworth, much wisdom; but the world, perhaps even more wisely, refuses to judge a poet by his theory, which (however admirable) seldom yields up his secret. Yet Arnold had a considered view of what the poet should attempt and what avoid; and that he followed it would remain certain although much evidence were accumulated to prove that he who denounced 'poetry's eternal enemy, Caprice,' could himself be, on occasion, capricious. He leaves the impression that he wrote with difficulty; his raptures, though he knew rapture, are infrequent. But through all his work there runs a strain of serious elevated thought, and on it all there rests an air of composure equally serious and elevated—a trifle statuesque, perhaps, but by no means deficient in feeling. No one can read, say, the closing lines of *Mycerinus* and fail to perceive these qualities. No one can read any considerable portion of his work and deny that they are characteristic. Nor, we think, can any one study the poetry of 1850 and thereabouts without being forced to admit that it needed these qualities of thoughtfulness and composure which Arnold brought to it. He has been criticised for discovering in Tennyson a certain 'deficiency in intellectual power.' But is he by this time alone in that discovery? And if no lack of thoughtfulness can be charged against Browning—as it cannot—is not Browning violent, unchastened, far too often energetic for energy's sake? Be it granted that Arnold in poetical strength was no match for these champions: yet he brought to literature, and in a happy hour, that which they lacked, insisting by the example of his verse, as well as by the precepts of his criticism, that before anything becomes literature it must observe two conditions —it must be worth saying, and it must be worthily written.

Also he continued, if with a difference, that noble Wordsworthian tradition which stood in some danger of perishing—chiefly, we think, beneath the accumulation of rubbish piled upon it by its own author during his later years. That which Matthew Arnold disinterred and re-polished may have been but a fragment. His page has not, says Mr Watson, 'the deep, authentic mountain-thrill.' We grant that Arnold's feeling for Nature has not the Wordsworthian depth: but so far as it penetrates it is genuine. Lines such as

> While the deep-burnish'd foliage overhead
> Splintered the silver arrows of the moon...

may owe their felicity to phrase rather than to feeling. The Mediterranean landscape in *A Southern Night* may seem almost too exquisitely elaborated. Yet who can think of Arnold's poetry as a whole without feeling that Nature is always behind it as a living background?—whether it be the storm of wind and rain shaking Tintagel—

> I forgot, thou comest from thy voyage—
> Yes, the spray is on thy cloak and hair...

or the scent-laden water-meadows along Thames, or the pine forests on the flank of Etna, or an English garden in June, or Oxus, its mists and fens and 'the hush'd Choras-mian waste.' If Arnold's love of natural beauty have not those moments of piercing *apprehension* which in his mas-ter's poetry seem to break through dullness into the very heaven: if he have not that secret which Wordsworth must have learnt upon the Cumbrian mountains, from moments when the clouds drift apart and the surprised climber sees all Windermere, all Derwentwater, shining at his feet; if on the other hand his philosophy of life, rounded and complete, seem none too hopeful, but call man back from

eager speculations which man will never resign: if it re-
press, where Browning encouraged, our quest after

> Thoughts hardly to be pack'd
> Within the narrow act,
> Fancies that broke through language and escaped...

yet his sense of atmosphere, of background, of the great
stage on which man plays his part, gives Arnold's teaching
a wonderful *comprehension*, within its range. 'This,' we
say, 'is poetry we can trust, not to flatter us, but to sustain,
console.' If the reader mistake it for the last word on life
his trust in it will be illusory. It brings rather that

> lull in the hot race
> Wherein he doth for ever chase
> That flying and elusive shadow, rest.
> An air of coolness plays upon his face,
> And an unwonted calm pervades his breast;
> And then...

(if after protesting against italics in poetry we may italicise
where, for once, Arnold missed the opportunity)

> he *thinks* he knows
> The hills where his life rose,
> And the sea where it goes.

# SWINBURNE

## I

*How were the roses so fresh and so fair!*

I do not suppose that anybody now alive (I speak of lovers
of poetry) who was not alive in 1832 and old enough then to
enjoy the first perfect work of Tennyson, has had such a
sensation as that which was experienced in the autumn of 1866
by readers of Mr Swinburne's *Poems and Ballads*. And I am
sure that no one in England has had any such sensation since.

THUS wrote Mr George Saintsbury, some twenty-
two years ago, in a volume called *Corrected Impressions*: and it is certain that no one survives today to compare the emotional experiences of 1832 and 1866, to
report to us. Indeed of the men who in 1866 were old
enough to wage war over *Poems and Ballads* the greater
number pre-deceased its author, and by this time a very
few remain. Mr Saintsbury, who happily survives (but
will not be called 'Doctor'), was an undergraduate in
1866. He tells us:

The autumn must have been advanced before [the book]
did come out, for I remember that I could not obtain a copy
before I went up to Oxford in October, and had to avail myself
of an expedition to town to 'eat dinners' in order to get one.
Three copies of the precious volume, with 'Moxon' on cover
and 'John Camden Hotten' on title-page, accompanied me
back that night, together with divers maroons for the purpose
of enlivening matters on the ensuing Fifth of November. The

book was something of a maroon in itself....We sat next afternoon, I remember, from luncheon time till the chapel bell rang, reading aloud by turns in a select company *Dolores* and *The Triumph of Time*, *Laus Veneris* and *Faustine*, and all the other wonders of the volume.

The hubbub raised over *Poems and Ballads* in 1866 still, after half a century, interrupts criticism with an echo too loud for its real importance, even for its historical importance. It was not, to be sure, a mere hubbub of the market-place, and for much of it that sounded in the market-place Swinburne and his friends were largely to blame. The Pre-Raphaelites had a tribal way of shouting their wares before producing them. In Goblin Market 'Come buy! Come buy!' habitually dinned as noisily as in any vulgar one, and Alexander the coppersmith could colourably plead, nine times out of ten, that he had not started the tumult. Dante Gabriel Rossetti in particular had always a nervous sense of the public opinion it was proposed to offend; his own poems appeared in circumstances (creditable enough if hidden) which, made public, to an uncharitable world suggested *réclame*. There can be no doubt, we think (after reading many Memoirs), that his friends did Swinburne little service together with much disservice by puffing his book beforehand. 'Now we were told, first, that a volume of extraordinarily original verse was coming out; now, that it was so shocking that its publisher repented its appearance; now, that it had been re-issued, and was coming out after all.' Nor can it be said that, when the storm burst, Swinburne either handled his craft or comported himself in a way to make easy weather. The book *did* challenge the world: it *did* contain matter of offence—and he well knew it. When we have allowed everything for the sensitiveness of a poet, it remains true that a man who throws down a challenge should be prepared to keep his head when the glove is taken up.

But the real marvel of *Poems and Ballads* lay, of course, in its *poetry*, as in that lay the real innovation. Other poets had been scandalous—plenty of them—before Swinburne; and the possible changes that true poetry can ring on the libidinous are, after all, pretty few. But here was a man who, five hundred years after Chaucer, in the long line of descent which already boasted Shakespeare, Milton, Dryden, Pope, Wordsworth, Shelley, Byron, Tennyson, Browning—all so great and all so different—had suddenly discovered a new door and thrust it open upon what seemed endless vistas of beauty. Here was a man who, coming after these mighty inventors, could take the language in which they had wrought and convert it to a music as unlike any of theirs, as absolutely fresh and original, as it was patently the music of a peer. Swinburne constantly held that all great poets must be conscious of their greatness. He himself could be as arrogant as any one, when provoked; but although self-centred, he was too noble a gentleman to be arrogant by habit—he was even over-prone to abase himself before the greater gods of Parnassus: and in the following anecdote he is made to assert a claim which many will think not overweening.

He was not disinclined, on occasion, to refer to himself with an engaging frankness, as if he were speaking of someone else. At Jowett's dinner-table R. W. Raper once asked him which of the English poets had the best ear. Swinburne replied with earnestness and gravity: 'Shakespeare without doubt; then Milton; then Shelley; then, I do not know what other people would do, but I should put myself.'

Although our memory reach short of Mr Saintsbury's, we can bring a small illustration of the sway this genius

held over young men in 1880. The wave of enthusiasm
had fallen into a trough with *Bothwell*. The splendid
choruses in *Erechtheus* had lifted it a little; but *Erechtheus*
as a whole failed to 'amuse,' and the worshippers had an
uneasy sense that their master was fumbling in an art for
which he lacked instinct as well as tact; that, when prolixity should have warned him as the surest signal of a mark
missed, Swinburne had not even the eyes to see that his
prolixity was prolix. But in 1878, with *Poems and Ballads,
Second Series*, on the wonderful crests of such lyrics as *The
Year of the Rose, A Forsaken Garden, A Wasted Vigil*,
and the supreme *Ave atque Vale*, the wave surged up anew
to its summit: and if we missed the adventurous feeling of
naughtiness, that too was restored to us, after a fashion, in
1880, by *Heptalogia*—for youth loves parodies, and to see
fun poked at pontifical seniors. Memory recalls a night
in the autumn of that year, a set of rooms in Balliol—but
men dropped in from other colleges and stayed until close
upon midnight—a voice chanting the *Heptalogia* to wild
shouts of laughter, the company taking fire and running
back, like flame over stubble, to race through the audacities
of *Poems and Ballads* even back to the Circean choruses of
*Atalanta*—'hounds of spring on winter's traces':

> And Pan by noon and Bacchus by night,
> Fleeter of foot than the fleet-foot kid,
> Follows with dancing and fills with delight
> The Maenad and the Bassarid;
> And soft as lips that laugh and hide
> The laughing leaves of the trees divide,
> And screen from seeing and leave in sight
> The god pursuing, the maiden hid.

And then, almost suddenly—even in breasts that continued
to echo the memory of it—all this enthusiasm had died

down; and while Swinburne went on writing, writing, of stars and love, and waves and flames that were deathless or breathless or tattered or battered or shattered, none of them mattered, none of them contained any longer any hope; all were galvanic—reflex action of genius after death.

*That* is the real tragedy which has to be explained in the biography of a man whose life yields the picturesque biographer very little—or very little that can be told—of incident for escape or resource. It would still be the real tragedy and kernel of the whole matter had Swinburne's life been crowded with spirited actual adventure. Swinburne was a tremendous force in poetry: the force died; the man outlived it, and died, many years later, solicitously tended. He had in his day the hearts of all young lovers of poetry at his feet. He has left an indelible mark on English verse: and for this, to the end, the younger generation venerated him as a great figure, a spent god and asleep under the pines (Putney). He was the last man in the world to leave a cause for a ribbon or a handful of silver. But he who had inspired parodists innumerable and many pale imitators, has left us no school of poets. Upon the literature of Victorian England he made an amazing irruption, and passed.

## II

It is always a pleasure to read a book by a man who knows how books should be written, and Mr Gosse's eagerly awaited *Life of Swinburne* tells the tale vividly, tactfully, adequately, in that excellent prose which, although one takes it for granted in the author of *Father and Son*, still gives so much pleasure that it were ungrateful to omit the *benedicamus*. Moreover the tale not only gives truth of fact, so far as our knowledge enables us to test this, but by nicely apportioning the whole to its subject, and its casual with its more significant and important parts, conveys an impression of truth scarcely less valuable. It omits, to be sure, the one word (of five letters) which, if uttered, might have saved the skilful artist a deal of trouble; but it does this in obedience to a tradition which makes, no doubt, for literary as well as for parliamentary decency; and we shall amuse ourselves by copying Mr Gosse's reticence.

The genius of Swinburne was something elvish, always and throughout. He had all the precocity of an elf, with no little of its outward guise. Like an elf, he never grew up. Like an elf, he suddenly gave signs of arrested growth, was an old man prematurely, and continued to be an old man for many years, until the moment when he peacefully faded out. There was one reason which in ordinary men would account well enough for this arrested development, but it will not account for Swinburne.

Even his birth is an elfin mystery. Who could predict—who can account for—this child as springing from the union of a British Admiral with a daughter of the third Earl of Ashburnham? The ancient and honourable families of Swinburne and Ashburnham have nothing in their records which begins to explain him. He himself has stated that he was born 'all but dead, and certainly was not expected to live an hour.' Of this circumstance (probably apocryphal) exact memory can hardly be demanded of him; but again and again his most definite recollections of his childhood (given in later years in all honesty by one who abhorred falsehood all his life) are shown to be legendary, to say the least—'intimations of immortality' rather than slavish records of fact. The fact of importance is that his childhood alternated between two homes—his parents' at East Dene, Bonchurch, in the Isle of Wight,

and Capheaton on the Northumbrian coast, where his
Border ancestors had settled in the reign of Elizabeth and
where his grandfather, Sir John Swinburne, sixth baronet,
kept house as head of the family. The seas off the Wight to
swim in—the Northumbrian coast to gallop along, chanting
verse against the rush of the wind in his face—chanting
(say) *Gastibelza*, 'the song of songs which is Hugo's'—
these, heaven to the boy's childhood, were cherished by
him to the end as his heavenliest experiences. Only the
coasts of Cornwall (Tristram's coast) and of Sark ever
competed in his affection with Bonchurch and Capheaton,
where

> Through fell and moorland,
> And salt-sea foreland,
> Our noisy norland
>     Resounds and rings.

As he never swerved from these first loyalties to place
and kindred, so, while pretending to grow up, he but
altered, without changing, the strange elvishness of his
personal appearance. His cousin, Lord Redesdale, thus
describes his first arrival at Eton (in the summer half of
1849) at the age of twelve:

What a fragile little creature he seemed as he stood there
between his father and mother, with his wondering eyes fixed
upon me! Under his arm he hugged his Bowdler's Shakespeare, a very precious treasure bound in brown leather with,
for a marker, a narrow slip of ribbon, blue I think, with a
button of that most heathenish marqueterie called Tunbridge
ware dangling from the end of it. He was strangely tiny. His
limbs were small and delicate, and his sloping shoulders looked
far too weak to carry his great head, the size of which was
exaggerated by the tousled mass of red hair standing almost at
right angles to it. Hero-worshippers talk of his hair as having

been a 'golden aureole.' At that time there was nothing golden
about it. Red, violent, aggressive red it was, unmistakable red,
like burnished copper. His features were small and beautiful,
chiselled as daintily as those of some Greek sculptor's masterpiece. His skin was very white—not unhealthy, but a trans-
parent tinted white, such as one sees in the petals of some roses.
His face was the very replica of that of his dear mother, and
she was one of the most refined and lovely of women. His red
hair must have come from the Admiral's side, for I never
heard of a red-haired Ashburnham.

Against this for a pendant, let us set Mr Gosse's description of the mature man:

Algernon Swinburne was in height five feet four and a half
inches. He carried his large head very buoyantly on a tiny
frame, the apparent fragility of which was exaggerated by the
sloping of his shoulders, which gave him, almost into middle
life, a girlish look. He held himself upright, and, as he was
very restless, he skipped as he stood, with his hands jerking or
linked behind him while he talked, and, when he was still, one
toe was often pressed against the heel of the other foot. In this
attitude his slenderness and slightness gave him a kind of fairy
look, which I, for one, have never seen repeated in any other
human being. It recurs to my memory as his greatest outward
peculiarity.

His head was bigger than that of most men of his height; as
Sir George Young tells us, when he entered Eton at twelve
years old his hat was already the largest in the school. Mr
Lindo Myers, who came over with him from Havre in the
autumn of 1868, writes to me that, Swinburne's hat having
been blown overboard, 'when we got to Southampton, we
went to three hatters before we found one hat that would go
on, and then we had to rip the lining out. His head was
immense.' In the late Putney days, when he became bald, this
bigness of his head was less noticeable than when it had been

emphasised by the vast 'burning bush' of his red hair, which in early days he wore very much fluffed out at the sides....The orb of this mop reduced the apparent thickness of his neck, which, looked at merely in relation to his falling shoulders, was excessive, yet seemed no more than was necessary to carry the balloon of head and hair.

But we must go back to Eton, where 'Grub' Brown, the librarian, would point the boy out to visitors as one of the sights of the place, 'where he sat, day after day, in a gallery window of the library with a folio across his knees.' He devoured the English poets at this time: the Elizabethan and Jacobean dramatists with a quite amazing voracity. Years afterwards, in 1885, he wrote that the plays of Marston had dwelt in his memory since 'I first read them at the advanced age of twelve'; and in 1887 that those of so obscure a writer as Nabbes had been familiar to him 'ever since my thirteenth year.' Thirty years later, too, looking over his bookshelves, he took down a copy of Lamb's *Specimens of the English Dramatic Poets* and remarked, 'That book taught me more than any other in the world —that and the Bible.'

There are some of us who hold (with all reverence for Lamb) that he—and Swinburne after him—in their enthusiasm have exalted these obscurer Elizabethans quite disproportionately and out of perspective, diminishing for the unlearned or unwary reader the true eminence of Shakespeare above them all. But we pass this by: the point for us, just here, being that in his literary loves, as in almost everything else, this fay-like creature never really grew up, never developed as other men develop. 'It is particularly important to notice,' says Mr Gosse, 'that almost all Swinburne's literary convictions were formed while he was at school'; and later we read, 'From the earliest record of his childhood to that of his last hours at Putney we see him unchanged by conditions and unaffected by opinion. This gives his career a certain rigidity....' In 1892, when Tennyson's death left the laureateship vacant and Queen Victoria is reported to have said to Gladstone, 'I am told that Mr Swinburne is the best poet in my dominions,' Swinburne gave it as his private conviction that Canon Dixon, author of *Mano*, had the highest claim for the post, and, failing him, Lord De Tabley. 'It will be observed,' Mr Gosse points out, 'that each of these poets was older than Swinburne, who had little knowledge of the verse of men born after 1850, and even less curiosity about their careers.' His attitude to old men of genius was 'adorable in humility—to Victor Hugo, to Landor—even to old men of talent, such as Barry Cornwall and Wells of *Joseph and his Brethren*'; but he had learned to worship them at school and each lived to a ripe age to retain his loyalty. Of young men he was incurious: which begins to explain why this innovator never founded a school.

It was the same with his politics. He sang of Italian liberty, sitting at the feet of Mazzini. Sitting at the feet of Victor Hugo he cursed Napoleon III as never man cursed save his master. He hailed the French Republic: to the end he could preach tyrannicide as a duty, like a schoolboy, academically wreathing his sword in myrtle bough. Yet again we come back upon ossification, both in hate and in hope.

When Napoleon III died, in pain and obscurity, at Chisle- hurst, having ceased for three years to be a power for good or for evil, France partly forgave him, and even Victor Hugo forgot him. Yet Swinburne neither forgot nor forgave, and to him it seemed as just to continue to execrate this miserable man six months after his death as it had been to abuse him six months before it....The essence of the series of sonnet-curses, *Dirae*, was ecstasy that 'we have lived to say The dog is dead.'

So he could sing for Italian liberty like a very Simonides ('the emotion of the poet...gave to the noblest parts of *Songs before Sunrise* an intensity unique in English literature, and probably to be compared with nothing else written since the Greeks produced cosmological hymns in the fifth century B.C.'), and, when that liberty was won, could drop all interest in Italy and Italy's future; as, after passionately acclaiming the French Republic, he averted his face and took no further interest in what happened to France. Yet, after all, what worth is either a new monarchy or a new republic, save as an instrument for furthering new political hopes?

## III

Having to do with a genius so precocious and so prematurely ossified, we need make no apology for switching from Eton to Putney and back. Mr Gosse opines that at Eton, where his physical strangeness invited it, 'he was preserved from bullying by a certain dignity and by his unquestionable courage.' His courage, then and through life, was beyond question, and indeed it would be strange if any scion of Swinburne and Ashburnham lacked *that* quality. Algernon Swinburne possessed it, at all events. At the age of seventeen he entertained a boyish notion of attaining eminence in life as a cavalry officer, and attempted the climb of Culver Cliff in the Isle of Wight (believed to be impregnable) 'as a chance of testing my nerve in the face of death which could not be surpassed.' He performed the feat, which had to be confessed to his mother.

Of course she wanted to know why I had done such a thing, and when I told her she laughed a short, sweet laugh most satisfactory to the young ear, and said, 'Nobody ever thought you were a coward, my boy.' I said that was all very well, but how could I tell till I tried? 'But you won't do it again?' she said. I replied, 'Of course not—where would be the fun?'

As a swimmer he was intrepid, and his rashness twice brought him near to drowning; but on each occasion he saved himself, having no great strength of stroke, by his indomitable persistence. When he was an elderly man, some hulking poetaster, half-mad with vanity, who had sought in vain to drag Swinburne into a correspondence, waylaid him with a big stick on one of his lonely walks. 'The antagonist was a powerful man, his victim a sort of fairy; but Swinburne cowed him by sheer personal dignity and serenely continued to walk on, with the blusterer growling behind him.' Theodore Watts-Dunton was alarmed, and took out a warrant against the man (had it been legally possible he would have done better to take out a warrant against a few London street-crossings, through the murderous traffic of which Swinburne would plunge and dance, heedless as a child, having a charmed life). Swinburne merely laughed at the affair: he did not even copy Dr Johnson's procedure (with Macpherson) and write a letter to the bully—which was just as well, perhaps, for we very much doubt if the serenity shown during the actual incident would have translated itself in ink upon paper.

In spite, however, of his constant and unquestioned courage, evidence could be collected, we fear, that Swinburne *did* suffer bullying at Eton. The late Viscount St Aldwyn, who had been his contemporary there, answered

Mr Gosse's application for a few reminiscences with 'a horrid little boy, with a big head and a pasty complexion, who looked as though a course of physical exercise would have done him good': and he who has known the inside of a public school will ponder this unfaltering pronouncement and shake his head. Anyhow the little victim refused to play, preferring to read. He had a trick, too, then and all his life, of jerking his arms and fluttering his hands violently when excited. It resembled 'St Vitus' dance,' and is not the sort of thing that makes sympathetic appeal to the average senior and stronger school-fellow. His parents consulted a specialist, who 'after a close examination,' reported that these motions resulted from 'an excess of electric vitality.' Electric or not, as the boy grew and reached sixteen, this vitality put forth symptoms of turbulence and insubordination, and at the end of the summer half he was withdrawn from Eton 'in consequence of some representations.'

This happened in 1853. In January 1856—after two years and a half spent in out-of-door exercise and desultory private tuition—he went up to Oxford, matriculating at Balliol. Scott was then Master. Jowett, who had been passed over in the 1854 election for headship, was Regius Professor of Greek, but the heresy-hunters still laid their scent upon him and his plans for university and college reform. This persecution of one who became his wise and enduring friend may account in some part for Swinburne's dislike of Oxford, which became inveterate. He resided for three years and a half, and left without taking a degree or having (so far as his contemporaries tell us) excited any particular attention among dons or undergraduates. But:

It is much to be observed that in later life, though he spoke often and in affectionate terms of Eton, Swinburne was never betrayed into the smallest commendation of Oxford. He was indeed unwilling to mention the University....Long afterwards, in late middle life, he railed against Matthew Arnold for his 'effusive Oxonolatry,' and earlier he had contrived to analyse and commend *The Scholar-Gipsy* and *Thyrsis* without so much as naming the 'sweet city with her dreaming spires' which is the very substance of those poems.

He made friends—some good for him, some rather obviously the reverse: he competed for the Newdigate (subject—'The Discovery of the North-West Passage') and failed, having sent in a composition far better than that which took the prize; he learned to be a frantic Republican, bought a portrait of Orsini—would-be assassin of Napoleon III—hung it up in his sitting-room, opposite that of Mazzini, and 'pirouetted in front of it in ecstasies of enthusiasm.' How much Jowett knew of this does not appear, nor how Swinburne managed to tolerate in Jowett (whose weakness, if he had one, was for apparent worldly success) a certain admiration for the third Napoleon. But there was never a break in their intimacy, which Swinburne after Jowett's death commemorated in a chapter of reminiscences, beginning

Among the tributes offered to the memory of an illustrious man there may possibly be found room for the modest reminiscences of one to whom the Master of Balliol was officially a stranger and Mr Jowett was an honoured and valued friend.

Other gracious seniors attempted to take the somewhat graceless young man in hand; notably Dr (afterwards Sir Henry) Acland, who asked Swinburne to his house. Acland was—we can corroborate Mr Gosse's description—'the soul of urbanity,' but all the more and none the less an Acland.

Swinburne was particularly annoyed because Acland, in his

boundless sympathy, wished to share 'the orgies and dare-
devilries' of their little group; and on one occasion they all
fled to London, to avoid having tea in a meadow with Acland
and his children. They behaved very badly, and like shy and
naughty boys, to excellent Dr Acland, whom they privately
called, I do not know why, 'the Rose of Brazil'; but the
biographer has to admit, with a blush, that Swinburne behaved the worst of all. On one occasion, when Dr Acland
was so kind as to read aloud a paper on Sewage, there was a
scene over which the Muse of History must draw a veil.

Against this we may, skipping forward a little, match an
equally unhallowed scene of the year 1862 when Swinburne, preparing his *Poems and Ballads* for the press, was
given to trying the effect of them on any private audience
he conceived as likely to be sympathetic. The occasion of
the following experiment was a visit to Monckton Milnes
(Lord Houghton) at Fryston:

In the summer of 1862 a distinguished party assembled at
Fryston: it included Venables, James Spedding, the newly-
appointed Archbishop of York (William Thomson), and
Thackeray, the latter having brought his two young daughters,
afterwards Lady Ritchie and Mrs Leslie Stephen. Lady Ritchie
recalls for me that the Houghtons had stimulated the curiosity
of their guests by describing the young poet....On Sunday
evening, after dinner, he was asked to read aloud some of his
poems. His choice was injudicious; he is believed to have recited
*The Leper*; it is certain that he read *Les Noyades*. At this the
Archbishop of York made so shocked a face that Thackeray
smiled and whispered to Lord Houghton, while the two young
ladies, who had never heard such sentiments expressed before,
giggled aloud in their excitement. Their laughter offended the
poet, who, however, was soothed by Lady Houghton's tactfully
saying 'Well, Mr Swinburne, if you *will* read such extraordinary things, you must expect us to laugh.' *Les Noyades*

was then proceeding on its amazing course, and the Archbishop was looking more and more horrified, when suddenly the butler—'like an avenging angel,' as Lady Ritchie says—threw open the door and announced, 'Prayers! my Lord!'

But our extracts run ahead of the story. In his third year at Balliol 'turbulence' again began to exhibit itself, and Jowett expressed a fear that his young friend might be sent down. To protect him from this disaster Algernon was consigned for a term to read history at Navestock in Essex with the Reverend William Stubbs, afterwards Bishop of Oxford and most renowned of historians, but then vicar of an agricultural parish and almost unknown to fame. Stubbs, who had a sly twist of humour and no mean capacity for telling a story, was used in later days to draw freely on his recollections of this amazing guest's descent upon his country cure. There is no doubt that he and Mrs Stubbs made the stay a happy one; but soon after Swinburne's return to Oxford his landlady lodged complaint against 'late hours and general irregularities,' and on the 21st of November 1859 Swinburne left Oxford, as he had left Eton, prematurely. 'My Oxonian career culminated in total and scandalous failure.'

## IV

At Oxford he had made friends with Rossetti, Burne-Jones, and Morris during their famous visit in which they painted frescoes around the debating-hall (long since converted to library) of the Union. They had gone back to London, and thither (after patching up the quarrel with his father, who was naturally incensed over the Oxford fiasco) Swinburne followed them. There he fell easily into the Pre-Raphaelite circle and talked red-republicanism to them. They never doubted his genius or his capacity to express it in poetry if he would choose to try. Rossetti, then their real leader, took from the first the line of elder brother. He 'adopted, with a full and almost boisterous appreciation of the qualities of Swinburne, and a tender indulgence to his frailties, a tone of authority in dealing with "my little Northumbrian friend," as he used to call him, which was eminently wholesome.' And Swinburne chose to try. In 1860, while writing at *Chastelard*, he published his first book, *The Queen Mother and Rosamond*. The insuccess of the venture was conspicuous. 'Of all still-born books,' said Swinburne afterwards, 'it was the stillest.' Says Mr Gosse, 'Nobody read it, nobody saw it, nobody heard of it.'

*The Queen Mother* might be turgid and *Rosamond* a pale study in Pre-Raphaelitism, but the young poet meanwhile was mewing a mighty youth over such lyrics as *The Triumph of Time*, and for a sample:

> I will go back to the great sweet mother,
>   Mother and lover of men, the sea.
> I will go down to her, I and no other,
>   Close with her, kiss her and mix her with me;
> Cling to her, strive with her, hold her fast:
> O fair white mother, in days long past
> Born without sister, born without brother,
>   Set free my soul as thy soul is free.
>
> O fair green-girdled mother of mine,
>   Sea, that art clothed with the sun and the rain,
> Thy sweet hard kisses are strong like wine,
>   Thy strong embraces are keen like pain.
> Save me and hide me with all thy waves,
> Find me one grave of thy thousand graves,
> Those pure cold populous graves of thine
>   Wrought without hand in a world without stain.

It was not until 1865, however, that, with *Atalanta in Calydon*, he made a second attempt on the public. The Pre-Raphaelites indeed had made some impression by this time with their paintings, but as poets they and their friends had met with the chilliest of receptions. Meredith's first attempt in 1851, his second in 1862, Morris's first in 1858, Swinburne's own in 1860, D. G. Rossetti's in 1861, had missed fire, one and all and completely. It was not until 1862 that Christina Rossetti scored the first success with *Goblin Market*—'Christina,' said Swinburne, 'was the Jael who led our host to victory.' So the publisher (Bertram Payne, of the firm of Moxon) had small confidence, rested his only hope on making the book beautiful in outward appearance, and, confining the first edition to a hundred copies or so, spent pains to cover them in ivory-white buckram adorned with mystic golden spheres. It must have been a high moment in April 1865 for one or two who opened these covers and came, first, upon the Greek elegiac dedication to Landor:

οὔποτε σοῖς, γέρον, ὄμμα φίλοις φίλον ὄμμασι τέρψω,
σῆς, γέρον, ἁψάμενος, φίλτατε, δεξιτερᾶς...

and then upon the exquisite opening of the poem itself:

Maiden, and mistress of the months and stars
Now folded in the flowerless fields of heaven....

Here was writing truly Hellenic, of the right line of tradition, and we should despair of the future of our literature—watered as it has ever been and renewed from Mediterranean springs—if we believed that England will soon lack men of an intellect ready to recognise *that*, to hail and salute it. No such curse, at all events, had descended upon our nation in 1865. *Atalanta*, and Swinburne with it, soared into sudden fame. It was a song before sunrise, a shaft of morning after long watches, lighting the hearts of the faithful with hope:

> And hope was strong, and life itself not weak.

## V

We have hinted at the rest of the story in previous pages, and need not dwell on it here nor tell it at length. In particular we would skirt quickly around the throng which vociferated about *Poems and Ballads* in 1866, because it not only missed infinite good for the sake of a little evil, but, even in so far as it happened to be right, mistook the symptom for the disease.

The true danger, for poetry, was not so much that Swinburne had fallen into bad courses, as that he might fall into pedantry. Now there is—as every student of literature, and especially every student of medieval literature, must know—a pedantry which relaxes, as well as a pedantry which binds. The actual disease is a withering up of the man within, by which he loses sense of literature as a grace of life and comes to mistake it for an end in itself, even for life itself.

Now we make no doubt that Swinburne's way of life helped towards that ossification which overtook his genius. It *must* have acted so, since (as Burns knew and noted) the true tragedy of profligate living is that 'it hardens a' within, *and petrifies the feeling.*' But we think George Meredith came nearer to diagnosing the real trouble when he wrote, 'I don't see any internal centre from which springs anything that he does. He will make a great name, but whether he is to distinguish himself solidly as an artist I would not willingly prognosticate.' Meredith touched the secret. In this elfin genius, when the rush of fire had spent itself over the twigs, there was no log left 'leaning back,' in his master Landor's image, with a male, slow, generating core of fire. Set apart *Hertha*, that glorious poem, Swinburne's own best-beloved, and all the blazing rhetoric of *Songs before Sunrise* falls short of convincing us that Swinburne ever understood that greatest of all maxims, 'Look into thine heart, and write,' or even that he had a real heart to look into. It has the fatal chill of a *parti pris*: it fails to persuade, having neither sap nor growth nor any fecundity: it neither kindles us, where it is right, to passionate assent, nor moves us to forgive where it is wrong. Over it all lies the coming shadow of pedantry.

So, to speak generally, it is with *Bothwell* and with almost all his verse after *Poems and Ballads, Second Series*. Pegasus seems to be at a gallop all the while, but his hoofs are for ever coming down in the same place: and while monotony (as in *The Faerie Queene*) can be pleasant enough, nothing in the world is more tedious than a monotony of *strain*.

Nor, in the middle years, could Swinburne search into himself, to criticise. Having written the opening scene of *Bothwell* (1871) he gave it over to Jowett to read.

Jowett pronounced it much too long. Swinburne was surprised, but having a great respect for Jowett's judgment, took the criticism very seriously. Accordingly next day—they were living in the hotel at Tummel Bridge—Swinburne stayed in bed all the morning to work on the scene. He produced it triumphantly at luncheon, when Jowett dryly observed that it was three lines longer than it was before....Later on, at one of Jowett's reading-parties at West Malvern, R. W. Raper saw Swinburne suddenly fling himself on the floor at Jowett's feet, and heard him say, 'Master, I feel I have never thanked you enough for cutting *four thousand* lines out of *Bothwell*.'

Thus, while still essaying sustained work for which his genius—more and more declaring itself to be merely lyrical—was unfitted, essaying work for which at least that genius should have been put to hard schooling, he could never learn that a great poem requires structure based on stern preparation in anatomy, nor see the need of learning. For *A Song of Italy*, as later for *Balen*, he was capable of choosing a lyrical measure which, pleasant enough for a snatch of song, maddens the ear by repetition over seventy or a hundred or two hundred pages. His critical odes, such as the *Song for the Centenary of Landor*, came to have no proportions at all; and *Tristram* itself (after the magnificent prologue) hag-rides the reader into utter weariness. Swinburne, who delighted to recite, or intone, his own works, could never understand that his auditor might at any point tire of listening. In 1895 he read *Balen* through at a sitting to the Dutch novelist Maarten Maartens, who 'did not unreservedly admire his delivery':

It was too subjective an outpour, and wearisomely impassioned, like a child's jump against a wall....At the first moment, however, when he ceased, I felt a poignant grief that it was over....It had been very beautiful...all the difference between seeing a beautiful woman and feeling her embraces.

When we read Keats's *Endymion* we sigh over the premature death of one who, had the gods seen fit, might have lived to build with his material. Swinburne lived and never built, never arrived at seeing that architectonic is necessary.

## VI

In London, as at Oxford, Swinburne made friends good and bad for him. Among the latter must be counted the much-travelled Richard Burton, translator of *The Arabian*

*Nights.* 'Burton, a giant of endurance, and possessed at times with a kind of dionysiac frenzy, was no fortunate company for a nervous and yet spirited man like Swinburne'—who, it may be told, had already, by his excesses, superinduced a kind of epilepsy upon his habitual twitch.

It took the form of a convulsive fit, in which, generally after a period of very great cerebral excitement, he would suddenly fall unconscious. These fits were excessively distressing to witness, and produced a shock of alarm all the more acute because of the death-like appearance of the patient. Oddly enough, however, the person who seemed to suffer from them least was Swinburne himself. The only real danger appeared to be that he would hit himself in his fall, which indeed he repeatedly and severely did. But his general recovery after these fits was magical, and it positively struck one—if it is not absurd to say so—that he was better after them, as after a storm of the nerves.

So it happened again and again. The Admiral would be hastily summoned to London to take his son home to the country. In two days' time Algernon would be out and about, a 'good boy' chastened, affectionate, extremely docile. Then after some weeks would come the return to London, and in due course more 'irregularity,' more irritability, more quarrels with his best friends, another fit, another telegram to the Admiral, another swift recovery. It seemed to work out like a sum with a recurrent decimal; but actual life is less tolerant of recurrent 'irregularity' than is mathematics. In actual life you may expel nature with a thyrsus—*tamen usque recurret*. The crash came in August 1879. He had lost his father; he had alienated his friends; he had a fancy for a while to have nothing to do with his family, even with his mother. He lived lonely in his rooms in Great James Street, 'in a state of constant

febrility and ill-health.' There an illness took him and
carried him to the very doors of death, just outside of which
Mr Theodore Watts (afterwards Watts-Dunton) entered
upon the scene and saved him.


## VII

Mr Watts, a solicitor of St Ives in Huntingdonshire, had
come up to London in the year 1872 or thereabouts with
an ardent enthusiasm for the group of Pre-Raphaelites, and
had been baffled in a first attempt to make Swinburne's
acquaintance. Towards the end of the year, however,
Madox Brown advised Swinburne, whose business affairs
he knew to be in a tangle, to place them in the hands of
Theodore Watts; which he did, with very happy results.

In September 1879, then, armed with the approval of
Lady Jane Swinburne, Watts called at 3 Great James Street
and, finding the poet in a truly deplorable condition,
carried him almost by force to his own rooms, close by,
and thence, after a week or two, to the upper storey of a
semi-detached villa at Putney, hired for the purpose.
Again Swinburne made an amazing recovery. By the
middle of October he was able to resume his correspondence, to read, and even to walk out of doors. But he had
been near enough to the grave to look into it: and hence-
forth he put himself into Watts's tutelage with a childlike
and most pathetic trust. A lease was taken of 'The Pines,'
Putney, and there the two lived together for nearly thirty
years. Watts supervised the poet's food and drink, ad-
ministered his moneys, kept away callers (with the help of
an inexorable maidservant), and mapped out his days with
almost mathematical precision. Towards the middle of
every morning Swinburne, no matter what the weather,

took a long walk 'generally up Putney Hill and over the Heath, but sometimes along the Richmond Road to the Mortlake Arms, and then through Barnes Common as far as Barnes Green and the Church.' At the corner-shop of the Misses Frost, going into Wimbledon, he bought his newspapers and ordered his books.

In storm and rain, always without an umbrella, the little erect figure, with damp curls emerging from under a soft felt hat, might be seen walking, walking...so that he became a portent and a legend throughout the confines of Wandsworth and Wimbledon. He always returned home a little while before the midday luncheon, or dinner; and at 2.30, with clockwork regularity, he 'disappeared to enjoy a siesta,' which sometimes lasted until 4.30. Then he would work for a while....In the evening his regular habit was to read aloud....In these conditions his health became perfect; he developed into a sturdy little old man without an ache or a pain; and he who had suffered so long in London from absence of appetite and wasting insomnia, for the last thirty years of his life at Putney ate like a caterpillar and slept like a dormouse.

* 'Walking, walking,' for thirty years. But that which walked was the ghost of the poet who had written *Atalanta* and *Poems and Ballads*. It is pretty safe to say that Watts had saved Swinburne's life: it is certain that he had averted a tragedy: and against this positive deed of friendship and thirty years of devotion little is set by sneering at Watts as 'a pedicure of the Muses'—which, we believe, was Meredith's phrase for him. It must be allowed, however, that Watts averted tragedy only by turning these thirty years into comedy, and rather absurd comedy. The worst was not that Watts, in the jealousy of his sway, allowanced the supply of other friends even more sternly than he cut down 'The Bard's' liquor; nor that, as elderly ladies succumb

to the wiles of the tramp, he and Swinburne, while mostly inaccessible to real authors, were given to open their door to any who oiled its key with praise of Watts's own preposterous novel *Aylwin*. Nor was it even the worst that, happening in his own way to dislike such faulty but full-blooded poets as Byron and Walt Whitman, he drew Swinburne to abuse both, whom he had formerly admired, and recant noble praise in terms of scurrility. The unpardonable fault was that, admiring the rhetorical aptitude which had always been Swinburne's bane, he encouraged him to substitute rhetoric for poetry and rhetoric for prose: and so, while Swinburne wrote much in these thirty years —especially on Shakespeare—that was marvellous; though Swinburne himself be to blame that the more he learned of Mary Queen of Scots the more it got in the way of poetry about her; old lovers of his verse and prose cannot help feeling that 'the rest is silence' may be, after all, a better epitaph than 'the rest is—rhetoric.'

We will not quote for disparagement the worst passages which deal with Byron and Whitman in *Miscellanies* and *Studies in Prose and Poetry* (1891 and 1894); but we will append a passage on Byron, written in 1866, to show what a prose-writer was lost in Swinburne:

His work was done at Missolonghi; all of his work for which the fates could spare him time. A little space was allowed him to show at least a heroic purpose, and attest a high design; then, with all things unfinished before him and behind, he fell asleep after many troubles and triumphs. Few can ever have gone wearier to the grave; none with less fear. He had done enough to earn his rest. Forgetful now and set free for ever from all faults and foes, he passed through the doorway of no ignoble death out of reach of time, out of sight of love, out of hearing of hatred, beyond the blame of England and

the praise of Greece. In the full strength of spirit and of body
his destiny overtook him, and made an end of all his labours.
He had seen and borne and achieved more than most men on
record. 'He was a great man, good at many things, and now
he had attained his rest.'

## VIII

We have indicated what we think the worst to be
lamented of those last thirty years, and, for all our debt to
the memory of Mr Watts-Dunton and our gratitude for
the work Swinburne accomplished in those years, it remains lamentable. Desperate causes may require desperate
remedies: the devotion which applied these and kept a
friend alive and happy cannot, must not, be slighted. But
as little can its effect be gainsaid—that a biography of
Swinburne must, to be true, overbalance the end with the
beginning and can hardly, to be told well, escape being
told with a touch of ironic humour, of laughter amid tears
for humanity and its ways. Mr Gosse has written it so;
written it with infallible tact; written it just as well as it
could be written. But it is so, and the pity is it should be
so. *How were the roses so fresh and so fair!*...This man,
who succumbed to frailty, was a splendid poet, and his
verse will yet avenge him on Time. Meanwhile

> Who shall seek thee and bring
>     And restore thee thy day,
> When the dove dipt her wing
>     And the oars won their way
> Where the narrowing Symplegades whitened the straits of
>     Propontis with spray?

# CHARLES READE

CHARLES READE was born a hundred years ago, on the 8th of June 1814; he died on Good Friday, April 11, 1884. Then, or about then, Walter Besant could write as follows of

the position occupied by this writer, which is—and has been, since the death of Thackeray and Dickens—alone in the first rank. That is to say, alone because he resembles no other writer living or dead—not alone because there has been no other writer in line with him. His merits are his own, and they are those of the first order of writers. He cannot be classified or compared; in order to be classified, a man must be either a leader or one of a following. Reade certainly cannot be accused of following. One can only say that he stands in the front rank and he stands alone. One can only say that this great writer —there is no greater praise—paints women as they are, men as they are, things as they are...

all of which is skimble-skamble thought in slipshod language; a confusion of platitude, falsity, and nonsense stark but inarticulate. (Also George Eliot survived Thackeray and Dickens by some years.) Still it is obviously trying, under a spell of admiration, to say something about Charles Reade; and the mischief—for those of us who admire Reade, albeit differently—lurks in a little devil of a doubt that anyone, a hundred years hence, will care either for the something Besant wanted to say or for the reservations we think worth while.

Reade as a novelist had merits we can hardly believe

to be perishable. To take the most eminent: when he 'got going' upon high, straight epic narrative—Gerard's odyssey, the last voyage of the *Agra*, the bursting of Ousely dam, the storming of the Bastion St André—no one of his contemporaries could touch him; no English writer, at any rate, could get near him. Nor were these efforts mere spurts of invention; but long, strong, masterly running, sustained right to the goal over scores of pages. Could one but pluck these chapters out of his books, blot the residue out of existence, and holding them out to posterity (they would make no mean handful either) challenge it to refuse Reade a place in the very first rank, there could be no answer. He had other great merits too; but with them a fatal talent for murdering his own reputation, for capping every triumph with an instant folly, either in the books themselves or in his public behaviour; and these follies were none the less disastrous for being prompted by a nature at once large, manly, generous, tender, incapable of self-control, constitutionally passionate, and in passion as blind as a bat.

He started in life as the youngest of eleven children; son of a high Tory squire (of tall and noble presence) and a lady who had descended upon Ipsden in Oxfordshire out of the inner social circle of Buckingham Palace and the Regency. To quote the official *Memoir* into which Reade's luck followed him (it fills two volumes worthy to survive for brilliance of fatuity even when their subject shall be forgotten), 'Charles Reade was born into a refined family circle, for his mother had the *bel air* of the Court, and his father was a gentleman of the old school.' Further, the mother 'was no common woman. Born under the torrid sun of Madras, immersed while yet a girl in the life of politics, society, and the Court, she was before all things a lady [!]. Haydn taught her music, and Sheridan epigram and repartee. Her manner was perfect, and her conversational powers so extraordinary as to have fascinated so superior a master of rhetoric as Samuel Wilberforce.' In the country she imbibed religion (Calvinism) from a divine who, 'though a splendid preacher and a Hebrew scholar, never attained to the semblance of a gentleman. In his old age a long pipe and a spittoon were his inseparable companions.' Environed by this Arcadian simplicity, Mrs Reade lived and did her work industriously and happily. She was at once domestic and social, with an aptitude for cultivating the great of the earth.

Lord Thurlow was godfather to her eldest son; Barrington, the Prince-Bishop of Durham, who resided at Mongwell Park, three miles off, became sponsor for her fourth; and Warren Hastings for her youngest daughter. 'My dearest Lady Effingham' was the friend of her life-time until that lady in her eighth decade ran away with a Scripture-Reader, when the note changed and she was styled 'That horrid old woman.'

She was a daughter of Major John Scott (afterwards Scott-Waring), M.P. for the old borough of Stockbridge, Hants —a figure in the polite and the party memoirs of his age; and, like most women trained in its high politics, she had a sharp eye for 'openings.' 'Her influence with the Board of Directors of the Old East India Company was virtually paramount. She obtained no less than three writerships [i.e., appointments in the Civil Service], together with two cavalry cadetships, for her sons, and an infantry cadetship for a connection by marriage.' The elder sons had been sent to public schools—Rugby, Haileybury, Charterhouse; but she had a whim to subject Charles, her youngest and her darling, to private tuition.

## I

This was the child's first misfortune, and no slight one. Though the public schools of this land have pretty steadily evolved some four-fifths of its admitted genius, their reputation for discouraging genius is saecular and shall not be disputed here; but at all events they discourage those abnormalities of temper and conduct to which genius is prone, as by their stern correction it is not infrequently bettered. Reade was committed to a flagellating minister at Iffley, who taught him the Latin irregular verbs; if of a hundred he could repeat all correctly, he escaped; if but nine-and-ninety, he was caned and—being all unlike an elder brother who in the midst of a furious whacking observed pleasantly, 'I say, if you keep on at this much longer you'll *hurt*'—Charles was not cured of a sensitive skin by this method of grafting-on the classics. After five years of penal servitude his parents removed him to a far humaner school at Staines; a change which, in the words of the *Memoir*, 'can only be compared to one from a diet of gall to one of champagne.' Even that (one conjectures) would not suit all stomachs; and the boy, though happier at Staines, missed the right regimen of health for his character. Next came Oxford. His father the squire, who had been at Rugby and Oriel, could not see that Oxford fitted a man for life. (He kept a pack of harriers.) But Mrs Reade insisted, and Charles went up to stand for a demyship at Magdalen: which he won in the teeth of all probability, not because he sent in a good essay (which he did), nor through parental wire-pulling, but because one of the eight nominee candidates whom the Fellows proposed to job in failed so conspicuously that old Dr Routh refused to have him and preferred to admit the outsider who came of good family and could write sound English. Luck and ability combined again, four years later, to win him his fellowship. A demy of Magdalen in those days could only succeed to a fellowship on his particular county, and then only if he had taken his degree before the day of St Mary Magdalen next ensuing after the vacancy. Reade, though privately tutored by no less a man than Robert Lowe (afterwards Lord Sherbrooke), may have been indolent; at any rate in the early summer of 1835 he was unprepared for 'Greats' when quite unexpectedly a vacancy occurred in Oxfordshire, his own county. The month was June, and he had twenty-four hours in which to decide between entering his name for a pass or for honours. For the pass he would have to sit at once; and, though the examination was light as compared with the other, a total ignorance of the books offered would hardly be covered by autoschediastic brilliancy. He therefore entered his name for honours, and in the three weeks' respite read furiously. Thirty-six hours before the examination he began upon the Thirty-nine Articles, which all candidates had to commit to memory —rejection on this test invalidating success in all the others. He had a bad memory (ruined, as he always maintained, by ferocious overtaxing at his first school). Lo! when he started upon this task, which he had left to the last, his memory collapsed. To make matters worse, the three weeks' strain had brought on a racking neuralgia. He walked up to the examination table knowing just three Articles by rote; his mind, for the remaining thirty-six, a blank. The Article chosen by the examiner chanced to be one of the magic three. Reade repeated it pat, won his degree, and inherited his fellowship.

Later, and having in the meantime entered at Lincoln's Inn and begun to study law, he achieved the Vinerian

Scholarship, less by luck than by good management. The Masters of Arts elected to this scholarship; and the Fellows of Magdalen, though etiquette forbade them to vote or canvass against one of their Society, had by this time been chafed more than a little by Reade's 'nodosities' and angularities of temper, and would help him to no university backing. It occurred to Reade that, with his father's influence in the shire, he might whip up a number of county gentlemen who happened to be M.A.'s and surprise, perhaps even swamp, the resident voters.

His mother canvassed the clergy; and, when favourable answers were obtained, offered conveyances free of cost. On the day of election Oxford swarmed with squires and parsons whipped up for Charles Reade, and thus when he came in head of the poll by a substantial majority, some chagrin found expression within the bosom of the college.

In truth, this contentious, irascible man was no easy fellow for any collegiate society, let alone that of Magdalen under Dr Routh. His colleagues found him gey ill to live with; while he, smarting as he did under every petty wound, real or imaginary—and, for a real one, there had been an attempt to oust him save on a condition of his taking orders —saw no more of them than he was obliged. He rarely dined in hall: but he swore by the college cook (who swore by him), and in later years even bought himself a set of silver dishes in which his dinners were conveyed from Magdalen to London! But he wished to be quit of college business, though he duly served his term as Dean of Arts —in a green coat with brass buttons, a costume at which the late Goldwin Smith took deep umbrage.

## II

In 1839 Reade left Oxford for a sort of grand tour, Paris and Geneva being the chief resting places. Thereafter for a few years he wandered a great deal, especially in Scotland—as the *Memoir* puts it: 'between the years 1837 and 1847 his visits to the land of cakes were chronic.' When at home he had, so to speak, three homes—Ipsden, Magdalen, and some chambers he rented in Leicester square—nor was either of them warned when to expect him: for he kept a separate wardrobe at each, travelled without luggage, and probably would have disdained the telegraph had it been invented. His rooms in Leicester square swarmed with squirrels which he imported from Ipsden. He started a craze for violins; collected Cremonas, plunged into the secrets of their manufacture, almost desperately offended his father by spilling varnishes from his window-sill over the white front of Ipsden; bolted in a huff for the continent and Paris; almost lost his life as a hated Englishman in the Revolution of 1848; escaped in a cab under a truss of straw; and arrived back at Ipsden travel-stained but cool, as he could be when not enraged by trifles. 'My dear Charles,' was the greeting, 'you have had a narrow escape of your life.'—'I have. They put me into a damp bed at Boulogne.'

We come now to that turn in Reade's fate which, if but for it he had never been a writer, must be accounted a blessing, as to the last he loudly and sincerely proclaimed it. But if primarily a blessing, in a dozen ways (or we are grievously mistaken) it proved to be a steady curse, though the woman responsible was innocent of all conscious harm. He had always been attracted by the stage. He reckoned drama to be the first of the arts. He left orders to be written on his tomb: 'Charles Reade: Dramatist, Novelist, Journalist'—in that order. About this time, 1849, when 'his fine old sire paid the debt of nature' (*Memoir*), he wrote a play—many plays. He took it to 'a distinguished comedian, Mrs Seymour,' then acting with Buckstone at the Haymarket. 'She was magnanimous and appreciative and, like many women of her calibre, could recognise the difference between a real and a sham gentleman. Ladies whom the voice of scandal has spared have been less warm-hearted,' &c. (*Memoir*). 'It may, however, be safely predicted [*sic*] that he (Reade) stood alone in believing her to be a really great artist.' He asked for an interview. 'The response was in the affirmative' (*Memoir*). She did not think much of the play, and showed that she didn't. Reade had called 'hat in hand'; 'politely, and without any show of the offence he felt he bowed himself out.' She felt sorry, pitied 'a fine man with the *bel air* of one accustomed to society,' jumped (mistakingly) at the guess that he was hard up for money, sat down and wrote a letter. It fetched Reade back with an explanation.

What passed at that interview is not known. Each had learnt in a moment to respect the other, and we may be sure that a friendship thus commenced was from the outset regarded as sacred. It had moreover to develope....It must, however, be categorically asserted [*sic*] on the individual authority [*sic*] of the late Mr Winwood Reade, who was a constant inmate subsequently of their house in Bolton Row, that the friendship between these two was platonic.

To have done with this egregious *Memoir*.—No one doubts that Mrs Seymour was an honest lady, or that she started Charles Reade upon writing novels, or that she gave him some sound practical advice by the way. But the crucial test of such a partnership as this (and there have been not a few in the history of letters) is only passed when the silent partner supplies that self-criticism which the active partner lacks. Unless the two are thus complementary—if the silent one merely encourages the active performer to the top of his bent—the momentum but drives forward an inordinate mass to topple by its own weight; as Lewes drove George Eliot from *Scenes of Clerical Life* to *Deronda*. Now Mrs Seymour, a woman of little cultivation, was quite incapable of correcting, because incapable of perceiving, those defects of taste and temper to which Reade was prone. If she did not foster them she at least left these idiosyncrasies to mar his work. Worse even than this— she was an actress, and not a first-class actress, of a very bad period. She saw everything 'literary' in the light of the stage, and her stage was of the stagiest. By ill-luck Reade, too, suffered from this false stage-eye. He too *saw* all his novels first as plays. His earliest, *Peg Woffington*, was adapted straight from a short play, *Masks and Faces*, which still holds the boards in spite (or by virtue) of what Swinburne called 'the preposterous incident' of the living portrait. Rightly classing this with the burlesque duel in *Christie Johnstone*, Swinburne rightly adds that 'in serious fiction they are such blemishes as cannot be effaced and can hardly be redeemed by the charming scenes which precede or follow them.' The tedious conclusion of the first of the long novels, *It is Never Too Late to Mend*, with its avenging Jew and its Wicked Bridegroom foiled at the church-door, is but stage-grouping and melodrama carried to the $n$th power: the same bag of tricks being produced again to affront the reader's intelligence in *Put Yourself in His Place*. Reade had written *The Cloister and the Hearth*, *Hard Cash*, and *Griffith Gaunt* in the interval between these two, and yet *Put Yourself in His Place* would seem to prove that he had learnt (or, rather, had unlearnt) nothing. The devices by which the hero is made to vanish and to keep his betrothed without news that he is alive would not impose on a child, and the sawdust puppet Squire Raby becomes almost a thing of horror when we reflect that Reade probably intended him for a portrait of his own father!

Few men can have written a critical sentence wider of the truth than Besant's 'One can only say that this great writer...paints women as they are, men as they are, things as they are.' That was just what Reade could not learn to do for any length of time, save now and then when left alone in his rooms in Magdalen. When he saw men and women with the help of Mrs Seymour, or of such playwrights as Tom Taylor and Dion Boucicault, he saw them as dolls making their exits and their entrances behind footlights. He wrote *Foul Play* in collaboration with Dion Boucicault, which is another way of saying that he submitted his true epical daemon, though it broke loose for a long run in the splendid adventures of the castaways, to be caught and reconsigned to a prison of cardboard. He wrecked *Griffith Gaunt*, which was coming near to be his best novel, as Shakespeare wrecked *The Two Gentlemen of Verona* (but Shakespeare lived to learn better), by making his hero for purely stage purposes suddenly renounce his nature and behave like a quite incredible cad; nor could we readily find by searching the old pages of *Bow Bells* or *The London Journal* theatricality stalking in such nakedness as in *A Terrible Temptation*, one of Reade's later works.

## III

The pity is the greater because he took enormous trouble to be true to fact, and above everything prided himself upon being *therefore* true to Nature (whereas the two are different things). His method of work, his method of preparation for it, his material and appliances—documents, blue-books, note-books, newspaper files, indexes—will be found described as accessories to that full-length portrait of himself which (for no artistic reason) he thrusts into *A Terrible Temptation* along with a picture of his work-room:

...an empty room, the like of which Lady Bassett had never seen; it was large in itself and multiplied tenfold by great mirrors from floor to ceiling, with no frames but a narrow oak beading; opposite her on entering was a bay window, all plate glass, the central panes of which opened like doors upon a pretty little garden that glowed with colour and was backed by fine trees....The numerous and large mirrors all down to the ground laid hold of the garden and the flowers, and by double and triple reflection filled the room with nooks of verdure and colour.

He used this device in his rooms at Magdalen, which looked upon the college deer park; by mirrors contriving to bring it indoors and around him while he sat, like Chaucer in Longfellow's sonnet 'in a lodge within a park':

> The chamber walls depicted all around,
> [Not] With portraitures of huntsman, hawk, and hound
> And the hurt deer...

but with the deer alone, unhurt, browsing under green branches.

Underneath the table was a formidable array of notebooks, standing upright and labelled on their backs. There were about twenty large folios of classified facts, ideas, and pictures, for the very wood-cuts were all indexed and classified on the plan of a tradesman's ledger....Then there was a collection of solid quartos and of smaller folio guard-books called Indexes. There were *Index Rerum et Journalium—Index Rerum et Librorum—Index Rerum et Hominum*—and a lot more; indeed so many that, by way of climax, there was a fat folio ledger entitled *Index ad Indices*. By the side of the table were six or seven thick pasteboard cards, each about the size of a large portfolio, and on these the author's notes and extracts were collected from all his repertories into something like a focus for a present purpose. He was writing a novel based on facts—facts, incidents, living dialogues, pictures, reflections, situations, were all on these cards to choose from, and arranged in headed columns....

One thing this method taught him at any rate—to exert his style upon concrete objects. He might, indeed, distort men, women, things; he did so as often as not; but he ever saw them as tangible, and detested all writing that was nebulous, high-faluting, gushing. His style is ever lively and nervous. It may irritate even the moderately fastidious; it abounds in errors of taste; but is always vigorous, compelling—the style of a man. We feel the surer that our account of it does no real injustice to poor Mrs Seymour's influence on observing that Reade's masterpiece *The Cloister and the Hearth* and *Hard Cash* (which many rank next) were written at a remove from her, in his college rooms. Anyhow she did not know enough of the times or the materials handled in *The Cloister* for her opinion to have had even a plausible value, and in fact he seems to have done without it. On the other hand, we do her memory the justice to doubt if any tact, any skill, could have taught Reade tact, cured his combativeness, or alleviated his wrathful knack

of putting himself in the wrong. He was not only hasty in
a quarrel; being in it, he might be counted on to make his
friends blush and the cool observer smile. The *Memoir*
contains a letter, written before he commenced author,
extending over many pages, addressed to the officials of the
Treasury and haranguing them in this fashion because he
had been charged what he thought an excessive import
duty on some old violins:

Merit never comes to bear until first filtered through the
consideration of name. If then a Man looks at twenty old
fiddles, the merits of which he can see, but does not know who
made each and how that Maker ranks in the Market—where
is he? and what is he?—a sailor on the wide Pacific without a
compass or a star is not more the sport of water and wind than
such a man as this is of flighty dreams and of brute chance....
Oh! my Lords, if you or the Commissioners would only con-
descend to look at the things....Malice is a blackguard, but
Ignorance is a Wild Beast, &c., &c.

This kind of thing may not have been ineradicable in
Reade, but it was certainly never eradicated. To the end
—for example when accused of plagiarising from Swift in
*The Wandering Heir*—he could never fit the word with
the occasion or keep any sense of proportion between the
argument and his temper. A similar tactlessness led him,
having accepted a commission from the firm of Cassell,
Petter and Galpin, to affront the readers of *Cassell's
Magazine* with *A Terrible Temptation*. Nobody could
have been more genuinely amazed and indignant than was
Reade at the reprobation it excited; but so recently as
twenty years ago a mischievous person in search of amuse-
ment could count on it if he walked into Messrs Cassell's
premises and pronounced the name of Charles Reade in a
voice above a whisper. Reade, to be sure, had usually

moral right on his side, and behind his excesses; and the amount of positive good he did, not only towards reforming social abuses by such works as *It is Never Too Late to Mend* and *Hard Cash*, but by pamphlets and letters championing individual victims of injustice, would amount to a fine total. But we are considering him as an artist, and the artistic side and the side of the angels are not conterminous, though they agree roughly.

The general verdict seems to be that, while *Griffith Gaunt* and *Hard Cash* are works of mastery (and the high seriousness of *Griffith Gaunt* cannot be denied), *The Cloister and the Hearth* was his masterpiece. With this verdict we entirely agree, and hold that, if there must be a first place among 'historical' novels, that work and *Esmond* are the great challengers for it. For artistry, grace of handling, ease, finish, the delicate rhythm of its prose, nice perception of where to restrain passion, where and how far to let it go, *Esmond* must carry every vote. *The Cloister and the Hearth*, moreover, tails out tediously, though the end, when it comes, is exquisite—a thing of human blood purified to tears and tears to divine balm.

'But now the good fight is won, ah me! Oh my love, if thou hast lived doubting of thy Gerard's heart, die not so; for never was woman loved so tenderly as thou this ten years past.'

'Calm thyself, dear one,' said the dying woman with a heavenly smile. 'I know it; only being a woman, I could not die happy till I had heard thee say so.'

In the depth of this, as through the whole story which it closes, shines a something which Thackeray could no more match than he could match the epic chapters wherethrough Gerard adventures with Denys of Burgundy, though between the two novelists, on the sum of their writing, there can be, of course, no comparison.

None the less, and through all his blindfold mistakes—even through his most amazing trivialities—Reade carries always the indefinable aura of greatness. Often vulgar, and not seldom ludicrous, he is never petty. 'No man,' said Johnson, 'was ever written down but by himself.' Reade, vain and apt to write himself down in the act of writing himself up, was all but consistently the worse foe of his own reputation. It will probably survive all the worst he did, because he was great in a way, and entirely sincere.

# PATRIOTISM IN ENGLISH LITERATURE. I.

## I

BY those who do not understand Socratic irony, or the delicacies of it as rendered by Plato, a great deal of obtuse criticism has been wasted upon the *Menexenus*, which is a dialogue purporting to be a true account by Socrates of a funeral oration composed to be recited over certain of the Athenian dead who fell in the Peloponnesian war. Let me sketch the introduction:

Socrates happens on his friend Menexenus, returning from the Agora. 'Where have you been, Menexenus?' 'At the Council, where they were to choose some one to pronounce the customary oration over the dead; for there is to be a public funeral. But the meeting adjourned without deciding on the orator.' 'O Menexenus, death in battle is a fine thing. The poor fellow, however poor he was, gets a costly funeral and an elaborate speech by a wise man who has prepared it long beforehand. He is praised for what he has done and for what he has not done—that is the beauty of it. And the speaker so steals away our souls, Menexenus, that I—standing and listening—feel myself a finer fellow than ever I have been; and, if there be any foreigners present, I am made conscious of a certain superiority over them, and they seem to experience a corresponding awe of me, and in fact it takes me about three days to get over it.' 'You are always poking fun at us,

Socrates. But what will the poor fellow—I mean the orator—have to say, at so short a notice?' 'Oh, that's easy. If a speaker had to praise Athenians among Peloponnesians, or Peloponnesians among Athenians, he might have some ado to gain credit. But where's his difficulty to win applause among the very people whom he is praising?' 'Could *you* do it, Socrates?'—'Well, yes, I have hopes I could praise Athenians to Athenians; and the more because I can recollect almost word for word a funeral oration I heard Aspasia compose, only last night, on these very dead, putting together fragments of the famous funeral oration which Pericles spoke, but (as I believe) she composed for him.'

Then follows the oration, carefully absurd in its dates, obviously travestied from Pericles' famous speech as conjectured for him by Thucydides. And the German scholars solemnly doubt (although Aristotle happens to quote the dialogue as Plato's) how the thing can be Plato's, seeing it is so very like Thucydides: and why Plato—a serious philosopher—should put it into the mouth of Aspasia, of all people! They incline to think it spurious, on internal evidence: which means, the evidence of their internals.

We must not suppose however, because Plato, speaking through the mouth of Socrates, lets his irony play like summer lightning around these patriotic encomia upon the dead, that therefore he was no true patriot, or anything less than a fervent one. For, first, observe that what he so gently derides is ready-made patriotism kept in stock and vended to order—the sort of thing that in a later age constrained Dr Johnson to utter suddenly in a strong determined tone the apophthegm, 'Patriotism is the last refuge of a scoundrel.' Plato more urbanely suggests that it appertains to the stock-in-trade of a good many humbugs. Now

it was a great part of the service rendered to mankind by the
Greek intellect (and specially by the Athenian intellect)
that it insisted on penetrating humbug, to see things as they
are, and so has helped men ever since to separate true
things from false.—'O Athenian stranger—mere inhabitant
of Attica I will not call you, but you seem to deserve rather
the name of Athene herself, because you go back to first
principles' (Plato, *The Laws*).  It does not follow, because
Plato slily derides the sort of stuff Archinus or Dion would
have turned out in imitation of Pericles, that he would not
be profoundly moved by the great oration which (put into
Pericles' mouth by Thucydides) has moved the souls of
men for two thousand years[1].  It does not follow from
Plato's irony that he was a man likely to be left unthrilled
by a speech which stands to this day as the *locus classicus*
of patriotism.  Rather, the contrary follows.  He is separating
the true from the spurious imitation served out by second-
rate rhetoricians.

Lastly, on this point let me recall to some of you a word
or two spoken in a previous lecture, on the subject of
parody.  If a man's mind be accustomed, as Plato's was, to
move reverently among holy things and so that his appreciation of them has become a second nature, he can afford

[1] Here may I interpose a warning that you do not hastily
take it, as some do, for Thucydides' own composition.  On
other speeches in the *History* he may have practised freely the
art of dressing-up to which he pleads guilty.  But of so glorious
a speech as that every sentence would sink into the hearers'
hearts.  Thucydides must have had a hundred memories from
which to collate it; and—what is more—he could not only
have found it hard, in the 'faking,' to rise so far above his
habitual style, but he could hardly have *dared* to foist new
sentences of his own in place of those which the occasion had
left 'familiar in men's mouths as household words.'

(whether he speak of poetry, or of art, or of religion) to play with his adored one even as a tactful lover may tease his mistress, and the pair of them find in it a pretty refreshment of love. For he knows exactly where to stop, as she what to allow. So—to come to modern times for an instance —you respond to every noble phrase in Abraham Lincoln's oration over the dead of Gettysburg:

We have come to dedicate a portion of that field as a final resting place for those who have given their lives that a nation might live. It is altogether fitting and proper that we should do this.

But in a larger sense we cannot dedicate, we cannot consecrate, we cannot hallow this ground. The brave men, living and dead, who struggled here have consecrated it far above our power to add or detract. The world will little note, nor long remember, what we say here; but it can never forget what they did here. It is for us, the living, rather to be dedicated here to the unfinished work which they who fought here have thus far so nobly advanced.

'The world will little note, nor long remember, what we say here; but it can never forget what they did here.' The more intimately you respond to this—the more sensitively you feel, with the thrill of the old Periclean antithesis, that here, after so many generations, the world has thrown up, in Abraham Lincoln, a man worthy to speak to it once again as Pericles spoke—with the lighter courage you can consign all spurious or second-rate imitations to the caressing raillery of Mr Dooley.

## II

It may seem a long way—even a longer way than to Tipperary—from the polite irony of Menexenus to the cheerful irony of the English private soldier, now fighting for us on the Belgian border. But I suggest to you that *his* irony too plays with patriotism just because he is at home with that holy spirit; so much at home that he may be called at any hour of the day or night to die for it. Precisely because he lives in this intimacy, he is shy of revealing it, and from shy turns to scornful when the glib uninitiate would vulgarise the mystery:

> Send for the army and the navy,
> Send for the rank and file—
> (Have a banana!)

A well-meaning scholar, having written, the other day, for the British infantry-man a number of ditties to which he will never march, protested that if he preferred to march to *this* sort of thing, his laureate should be the village idiot; which pleased me, who have always contended that the village idiot has his uses, and that Mr McKenna was far too hasty with his Mental Deficiency Act.

There is a real mental deficiency—and most of us who work on recruiting committees have bitter experience of it —in well-intentioned superior persons who, with no prospect of dying for their country, are calling on others to make that sacrifice. On platform after platform since August I have sat and seen the ardour of young men chilled by exhortations from intellectual speakers who lacked understanding, by middle-aged people—sentimental or patronising—who schooled their hearers in what they ought to feel. To the British soldier Tipperary was, if you will, just Tipperary: to some of us who heard him singing and know what he went forth to find, it remains a city celestial.

After this it was noised about that Mr Valiant-for-truth was taken with a Summons.... Then said he, I am going to my Father's; and tho' with great Difficulty I am got hither, yet now I do not repent me of all the Trouble I have been at to arrive where I am. My Sword, I give to him that shall succeed me in my Pilgrimage, and my Courage and Skill, to him that can get it. My Marks and Scarrs I carry with me, to be a witness for me, that I have fought his Battels, who now will be my Rewarder.

When the Day that he must go hence was come, many accompanied him to the River side, into which, as he went, he said, Death, where is thy Sting? And as he went down deeper, he said, Grave, where is thy Victory? So he passed over, and the Trumpets sounded for him on the other side.

(*The Pilgrim's Progress*)

But there are serious good folk who would paraphrase

> Good-bye, Piccadilly,
> Farewell, Leicester Square

into

> Good-bye, Self-indulgence!
> Farewell, the soft arm-chair!

and to these the British infantry-man responds

> Have a banana!

Yes; and truly (when one comes to think) it were hard to find, in few words, a better answer.

> Send for the boys of the girls' brigade
>   To set old England free:
> Send for my mother, and my sister and my brother,
>   But for heaven's sake don't send me!

That is 'merry England.' The enemy wonders that our men march—and so obstinately too—to this stuff while by rights they should be chanting *Rule, Britannia!*: and it would seem that not a few cultivated Englishman, who of late years have lent too much of their minds to Germanic ways of thought, suffer from an uneasy suspicion that we ought to be answering the perpetual *Deutschland über alles!* with a perpetual *Rule, Britannia!*. Nay, the late Professor Cramb—who felt the German hypnotism none the less for resenting it—conveys the reproach in passages like this:

It is hard for us in England to understand what the Rhine really means for a German, the enthusiasm which he feels for that River. Treitschke himself says of it, for instance, when he has to leave Bonn: 'Tomorrow I shall see the Rhine for the last time. The memory of that noble river'—and this is not in a poem, observe, but simply in a letter to a friend—'the memory of that noble river will keep my heart pure and save me from sad and evil thoughts throughout all the days of my life.' Try (writes Professor Cramb) to imagine anyone saying that of the Thames!

Well, I daresay some Old Etonians have felt something like that about the Thames, and have confessed it in private letters. But how could Professor Cramb have missed to see that when we Englishmen lift our thoughts to their stature, our Rhine is not the Thames? Come, I will answer for once with a *Rule, Britannia!*. Our Rhine, our king's frontier, is no Thames but the royal sweep of seven oceans. The waters of our baptism flow past Dover through the Straits of Hercules, down past the Cape of Storms, to divide again to reach, to coast, to claim Hindostan, Australia. *There* (if you will have it so) runs *our* Rhine: our Bonn and Bingen and Drachenfels are the Heads of Sydney, the ramparts of Quebec, the citadel rock of Gibraltar:

> rock which Hercules
> And Goth and Moor bequeathed us. At this door
> England stands sentry. God! to hear the shrill
> Sweet treble of her fifes upon the breeze,
> And at the summons of the rock gun's roar
> To see her red coats marching from the hill!

## III

But—to be fair—let us admit that we do not often open our hearts in this fashion. I suppose that if England ever bred a great 'imperialist' in days before our language had coined that unbeautiful word, his name was Sir Walter Ralegh: and he has left us, in noble verse, a reminder that

> Passions are liken'd best to floods and streams:
> The shallow murmur, but the deep are dumb.

I trust—as I believe—this to be the explanation why we, who seek in English literature for the passion of patriotism, have to pride ourselves on its being everywhere implicit. To be sure the patriotic orator can always quote to us the lines of dying Gaunt:

> This royal throne of kings, this sceptr'd isle,...
> This happy breed of men, this little world,
> This precious stone set in the silver sea,
> Which serves it in the office of a wall
> Or as a moat defensive to a house,
> Against the envy of less happier lands,
> This blessed plot, this earth, this realm, this England...

or the Bastard's equally famous conclusion:

> Come the three corners of the world in arms,
> And we shall shock them. Nought shall make us rue,
> If England to itself do rest but true.

Yet I think it observable that the one speech is put into the mouth of a febrile and dying man while the other rounds off a play with obvious declamation: and yet more observable that whereas the body of Shakespeare's work is a whole school in itself of patriotic thought and feeling, more than nine-tenths of it is implicit; after *King Henry the Fifth* almost the *whole* of it is implicit.

Certainly if we turn to the body of English poetry we shall find explicit, loud-mouthed patriotism even worse represented than is our pride in sea-power, that particular glory of our birth and state. When we happen to talk of our country, we are at one, or almost at one. It is only Bubb Dodington who can write:

> Love thy country, wish it well,
>   Not with too intense a care:
> 'Tis enough that, when it fell,
>   Thou its ruin didst not share.

It is true—nay, it is part of my argument—that when an Englishman talks of art, of literature, of philosophy (I fear me, even of theology), some solid sense of his country's dignity is usually discoverable at the back of his mind. We feel this solid background, for example, all the while we are reading Coleridge's *Biographia Literaria*; in a metaphysical passage of De Quincey, as through parted clouds, suddenly will come charging the British dragoons of Talavera; while Dryden opens his famous *Essay of Dramatic Poesy* with the sound of our navy's gunnery:

It was that memorable day, in the first summer of the late war, when our navy engaged the Dutch; a day wherein the two most mighty and best appointed fleets which any age had ever seen, disputed the command of the greater half of the globe....While these vast floating bodies, on either side, moved against each other in parallel lines, and our countrymen, under the happy conduct of his Royal Highness, went breaking by little and little into the line of the enemies; the noise of cannon from both navies reached our ears about the City, so that all men being alarmed with it, and in a dreadful suspense of the event which we knew was then deciding, everyone went following the sound as his fancy led him; and leaving the town almost empty, some took towards the park, some cross the river, others down it; all seeking the noise in the depth of silence.

He goes on to narrate how in company with three gentlemen, 'whom their wit and quality have made known to all the town,' he took barge down through the crowded merchant-shipping to Greenwich, where the four listened as the air broke about them in little undulations of sound 'like the noise of distant thunder, or of swallows in a chimney,' until, as 'by little and little' it fell more distant, one of the four, lifting his head, congratulated the others on that happy omen of victory, adding the devout wish 'that we might hear no more of that noise, which was now leaving the English coast.'

Thus Dryden prefaces a really profound conversation upon Poetry. Now you will not easily find a better combination of poet and true Englishman than in Dryden; and if you would seek the true patriotic in our literature, you must seek it in passages such as the one I have quoted; not in your hearty *Rule, Britannias!*, *Deaths of Nelson*, or *Battles of the Baltic*, where sentiment infallibly overstrains itself and on the azure main Britons do their duty for England, home and beauty, and the mermaid's song condoles, while the mournful billow rolls in a melody of souls, and the might of England rushes to anticipate the scene—Which is pretty, but whatever can it mean?

## IV

We have no great national epic like the *Aeneid*, none written to extol the British empire, the men who founded, built it, gave their lives for it. Our greatest epic, *Paradise Lost*, really has one point of resemblance with our old friend *Beowulf*, in that as Stopford Brooke once sagely observed 'there is not one word about our England' in either poem.

No: but wait! Let us (as I have preached to you more than once from this desk) constantly refer our minds back to Rome, habitually consult with Latin literature upon any question which puzzles us for the moment concerning our literature in character or origin.

We have no *Aeneid*. But open your Horace. You may or may not agree off-hand with what I am going to say: but to me Horace has always seemed far more patriotic in grain than Virgil—as it has always seemed to me that (Burke's rhetoric discounted) Horace Walpole was in his way as good a patriot as Burke and at least as clear-sighted. But open your Horace, and turn the *Odes*, page after page. Familiar as they may be to you, I think you will be amazed to note how thickly sown they are with names of nations, tribes, countries—east, west, south and north—Asia, Scythia, Parthia, Numidia, Dacia, Dalmatia, the passes of the Alps and the Tyrol—over which Rome was spreading conquest in Horace's day and establishing the *Pax Romana*. Nothing of foreign affairs would appear to escape him, and always his pride in Rome (unlike Virgil's) is quick, alert, practical: as not seldom it is lofty, and never less than absolutely sincere.

Why does Horace's patriotism ring so true? Because, if we search to the heart of it, we shall find that very heart, not in the Forum or the boulevard of the Via Sacra, but in his Sabine farm. The Forum and the Via Sacra intrigued him, as the French say; but as Piccadilly or Whitehall or his club in Pall Mall intrigues an Englishman, who yet knows all the while that these are but arteries; that for the true source that feeds them, the spirit that clarifies, he must seek home to a green nook of his youth in Yorkshire or Derbyshire, Shropshire or Kent or Devon; where the folk are slow, but there is seed-time and harvest and 'pure religion breathing household laws.'

I challenge you that here lies the heart of Horace's patriotism. He looks abroad (though he warns Quinctius against the habit) eagerly watching

> Quid bellicosus Cantaber et Scythes
> ......cogitet...

And what the Swede intend, and what the French...

but, for trust to confound their politics, he draws home to the Sabine lads—*rusticorum mascula militum proles*—shouldering logs for their mother's hearth; and to their mother herself, rustic Phidyle, paying her vows to the new moon, and her devoirs to the gods with a handful of meal and salt.

## V

Now as in a former lecture, Gentlemen[1], I warned you that to a Greek—even to an Aristophanes—his gods mattered enormously; as, coming to Rome, we saw that a Roman general on active service abroad would carry with him, packed in mule pannier, the *tessellae* of a small sacred pavement, that, wherever he encamped, his feet might rest on these holy pictures of his gods; so I warn you here that you will never understand what patriotism meant to a Roman unless you connect it with the old religious usage of Latium, with Lar and Terminus and other gods of field and garden, orchard and hearth:

> At mihi contingat patrios celebrare Penates,
> Redderoque antiquo menstrua thura Lari.

[1] *On the Art of Writing*, Pocket Edition, pp. 168–9, Cambridge University Press, 1923.

The feeling of this, should the originals be closed to you, you may yet find exquisitely conveyed in the first chapter of Pater's *Marius the Epicurean*, describing how the lad Marius attended the private annual rites of the *Ambarvalia*, of 'the religion of Numa,' in his country home, and how they impressed the boy's mind:

At the appointed time all work ceases; the instruments of labour lie untouched, hung with wreaths of flowers, while masters and servants together go in solemn procession along the dry paths of vineyard and cornfield, conducting the victims whose blood is presently to be shed for the purification from all natural or supernatural taint of the lands they have 'gone about.'...Early on that day the girls of the farm had been busy in the great portico, filling large baskets with flowers plucked short from branches of apple and cherry, then in spacious bloom, to strew before the quaint images of the gods—Ceres and Bacchus and the yet more mysterious Dea Dia—as they passed through the fields, carried in their little houses on the shoulders of white-clad youths, who were understood to proceed to this office in perfect temperance....The clean lustral water and the full incense-box were carried after them.

Then, Silence! *Favete linguis*, before the small homely shrines! No name in the great populace of the 'little gods' dear to the Roman home, was forgotten in the long Litany:

Vatican who causes the infant to utter his first cry, Fabulinus who prompts his first word, Cuba who keeps him quiet in his cot, Domiduca especially, for whom Marius had through life a particular memory and devotion, the goddess who watches over one's safe coming home.

*Favete linguis!* As the procession halted before each small shrine, Marius (we are told) strove to answer this impressive outward silence of the ritual by hushing his own boyish heart to that inward tacitness which religious Romans held due to holy things. And its comfort came back as he lay down to sleep that night after the long day's cere-monies:

To procure an agreement with the gods—*Pacem deorum ex-poscere*: that was the meaning of what they had all day been busy upon. In a faith, sincere but half-suspicious, he would fain have those powers at least not against him. His own nearer household gods were all around his bed.

'His own nearer household gods were all around his bed.' Hark, think for a moment, and catch the English echo, out of your own childhood:

> Four corners to my bed,
> Four angels round my head....

Follow that echo back, and tell me this. When you think of the real England in English poetry—of her heart, her meaning, her secret—nay even her glory—as our singers have come nearest to expressing one or the other or all of these, do you think of *Rule, Britannia!*, or *Ye Mariners of England*? Does not whatever is English in your heart lift rather to some casual careless line—maybe even some foolish-seeming line such as Chaucer's

> Wite ye nat where ther stant a litel toun
> Which that y-clepèd is Bob-up-and-down
> Under the Blee?

Or this:

> Me liketh ever, the longer the bet
>     By Wingestre, that joly citè;
> The town is good and well y-set,
>     The folk is comely for to se.
>                 *Benedicamus Domino!*

Or this of Robin Hood returning in old age to merry Sherwood:

> When he came to greenè-wood
>   In a merry mornìng,
> There he heard the notès small
>   Of birds merry singìng.
>
> 'It is far gone,' said Robin Hood,
>   'That I was latest here;
> Me list a little for to shoot
>   At the dunnè deer.'

Or again:

> O Brignall banks are wild and fair
>   And Greta woods are green.

Or:

> 'Tis pretty to be by Balinderry
>   'Tis pretty to be by Balindoon.

Or:

> The bells of Shandon
> That sound so grand on
>   The pleasant waters
>   Of the river Lea.

Or:

> Clunton and Clunbury,
>   Clungunford and Clun,
> Are the quietest places
>   Under the sun.

Or if it be a strip of meadow-land, with 'daisies pied and violets blue': or if a village 'where bells have knolled to church': or if it be but 'Scarlet town where I was born': or if it be London herself, 'of townes A per se':

> O! towne of townes, patrone and not compare

where John Gilpin keeps shop and Izaak Walton sallies an-angling, to stretch his legs up Tottenham, and all the way with the voice of the Psalmist running in his head:

He maketh me to lie down in green pastures: he leadeth me beside the still waters...

it is thus, and incurably thus, that we see England; as it was thus that Horace, the true Roman, saw Italy: and though in Britain

> Today the Roman and his trouble
> Are ashes under Uricon

we keep the lesson learnt. Other nations extend, or would extend, their patriotism over large spaces superficially: ours (or so much of it as, in Meredith's phrase, is 'accepted of song') ever cuts down through the strata for its well-springs, intensifies itself upon that which, untranslatable to the foreigner, is comprised for us in a single easy word—Home. We do not, in our true hours—as all our glorious poetry attests—brag of England as a world-power, actual or potential. Blame it who will upon our insularity, we do habitually narrow and intensify our national passion upon the home and the hearths now to be defended. And I say this, who said just now that our Rhine was seven seas.

# PATRIOTISM IN ENGLISH
# LITERATURE. II.

## I

WE talked last time, Gentlemen, of a certain shyness —often translating itself into irony—shared by our nation with great nations of the past when it comes to talking of that sacred emotion, love of one's country. In ordinary social life we know that a well-bred man naturally inclines to let his ancestry (or his rank; or his riches, if he have them; or any personal distinction he has won) go silently for granted; not undervaluing them, but taught to see them in their true value as gifts at the best held in trusteeship from the gods. We know the instinct of such a man towards his fellows; that it is constantly courteous, that it never says or seems to say, 'I am as good as you,' but always prefers the implication, 'You are as good as I.' We know that he keeps his heart as a mirror for other men's feelings, lest he should wound them; that even in controversy (as Newman says) his disciplined intellect is candid, considerate, indulgent, since he throws himself into the minds of his opponents and accounts for their mistakes.

So a nation such as France, or England, whose title-deeds time can no longer question, may cherish indeed certain inveterate foibles—even certain inveterate vices of character—which its fellows will smile at or deplore: but it will long ago have realised that it cannot have the moon, that (as the saying is) all sorts go to make a world, that civilised men must give and take. It will long ago have rid itself of bumptiousness, of that itch for self-assertion which is the root-bane of good manners.

Now the general good manners of Europe have been vexed for a generation by a people, raw in character and uncouth of speech, which has prospered by dint of bravery to a very high degree. Having prospered beyond hope by this pugnacious self-assertion, it has set itself since 1870 not only to philosophise its primitive instincts but to impose that philosophy upon the civilised nations into whose circle it had so complacently forced a seat.

'The be-all and end-all of a State is Power'—'True Patriotism consists in Self-assertiveness'—'What we want, it follows that we must have'—I will not weary you, today, Gentlemen, with confuting this doctrine. Long ago, on a hot day in a courtyard in Athens, Thrasymachus announced it, rehearsing all the advantages of the unjust man; and was laid on his back, wondering what had happened.

## II

The high teaching of the world was not to be put down by Thrasymachus, in his day, and is not to be put down in ours by the neo-Darwinists who teach that life, for nations as for individuals, is a kind of dog-fight, and its object self-assertion. Christ at any rate taught that he who would save his soul must first lose it: and that doctrine informs good literature, even down to the artless self-surrender of our own Nut Browne Mayde:

> Sith I have here been partynere
>     With you of joy and bliss,
> I must alsò part of your woe
>     Endure, as reason is:

> Yet I am sure of one pleasùre,
>   And shortly it is this—
> That where ye be, me seem'th, pardè,
>   I could not fare amiss.

In good literature, as in the Gospel, the self-assertor is, like Malvolio, a self-deceiver. 'What is a man profited, if he shall gain the whole world, and lose his own soul?' 'Love thy neighbour as thyself.' 'This law,' says a much-quoted German general, 'can claim no significance for the relations of one country to another, since its application to politics would lead to a conflict of duties.'

Believe me, a man who talks like that has been educated —that is to say, has had himself 'drawn out'—beyond his capacity to bear the strain. These are no times for men to make fetishes of tall words, even of words so tall as 'education' and 'religion.' These are times for clear sight into the values of things. Without clear thinking religion will not help us: for a stupid man, who cannot see clearly what he means by it, religion may easily be—and indeed not seldom is—the wickedest influence in the world. His heart will bleed over Louvain while he sacks it, and with gathering confidence he will promise, so he be allowed to do the same to Calais, to reward the Almighty (Who knows about crosses) with the decoration of an iron one. So with education: some men may as easily have too much education as too much religion. It is admittedly bad to have none; it is possibly, nay certainly, worse to have more than by character or intelligence you are adapted for. It has been the curse of Germany that, mistaking the human end of education and misconceiving what 'power' means in the saying 'Knowledge is Power,' she has strained herself to it beyond preparation of ancestry or manners.

### III

Now I propose to examine for a few minutes this morning, first the rationale, and afterwards some results, of this German self-assertiveness as it has invaded in our day the field of study with which we here are particularly concerned —I mean the study of English literature. Into what error soever the course of my examination may betray me, I at least commit none in starting from a fact which is one of common knowledge—that German professors and scholars have invaded that field with great assiduity.

You will not so readily agree—maybe you will not agree at all—with what I am going to say next. But I say it nevertheless. Every literature being written in a language —every great literature commanding a masterly style of its own language and appealing to an almost infinitely delicate acquaintance with its meanings, an almost infinitely delicate sense of its sounds, even to semi-tones and demi-semi-tones —no foreigner can ever quite penetrate to the last excellence of an unfamiliar tongue. I know this to be a hard saying: and I utter it very reluctantly because it is wormwood to me to own myself congenitally debarred—though it be in common with all modern men—from entering the last shrine of beauty (say) in a chorus of Sophocles. But I am sure that it is so. Lovely as we may divine the thrill to be (or rather to have been for those who had ears to hear)— educative as it may be even in tantalising our thirst—I am sure that no modern Englishman can ever quite reach back to the lilt of a Sophoclean chorus; still less to its play of vowel notes. I doubt even if by taking most careful thought he can attain to the last beauties of a sonnet by Leconte de Lisle or Heredia.

You may urge that, Latin and Greek being dead languages which we are agreed in various ways to mispronounce, this disability may apply to them, but does not extend to our modern Babel. I answer, first, that if only by structure of his vocal organs a German is congenitally unable to read our poetry; that his eye, perusing it, cannot translate it to any part of him capable of reproducing its finest sound. The late Philip Gilbert Hamerton once illustrated this from a few lines of Tennyson's *Claribel*.

> Where Claribel low-lieth
>    The breezes pause and die,
>       Letting the rose-leaves fall:...
>
> At eve the beetle boometh
>    Athwart the thicket lone:...
>
> The hollow grot replieth
>    Where Claribel low-lieth.

Now to an English critic with a musical ear the whole consonantal secret of that little poem resides in the labials, with their suggestion of moonlit lapsing water, and the low 'th' sounds in which one feels the very breath of eve softly wafted:

> At eve the beetle boometh
>    Athwart the thicket lone.

But a German simply cannot compass the soft 'th' sound. He *has* to introduce his own harsh hiss upon the twilit quiet where never a full sibilant was allowed. As this:

> At eve ze beedle boomess
>    Aswart ze zickhead lon

while as for the continuous hushed run of the soft guttural to lip and tooth ('Claribel,' 'throstle,' 'thick-leaved ambrosial,' 'the hollow grot') he must rest content with his ancestral habit which has not yet evolved even labials beyond the throat: 'Sick-leaved ambhrosial:

> Ze hollo ghrot hrepliez
>    Hwhere Chlaribel hlow hliez.

## IV

I say then that it must be extremely hard for any German to feel the last felicities of our language, to respond to its last, most delicate, harmonies. I think it must be impossible, for (to use a plain phrase) I don't see what he has to do it with. But I will content myself with maintaining that he must naturally find it very hard[1].

And this by no means exhausts the list of his natural disabilities. We know that many scholars have been able to write exquisitely in a dead language, or at any rate to write it in a way that to us seems exquisite. Cambridge is rightly proud of a long list of sons whose lips in her cradle the very bees of Hybla and of Hymettus have visited with their honey. Certain Frenchmen again (M. Jusserand is a notable instance) have written English 'as to the manner born'—nervous, elastic English, with an added grace of French charm. I doubt if the compliment can, save in politeness, be returned. Swinburne's French poetry, for example, is magnificently eloquent—but is it quite French? At all events the German who can write English of any quality has yet, I believe, to be found, unless we accept Max Müller's plastering for marble. To that whole nation —or, if you will, to that whole group of nations—our language is not only not living but something more than dead. This, when you consider it, throws back some merriment upon their claim that we are—or shall we say, have

[1] I believe that in a less, but yet a very high, degree, a Frenchman finds this natural difficulty with English, and an Englishman with French. Both of them are far more at home with the simpler pronunciation of Italian. This, further, seems to me a partial explanation of a fact which few will dispute— that (to speak only of us English) we have in the past *understood* Italians better than we have understood the French. In matters of art and literature this will hardly be denied.

been—in some sense cousins of theirs. It might appear that the claim has been set up on grounds not entirely unconnected with expectations of a legacy, and that our death has, as the lawyers say, by our amiable relatives been somewhat too hastily presumed.

Please understand that I am not belittling the mass of methodical and most helpful work done, during the last twenty or thirty—nay, the past hundred—years by German scholars upon that side of our literature which they are not congenitally precluded from understanding. When this war is over, I hope we shall retain no little gratitude for that service of labour, while able with clear eyes to see it in its real relationship to literature; that is, in its right place.

For (let us be fair) I do not say, nor do I believe for a moment, in spite of a long malignity now unmasked, the Germans have *of set purpose* treated English literature as a thing of the past or imposed that illusion upon our schools, with design to prove that this particular glory of our birth and state is a dead possession of a decadent race. My whole argument is rather that they have set up this illusion, and industriously, because they could not help it; because the illusion is in them: because this lovely and living art which they can never practise nor even see as an art, to them is, has been, must be for ever, a dead science—a *hortus siccus*; to be tabulated, not to be planted or watered.

But I do say that when they impose that hallucination upon the schools of English in our universities, whether they impose it deliberately or not, the effect is the same. And I do say it is in a high degree discreditable that English scholars, hypnotised (we must suppose) by contemplating the mere mountain of German false doctrine, have consigned to it alike in what they neglected and what they attempted.

Have it how you will, it disgraces somebody that an undergraduate of this university, from the sixth form of one of our best reputed public schools, coming to me the other day in his desire to know how English should be written (he wanted ardently to know this though, as he put the matter, 'it will be no good for me in the Classical Tripos')—that this boy should confess to me that in all his schooldays he had never been set to write one English essay, never taught to arrange two English sentences together.

## V

I have no blame for our enemies, as we must now call them. It is our fault that we treat our beautiful, breathing language as a dead thing. On all that side of the study which allowed them scope *they* have taken infinite pains, while the immensely more delicate, more significant, more difficult side—difficult to us, impossible to them—*we* have let go by default. Is it any wonder, then, that their general hallucination of culture has spread with a deeper infection of self-conceit, of self-deceit, over a study in which we have accepted them for taskmasters whom nature forbade to be more than hewers of wood for us and drawers of water?

I remember coming once—but cannot remember where —upon an ingenious theory that for a period of time in what we call the Dark Ages, everyone in Europe was more or less mad. At the time that seemed to me a cheerfully extravagant hypothesis, though it had the merit of illuminating quite a considerable number of facts the causes of which historians had left obscure. But in our day we are obliged to lay account with some explanation not very far short of this, seeing that the people of central Europe are at this very moment claiming—and, it seems, as one man

—to be apostles of a culture which the surrounding nations can only accept after a confession of insanity. Either we or they must be mad just now, and there can be no third way about it.

I daresay you read in your *Times* yesterday of a performance of *Twelfth Night* given in the Old Theatre at Leipzig on October 20th with a special prologue written by Ernst Hardt and put into the mouth of the Fool, who appeared in front of the curtain and thus delivered himself —I quote the English translation:

> Gentles, in very sooth I do appear
> A fool in semblance! And behind the curtain,
> Where now my world is built for your delight,
> I shall be truly—I can promise you—
> From my heart's depth and by my body's fashion
> A fool indeed! But here, and in these times,
> In front of you, how can I? Thorough-baked
> I stand as solemn as a whole meal loaf.
> My master, the great poet, who behind
> This curtain built his world, and therewith too
> Innumerous other worlds as marvellous—
> Ye[1] know him well, for near as man can climb
> To godhead, he won godhead by his works—
> Now this same poet hath commanded me
> In solemn earnest to declare you this:
> Ye unto him have been until today
> His second home; his first and native home
> Was England; but this England of the present
> Is so contrarious in her acts and feelings,
> Yea, so abhorr'd of his pure majesty
> And the proud spirit of his free-born being,
> That he doth find himself quite homeless there.

[1] 'Ye shall be as gods!'

A fugitive he seeks his second home,
This Germany, that loves him most of all,
To whom before all others he gives thanks,
And says: Thou wonderful and noble land,
Remain thou Shakespeare's one and only home,
So that he wander not, uncomprehended,
Without a shelter in the barren world!


# VI

Let us not deceive ourselves. The man who wrote that, meant it: and the man who spoke that, meant it. If I can read honest conviction in verse, honest conviction is there. These men do honestly believe our Shakespeare—Shakespeare nostras, as Ben Jonson affectionately termed him, whose language they cannot speak, cannot write, can but imperfectly understand (for those who can neither speak nor write in a language *cannot* understand it perfectly), our Shakespeare's spirit—has migrated to a nation whose exploits it benevolently watches in the sack of Louvain, the bestialities of Aerschot, the shelling of Rheims cathedral. These men believe it no less thoroughly than they believe that a telegram is all the better for being forged so that the forgery advantage them. Do not be surprised. As I warned you in certain lectures on *Macbeth*, a generation that has lived through the consequences of the Ems telegram and dabbled with a German professorial philosophy, which whether for the purpose or not does in fact excuse cheating at cards, cannot maintain that the mirage imposed upon Macbeth by the witches, the dream of winning all things by substituting evil for good, has lost its power to hallucinate the intellect, even the strong intellect.

So let us not blame these men, but ourselves, who

tamely suffered this imposture to grow. They could not understand, or understood only that they stood to profit. We had the birthright of understanding as well as the assurance that by allowing our intelligence to be enslaved we stood only to lose.

## VII

There is only one way, as we see now, of exorcising such a devil when he has been allowed to swell to full growth. The task then passes to the young—to the sword in the hands of the young—and they will lance this swollen tumour. But at what a cost of lives that might be building the next generation, and living and seeing good days—lost to how many through that default of ours!

Yes, it is good that the young have the salvation of this race in hand just now, and not our professors and lecturers. But when does ever a nation live, to whom its language is no longer a living thing? To the care of these professors and lecturers our language with its tradition of glorious energy was entrusted, to be treated at least as a living thing.

But it is ill for a country, Gentlemen—I fear we must acknowledge it—when her destiny passes into the guidance of professors. That lesson (if I mistake not) is going to be very painfully learnt by Germany in the course of this war; and it will be learnt less painfully by us only because our pedants have earned disregard by choosing to be abject —a doubly negative success. If our teachers of English had only—would only, even now—treat our mother tongue as a living tongue, our pride in it as a pride of practice, our use of it as a quick and perfectible art! How much can they yet do with their knowledge if they will repent and understand and become if not as little children then at least as men of the world!

As it is, the pricking of the bubble of arrogance is left to the clean instincts of our young men. I seem now to read the prophecy of this in two scenes, which suffer me to recall as they stand out now, bitten sharply on my memory—the one of Oxford, the other of Cambridge.

First then I recall a morning scene in Oxford in the early spring of 1912: the day bright, with a touch of frost, the air alive with the spirit of youth borne back—how poignantly!—to the heart of a passer-by, revisiting the familiar streets after many years. Under instructions I had posted myself at the corner of the Turl where it debouches into the High. Nor had I long to wait. Punctual as the many clocks competed in striking nine, by Carfax, around the end of St Aldates swung the head of a column of artillery—the O.U.T.C. returning from morning man-œuvres, out Radley way. They wheeled by Carfax into the High and came at a trot down that street of memories.

> Time like an ever-rolling stream
> Bears all his sons away...

doubtless: but for the moment at Oxford, all has past, everything even to the morning sunshine these tall boys commanded, for behind them they rattled the British guns. A sight to make the heart leap! But the heart in its exulta-tion cried out, 'If it must be, well....Yet not in our time, O Lord!'

And again, but the date is a year later—I see a cavalry troop of the C.U.O.T.C. clattering home over the bridge by Magdalene in a drizzle that at the shut of evening—her 'gradual dusky veil'—made their lighter Cambridge grey all but undistinguishable; these, also, taking charge of the road, calling to one another, as they wheeled by St John's, as if all Cambridge belonged to them—as now in retrospection one sees that it did. For these also were in their careless confident way preparing themselves.

They are gone. They have taken their cheerfulness out of Cambridge: and have left us to an empty university, to dull streets, the short days, the long nights. And we who, by age or for other causes, must stay behind, must needs question our heavy thoughts.

## VIII

Let me tell you—or remind you—of this, for a true history and a parable. In the year 1870, in the little village of Arbois in France and in a cottage close by the bridge that crosses the Cuisance river, there abode a small half-paralysed man, working at his books to a word which he constantly repeated—*Laboremus*. For his school in Paris was closed and he had been sent out of the city as an 'idle mouth' and indeed he was clearly unfit to carry arms. 'But sometimes,' says his biographer, 'when he was sitting quietly with his wife and daughter, the town-crier's trumpet would sound: and forgetting all else, he must run out of doors, mix with the groups standing on the bridge, listen to the latest news of disaster and creep like a dumb hurt animal back to his room,' where the portrait of his father an ex-sergeant of Napoleon's 3rd Regiment of the Line—'the brave amongst the brave'—hung to reproach him. 'Shall we not cry, "Happy are the dead"?' wrote this paralytic man to one friend; and to another, 'How fortunate you are to be young and strong! why cannot I begin a new life of study and work! Unhappy France, dear country, if I could only assist in raising thee from thy disasters!'

Now that man swore—in the depth of national defeat,

in the anguish of a brain active while the body was laid impotent—to raise France again to her rank among the nations and by work of pure beneficence. He would never forgive Germany: but he—a man warned of his end—would live to build this monument, for the glory of France, to shame by its nobility that vulgar excrescence raised by Germany over the Rhine. You may read it all in his *Life*; how the vow was taken, how pursued, how achieved. I, who quote this vow and its accomplishment, saw the wreaths piled five-and-twenty years later by all Europe—prouder trophies for a cathedral than stands of captured colours—on the grave of Pasteur.

'But that which put glory of grace into all that he did,' says Bunyan of Greatheart, 'was that he did it of pure love for his Country.'

# INDEX

Acland, Sir Henry, 245
Adoniram, 2
Alcuin, 14
Allen, Robert, 203, 205
*Ancient Mariner, The*, 207–211
Arnold, Matthew, 3, 179, 184, 218–231
*Atalanta in Calydon*, 249
Avignon, Bridge of, 17

Bacon, Francis, 153
Ballads, 22–47
*Beauty and the Beast*, 13
Bede, 14
Bentley, Dr Richard, 53
*Beowulf*, 283
Besant, Sir Walter, 258, 267
Blake, William, 72, 107
Blunt, Wilfrid (quoted), 279
Bossuet, 56
Bowles, William Lisle, 204
Brandes, Dr George, 77, 87
Bridges, Robert, 71
Bridgman, Sir Orlando, 142
Brooke, Christopher, 98
Brooke, Samuel, 98
Brooke, Stopford, 283
Brooke, W. T., 142
Broome, Alexander, 84
Brown, Thomas Edward, 185
Browne, Sir Thomas, 12
Browning, Robert, 54, 117–118, 162, 178, 221, 229

Bunyan, John, 277–278, 302
Burne-Jones, Sir Edward, 247
Burns, Robert, 250
Burton, Richard, 252
Byron, Lord, 178, 256

Campbell, James Dykes, 201, 203, 205
Campion, Thomas, 56, 57, 68
Carew, Thomas, 91
Carlyle, Thomas, 223
Cary, Lucius (Lord Falkland), 91
Cassiterides, The, 2
Champeaux, William of, 18
Chaucer, 17, 20, 74, 113, 183, 268
*Christabel*, 209–211
Churchill, Charles, 49
Clarendon, Edward Hyde, Earl of, 91
Cleiveland, John, 52
*Cloister and the Hearth, The*, 271
Coleridge, Samuel Taylor, 35, 103, 200–217, 281
Collins, William, 70, 82
Common Prayer, Book of, 65
Conington, John, 48, 50
Cory, William (Johnston), 181
Cowper, William, 53, 64
Crabbe, George, 53
Cramb, Professor J. A., 279

Crashaw, Richard, 154–156
*Cupid and Psyche*, 13

Daniel, Samuel, 68
Dante, 113, 114
Denham, Sir John, 82
De Quincey, Thomas, 200, 281
De Tabley, J. B. Leicester Warren, Lord, 241
Dixon, Richard Watson, 241
Dobell, Bertram, 143
Dobson, Austin, 65
Dodington, George Bubb, 281
Donne, Henry, 92, 93
Donne, John, 90–110, 122, 123, 124, 128, 145, 162
Dorset, Charles Sackville, Earl of, 63
Doughty, Charles M., 195
Drury, Sir Robert, 98, 99
Dryden, John, 52, 91, 103, 229, 281–282
Dunbar, William, 19, 20

Earle, John, 141
Ecclesiasticus, 40, 112
'Eliot, George,' 266
Ellesmere, Thomas Egerton, Earl of, 97
Emerson, Ralph Waldo, 13
*Essays in Criticism*, 222
Etherege, Sir George, 63
Evans, Mary, 203–205

Ferrar, Nicholas, 127
Fletcher, Giles, 146
Fletcher, John, 43
Fletcher, Phineas, 146
Froude, James Anthony, 221

Garnett, Dr Richard, 215
Gautier, Théophile, 85
Gibbon, Edward, 56
Gilbert, Sir William S., 55
Gladstone, W. E., 48, 56, 66
Godolphin, Sidney, 91
Goldsmith, Oliver, 53
Gorky, Maxim, 77
Gosse, Edmund, 236–257 *passim*
Gray, Thomas, 225
Grierson, Professor H. J. C., 91
Grimm, James, 22, 24
Grosart, Dr A. B., 127, 142
Gummere, Dr F. B., 25, 27, 35

Habington, William, 148
Hall, Bishop, 52
Hamerton, Philip Gilbert, 293
Hardt, Ernst, 297
Hardy, Thomas, 77, 178–199
Harvey, Christopher, 149, 153
Harvey, Gabriel, 67
Hazlitt, William, 158, 209
Henley, W. E., 152
Herbert of Cherbury, Edward, Lord, 123
Herbert, George, 77, 107, 123–135, 153, 154
Herbert, Sidney, 124
Herder, 22
Herodotus, 5
Herrick, Robert, 57
Hoccleve, Thomas, 45
Homer, 5, 84
Hood, Thomas, 128
Horace, 48–70 *passim*, 95, 283–284

Horn, sailing ships, 7

Houghton, R. Monckton Milnes, Lord, 246

Housman, A. E. (quoted), 287, 288

Hugo, Victor, 241

Ictis, Island of, 2

Job, Book of, 112

Johnson, Dr Samuel, 42, 91, 103, 106, 243, 272, 274

Jonson, Ben, 57, 74, 91, 298

Joubert, 218

Jowett, Dr Benjamin, 234, 244, 245, 251

Jusserand, J. J., 17, 294

Juvenal, 49

Keats, John, 182, 183, 252

Ker, Professor W. P., 27

King, Bishop Henry, 91, 146–148

Kipling, Rudyard, 35

Kittredge, Professor, 23, 25

*Kubla Khan*, 209, 210, 211

Lamb, Charles, 56, 160, 202, 206, 214, 240

Landor, Walter Savage, 65, 88, 241, 249

Lang, Andrew, 13, 95

Langland, William, 41

Lebanon, levy of, 2

Lincoln, Abraham, 276

Litany, The, 16

Locker-Lampson, Frederick, 54

London Bridge, 17

Longinus, 86

Louvain, 14

Lucian, 40

Lydgate, John, 45

Macaulay, Thomas Babington, Lord, 223

Macdonald, George (quoted), 120

Maartens, Maarten, 252

Maeterlinck, Maurice, 77, 140

Martin, Sir Theodore, 48, 66

Marvell, Andrew, 59, 62

Mazzini, Giuseppe, 241

Meredith, George, 74, 112–113, 157, 158–177, 181, 193, 250, 255

Milton, John, 45, 59, 62–63, 70, 74, 75, 113–114, 138, 191, 224, 228, 282

Molière, 183

Montaigne, 183

More, Sir George, 97

Morris, William, 180, 183, 247

Müller, Max, 294

Myers, Lindo, 239

Newman, John Henry, Cardinal, 56, 289

*Nut Browne Mayde, The*, 290–291

Oldham, John, 52

Paley, William, 119

Pascal, 16

Pasteur, Louis, 301–302

Pater, Walter, 285–286

Paul, Herbert, 220, 222

Peele, George, 56

Percy, Bishop, 36, 44

Pilgrim Fathers, The, 4
Plato, 109, 113, 197, 273–275
*Poems and Ballads*, 250
Poole, Thomas, 206
Pope, Alexander, 49, 53, 56, 75, 82–86, 103
Porter, Endymion, 91
Powell, F. York, 143
Praed, W. M., 65
Prior, Matthew, 63
Procter, Bryan Waller (Barry Cornwall), 241
Pythagoras, 113

Quarles, Francis, 150–153
*Quia Amore Langueo*, 150–151

Rabelais, 16, 56, 59
Ralegh, Sir Walter, 280
Raper, R. W., 234, 251
Reade, Charles, 258–272
Redesdale, Algernon Bertram Freeman-Mitford, Lord, 238
Remigius, 18
Richborough oysters, 1
Ritchie, Lady, 246
Roads, 15–16
Rochester, John Wilmot, Earl of, 152
Roman Colonists in Britain, 8
Rossetti, Christina, 249
Rossetti, Dante Gabriel, 233, 247, 249
Routh, Dr, of Magdalen, 261, 263

Sahara, The, 12
St Aldwyn, Michael Edward Hicks-Beach, Viscount, 243

Saintsbury, George, 222, 225, 232
Sappho, 11, 86
Schlegel, A. W., 24
Scott, Sir Walter, 35
Sedley, Sir Charles, 63
Shakespeare, 13, 72, 106, 162, 168, 191, 234, 280, 297
Shelley, Percy Bysshe, 72, 178, 213, 234
Shenstone, William, 44
Sherbrooke, Robert (Lowe), Viscount, 262
Sheridan, Richard Brinsley, 74
Simonides, 242
Skeat, Professor W. W., 114
Smith, Goldwin, 263
South, Dr Robert, 138–140
Southey, Robert, 205
Spenser, Edmund, 45, 67, 73, 74, 174, 251
Stevenson, Robert Louis, 61, 185
Stubbs, Bishop William, 247
Swift, Jonathan, 49
Swinburne, Algernon Charles, 180, 232–257, 266

Tarshish, navy of, 1
Tennyson, Lord, 6, 67, 178, 221, 226, 229
Thackeray, W. M., 56, 66
Thompson, Francis, 86, 150, 180, 182
Thucydides, 87
Tolstoy, 197
Traherne, Thomas, 107, 115, 117, 142–146
Tyrrell, Professor R. Y., 60

Universities, the early, 18

Vaughan, Henry, 107, 115–116, 130–136, 142
Vaughan, Thomas, 130
Vere, Aubrey de, 49
Virgil, 87, 207
Voltaire, 56

Walton, Isaak, 91–110 *passim*, 125–127, 287
Watson, Sir William, 226, 230
Watts, Dr Isaac, 69
Watts-Dunton, Theodore, 243, 254–257

Wells, Charles Jeremiah, 241
Whitman, Walt, 173, 256
Worde, Wynkyn de, 41
Wordsworth, Dorothy, 218–220, 224
Wordsworth, William, 56, 76, 107, 112, 122, 137, 138, 140, 184, 206–208, 211–217, 226, 229, 230
Wotton, Sir Henry, 56, 90
Wyat, Sir Thomas, 41, 56

Yeats, William Butler, 180, 182
Young, Sir George, 239

CAMBRIDGE: PRINTED BY W. LEWIS, AT THE UNIVERSITY PRESS